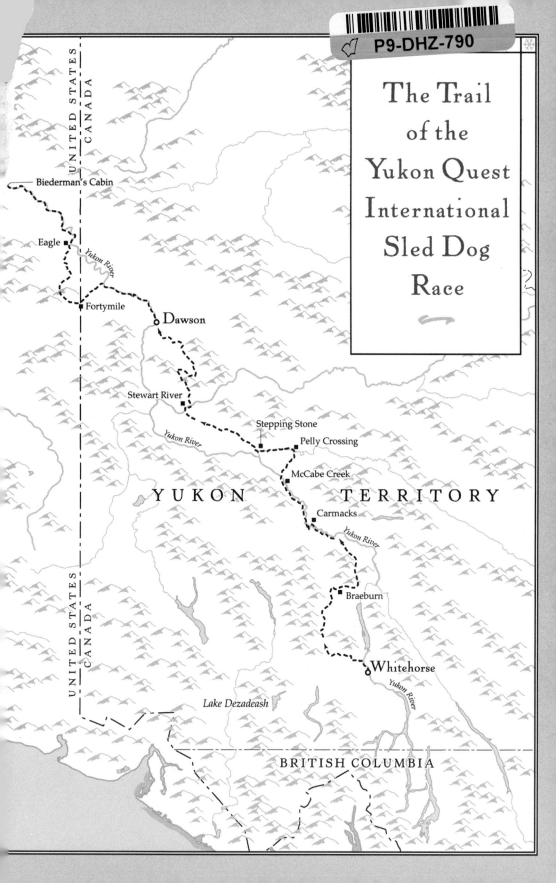

The Trail
of the
Yukon Quest
International
Sled Dog
Race

UNITED STATES
CANADA

Biederman's Cabin

Eagle

Yukon River

Fortymile

Dawson

Stewart River

Stepping Stone

Yukon River

Pelly Crossing

McCabe Creek

Y U K O N

Carmacks

Yukon River

T E R R I T O R Y

Braeburn

Whitehorse

Yukon River

UNITED STATES
CANADA

Lake Dezadeash

BRITISH COLUMBIA

Yukon Alone

YUKON ALONE

The World's Toughest

Adventure Race

JOHN BALZAR

Henry Holt and Company

New York

Henry Holt and Company, LLC
Publishers since 1866
115 West 18th Street
New York, New York 10011

Henry Holt® is a registered trademark of
Henry Holt and Company, LLC.

Copyright © 1999 by John Balzar
All rights reserved.
Published in Canada by Fitzhenry & Whiteside Ltd.,
195 Allstate Parkway, Markham, Ontario L3R 4T8.

Library of Congress Cataloging-in-Publication Data
Balzar, John.
Yukon alone: the world's toughest
adventure race/John Balzar. — 1st ed.
p.   cm.
ISBN 0-8050-5949-0 (hb : alk. paper)
1. Yukon Quest International Sled Dog Race. 2. Sled dog racing—
Yukon River Valley (Yukon and Alaska). 3. Balzar, John.
4. Journalists—California—Biography. 5. Mushers—Alaska—
Biography. I. Title.
SF440.15.B35A3   2000   99-10313
798.8′3—dc21   CIP

Henry Holt books are available for special promotions and
premiums. For details contact: Director, Special Markets.

First Edition 2000

Designed by Michelle McMillian
Cartography by Jeffrey L. Ward

Printed in the United States of America

1   3   5   7   9   10   8   6   4   2

Maps

The Trail of the Yukon Quest International Sled Dog Race (endpaper)
The Toughest in the World: Between Whitehorse, Yukon Territory, and Fairbanks, Alaska. A hardy few will venture into a frozen landscape of hardship and adventure. Here, old myths live on and nourish the rawboned spirit of the Far North.

Whitehorse to Pelly Crossing (page 10)
The Song of the Wild: Unchanged since the great Klondike Gold Rush, the trail leads along the frozen Yukon River and then bashes its way overland, through winding spruce forests and across chains of lakes. Encounters with people occur only at two tiny Indian villages, a ramshackle roadhouse, and a wilderness homestead.

Pelly Crossing to Dawson (page 104)
The Cold and the Lonely: Through remotest North America, the Yukon Quest trail climbs into hills and windblown mountains, en route to the small but still rollicking Gold Rush settlement of Dawson City. A poke of gold nuggets awaits the first to arrive. For others, a brief respite and a warm fire.

Beyond the Frontier: Huge jumbles of ice impede the path as the Yukon Quest trail aims toward Alaska. The route then climbs into forbidding mountains and to the snowbound outpost of Eagle. The trail then leads onto the exposed and stormy meanders of the Yukon River.

The Cruelest Climb: Once you're past a couple of old mining settlements, the finish beckons. But first the trail ascends to its most perilous challenge— an icy-steep and wind-scoured mountain summit. Then down a mill race of hills and through vast forests of spindly trees onto the Chena River and the hardscrabble community of Fairbanks.

Overhead a jagged hole recedes across the man's field of vision. He feels himself tumbling, cartwheeling slowly, heels over head, his eyes straining against greenish shadows to keep sight of this vital opening. But it is beyond grasp now and growing smaller. There is pressure against his eardrums yet he hears nothing, not after the sudden crack and wet shock of the splash. Naturally the man can no longer breathe down here either.

He detects the frantic pawing of his harnessed team of sled dogs, bubbles streaming from their muzzles. Wild-eyed, they look at him for instructions. Their trust has always been unconditional. Now he has failed them. He led them out on the mighty river. The ice gave way underfoot, and the whole team plunged into the deep flowing water. The jagged, disappearing circle is their only return through the blanket of ice overhead. For all their fury as they paddle, they cannot surmount the power of the current. They are swept downstream. The hole vanishes like a smoke ring.

Just before he drowns in the frigid, murky swirls of the Yukon River,

Rusty Hagan snaps awake, eyes wide, heart thumping. It is 4 A.M. and he gasps uneasily in bed, again.

He rubs his scabby knuckles, relieved to hear the panting of his own breath. He feels the familiar smoothness of bedsheets and the warmth of his sleeping wife nearby. But he does not relax. The creases draw tight on his leathery outdoorsman's face. In a few days, Rusty Hagan, rookie dog musher, will finish packing. He will draw on the ponderous, protective clothing of the Far North and will harness his team of fourteen huskies. He will say good-bye to his wife and a flag will drop. Behind these dogs that he has trained and loved for so very long, he will venture onto the icy wilderness of his dreams—and his nightmares.

Characters

DAVE DALTON: Fairbanks cabdriver. Clean-cut, friendly, and wholly devoted to mushing competition and the Quest.

RUSTY HAGAN: A weather-beaten, aw-shucks rookie musher from North Pole, Alaska. An inventor, a craftsman, and as nice a guy as exists.

WAYNE HALL: A fur trapper and wilderness guide from Eagle, Alaska. Burned and scarred in a plane crash, he lives on the edge of civilization. He was my guide into the most remote country of the Quest trail.

JIMMY HENDRICK: Former Colorado River runner and the wildest character in mushing. As tough and exuberant as they come. Lives outside Denali National Park, Alaska.

MIKE KING: A hand-to-mouth musher from Salcha, Alaska. Looks like Charles Manson but has a heart that won't quit. Give him ten dollars and he'll offer to take you to lunch. Incredible tolerance for cold.

BRUCE LEE: Handsome, relentless, and methodical. Previously finished second in the Quest, then spent years rebuilding his dog team after losing his kennel to a bad batch of vaccine. Lives on a bluff looking into Denali National Park, Alaska.

JERRY LOUDEN: As quiet as the remote woods where he is happiest. A second-year Quest musher from Two Rivers, Alaska. Hard as nails.

BRENDA MACKEY: Baby-faced teenager, Quest rookie, and daughter of Rick Mackey.

RICK MACKEY: Has spent a good part of his life on a sled running dogs. Winner of both the Yukon Quest and the Iditarod, and the son of an Iditarod champion, Dick Mackey. Smokes two packs a day and raises dogs in Nenana, Alaska.

JOE MAY: Former champion of the Iditarod, now retired from long-distance mushing. A race judge for the Yukon Quest and one of the grand spokesmen for mushing traditions. Lives in Trapper Creek, Alaska.

TIM MOWRY: Back home in Fairbanks, he's a scruffy newsman. On the trail, he's an experienced and determined musher who never quits. Everywhere, he looks to make life interesting.

ANDRE NADEAU: The stranger hereabouts—an unknown mid-distance musher from Quebec. Built like a fireplug. Gruff. A superb dog trainer.

GARY NANCE: The finest winter bush pilot I know. Lives in Fairbanks—and lives life to the hilt.

MARK AND LORI RICHARDS: Homesteaders deep in the bush of Alaska's Yukon River valley. Their family is among the last on the continent to carry on the great myth of living beyond the frontier. Way-stop hosts for Quest mushers.

PADDY SANTUCCI: The stuff of which legends are made. A mountaineer, bush pilot, wilderness wanderer, fierce competitor, and engaging friend. Lives in the bush outside Fairbanks.

JOHN SCHANDELMEIER: The finest of many great woodsmen of the Far North. A Quest champion, pilot, trapper, and fisherman from Paxson, Alaska.

FRANK TURNER: The only man crazy enough to have run all fifteen Yukon Quest races. Holds the record for the quickest finish. A fine defender of mushing. Looks like he stepped out of the 1890s. Lives in Whitehorse, Yukon Territory.

DAN TURNER: Made it only halfway during his first Quest. A rangy, handsome tax assessor from Haines, Alaska, shooting to go all the way this time.

ALIY ZIRKLE: A broad-shouldered beauty with a dazzling smile. Also tough as flint. She threw the hammer in college track and field and calls the wilderness home. Now a musher from Two Rivers, Alaska, and a rookie in the Yukon Quest.

Yukon Alone

Prelude

One thousand and twenty-three miles is approximately the distance from Los Angeles to Seattle. From New York to Daytona Beach, from Chicago to Denver, from Rome to Copenhagen. And the distance from Whitehorse, in the Yukon Territory of northern Canada, to Fairbanks, in the heart of Alaska. There is no other comparison between these realms. One is the present, familiar, comfortable: geography dense with people and shaped by their industriousness. The other lingers from an earlier time, a forbidding domain of riverways, mountain passes, and spruce forests big as entire states—wildlands settled only here and there, and even then barely settled at all.

From Whitehorse to Fairbanks, across 1,023 miles of this wildness, lies the route of the Yukon Quest International Sled Dog Race.

Here, with the proper gear, with a heavy helping of fortitude and specialized outdoor survival skills, the intrepid penetrate a porcelain world, white and hard. It is winter in the subarctic, season of ice, storm, and darkness, a shadowland where most of the day is night, where vast arcs of the aurora borealis flame green and pink overhead, where the snow underfoot is so crystalline hard it rubs like sandpaper, and every incoming breath burns like fire because the sting of deep, dry cold feels much the same as flame.

Here the age-old myths of the frontier endure. A handful of homesteaders, villages, and mining camps struggle on the far periphery of the territorial boundary of Western civilization. The restless dream that drove untold generations of settlers into the remote now belongs to them alone.

The Yukon Quest is one of two great sled dog endurance contests in the world, the other being the Iditarod, which courses from Anchorage to Nome. Farther north and deeper inland, the Quest is a colder journey: terrible and exhilarating cold. Temperatures routinely plunge to 40 degrees below zero, and even worse must be anticipated in these parts at this time of year. The mountain passes are higher, the intervals between checkpoints greater, the loads in the sleds heavier, the isolation more profound, and help farther away, usually impossibly far away. Because it occurs first, in the long darkness of February—the Iditarod follows in the emerging springtime of March—the Quest is a nighttime odyssey, run during a stretch of 17½-hour nights—a frightful prospect to those unfamiliar with the vastness of the subarctic, the cold, and the loneliness. A finisher's patch from either race will gain you heaps of respect up here, in places where respect does not come casually. But to those who run it, the Quest is the more demanding challenge, and truer to the independent spirit of the Far North.

Fifteen years ago the Quest was devised in counterpoint to the Iditarod. Because of network television coverage and the resulting growth of big-money sponsors, the successful few among Iditarod sled dog racers were starting to become professionals, as in Occupation: Dog Driver. Before long, elite mushers were breeding kennels of one hundred dogs or more in search of animals with an edge in speed and stamina. Those who could not devote themselves full-time to racing fell hopelessly behind. The big names in dog mushing even began to look, incongruously, like professional Formula One racers, in bright-clean overalls covered with embroidered patches. They brought with them hired handlers who wore the same uniforms.

A handful of traditionalists searched for some way to celebrate mushing as it had been done for more than a century up here, where men and women wore scruffy, functional, duct-taped, thrift-store gear because no right-thinking dog driver would wear anything else. They would gather not just for a race but for a full-blooded winter wilderness camping trip, a rendezvous with adventure, a commemoration of mankind's ancient bond with working dogs, a private testimonial to the values of the Far North without high-pressure commercialism. Here would be a contest for fur trappers, schoolteachers, bulldozer drivers. The old trails of the Klondike Gold Rush would inspire the choice of the route. Dawson City, bawdy capital of the 1898 Klondike, would serve as the midpoint way stop in the race. Along the way, here and there, the trail would intersect one of the far outposts of humankind—a native village, an old mining camp, the roadless log cabin of the last of North America's homesteaders. One year, mushers would start in Fairbanks and travel east to Whitehorse in the Yukon; the next year, the direction of travel would be reversed.

In 1998, in keeping with one-hundredth-anniversary celebrations of the Gold Rush, the Yukon Quest was scheduled to begin at the corner of First Avenue and Main Street in Whitehorse at 1:00 P.M. on Sunday, February 8. Thirty-four men, four women, and 530 rugged dogs were to pass through the starting chute. According to the rules, no Quest could ever be called off because of the severity of the weather.

I have been tromping across, writing about, and playing in the Far North for a decade now. As a wandering journalist, I joined an Eskimo crew as camp cook and went whaling in the Beaufort Sea—a first for a nonnative Outsider. I wrote of encounters with grizzly bears and wolves, as well as with gold miners, commercial fishermen, oilmen, renegades, adventurers, and bush pilots. As a boatman for a wilderness guide, I paddled tourists down the rivers of the northernmost mountains on the continent, the Brooks Range. I led backpack and river trips elsewhere in the state—not, I must add, because I knew so much, but because I had been so profoundly touched and felt I must share it with my friends.

Wherever I went, no matter how deeply I penetrated the country and culture, people told me I could go farther—someday maybe all the way to the Yukon Quest. There was a dreamlike quality to these conversations, as if this dangerous odyssey was a private wellspring from which the people of the Far North drew some of their rugged self-image.

Finally I set out to see for myself. As happened, none of my experiences prepared me for the intensity of the encounter: people and their dogs pushing across some of the planet's loneliest and most dramatic territory in the full bite of subarctic winter.

I arrived in Fairbanks a year ago. I carried a satchel of empty notebooks and what cold-weather clothing I could pull from the boxes of camping gear in my garage. Then I got lucky. Luck arrived in the form of simple advice from George "Skip" Brink, a seasonal construction worker who volunteers as a logistics expediter for the Quest. Over a beer at one of many swinging-door saloons in this sagging, permafrost town, Alaska's second largest settlement, Brink told me to put down my notebook and roll up my sleeves.

"Before you start telling everyone what they can do to help you, why don't you ask what you can do for them?" he advised.

In this part of North America, everyone who is from somewhere else is known as an "Outsider" and every other place is "Outside." Newspapers in Alaska offer the courtesy of capitalizing Outside, but it only serves to highlight the collective sentiment: Outsiders are them, not us. As for me, never mind that I've traveled more extensively here and for longer than many of those who call Alaska and the Yukon home. I'm still an Outsider, because I haven't given a commitment to the Far North and the scramble it requires to survive and make a living here. With a portfolio as a roaming feature writer from one of the largest Outside newspapers, the *Los Angeles Times*, I could easily be regarded by locals as another in the endless line of condescending, glib con men who come north to see what they can grab for themselves or the interests they represent—gold, perhaps, or timber or oil, or just stories to amuse those Outside. Often, maybe even most of the time, residents endure these exploiters, welcome them, smile, and pat them on the back, because they bring with them the promise of shared wealth, a promise only sometimes fulfilled. But at the time I didn't understand something, and I wouldn't for a while yet: when it comes to their private pursuits, like the Quest, Alaskans and Yukoners aren't always so acquiescent. So it proved exactly right to approach them by asking, What can I do to help? Who could turn down a graying man from L.A. who was willing to scoop up dog shit at the prerace veterinary check?

That was my first year with the Quest. I spent several hundred dollars adding layers to my clothing inventory, I bought Arctic bunny boots that weighed fourteen pounds a pair, and I started filling up the notebooks. For the race, I ended up working as an unpaid "vet tech," an errand boy for the team of volunteer veterinarians that travels from start to finish. The position got me inside the race organization and provided me with the logistical wherewithal to travel to some of the most remote, roadless way stops along the trail. It also got me close to the mushers and their dogs.

That first night I ventured up the trail and into a world beyond imagination:

It is 1:00 A.M. and the thermometer shows 24 below zero in the subarctic wilderness. Overhead, furious northern lights snake across one thousand miles of sky, great translucent belts and shivers of neon green, tinged in pink—unearthly luminescence known only to those at extremes of latitude. And beyond, colossal stars glint in shades of ruby and topaz and diamond. Crystalline snow underfoot catches the colors: flickers on an empty, quiet, cold vast shadowland.

For purposes of celebrating the Far North, the night is sublime. Perfect. God given, oh glory.

Something moves.

From out of a grove of frozen spruce, distant dogs come dancing. Silently puffing their own little vapor trails, they materialize in a bobbing double line: black dogs and yellow and white and brown and spotted dogs, floppy-eared and stand-up-eared dogs, shaggy and sleek dogs. They shoulder forward at a lope, not driven by the ponderously clothed human riding the sled behind them so much as driven from within. This is what they were born to do, what they plead to do, this is all they do and what they sometimes die doing. . . .

Photos of dog mushing often show throngs of people at checkpoints

and finish lines bathed in bright lights. But these are illusory. Almost all
the pursuit occurs alone, musher and dogs, in the darkness of 17½-hour
nights, traversing buckled ice crusts of rivers, through valleys of spindly
trees, over windblown summits. Faces caked in ice, they find companions
in wild nature and, for the mushers anyway, the perpetual twirl of
despair and euphoria in the mind. And the shhhhhhhish of the sled over
snow, and sometimes the howl of a wolf and the other strange voices that
speak to the exhausted. And always the cold . . ."

Somewhat to my astonishment, I realized that mushers and the larger oddball winter culture of the Far North had the power to fascinate—
and inspire. The terrain and nostalgic ways of life in the subarctic were
sources of mystique and, curiously, of hope. Boredom is the precursor
to despair, and I am not alone in believing that a chief source of boredom in our civilized, acquisitive, urban-crowded modern culture is the
absence of unknown places and peoples to inflame our imaginations.
In earlier times, the cartographer quaintly labeled unexplored spaces
on the map with the words *There Be Dragons*. No such terrain is left for
us now. It used to be that we described cultures we did not know with
words like *primitive* or *savage*. Now we call them "potential markets,"
as in customers for our consumer goods. We are comfortable knowing
that whatever their tribe, music, gods, heritage, or beliefs, they share
brand recognition for Coca-Cola and Marlboro. It was reassuring for
me to discover women and men who sloughed off the get-ahead mate-
rialism of our age, who lived in small cabins without running water or
electricity and spent every dime they earned on dog food, all for the
opportunity to journey into the dark and wild to enjoy the graceful
company of dogs, camp out, and explore a frozen landscape that
almost everyone else in the world regards as inhospitable.

As for the geography of our planet, what we haven't seen personally in this age of tourism has been brought into our homes by the
unblinking glass eye of television. Without my intending so, the Quest
put me in one of the few places in the world unspoiled and barely
explored by either tourism or television. Certainly in North America
there is nothing like it. For casual visitors, the winter climate is simply

too harsh. The clothing and gear you need to survive outdoors at these temperatures can easily cost $1,500, if by chance you know where to find them. The logistics of transportation, whether dog team or snow-machine or bush plane, are dangerous and more expensive still. Adherence to anything resembling a schedule is often a matter of luck, owing to the extremes of weather. Accommodations are nonexistent or so rough as to make Nepal or Central Africa seem comfortably appointed. So tourists tend to avoid the place in winter. TV cameras too: the light is lousy. And when you can see, vistas are perpetual black and white. Long-distance mushing, even at full throttle, occurs at the break-neck speed of barely ten miles an hour, usually less, which conveys hardly any drama through the camera. Dog teams are cumbersome things, and the personalities of the animals are slow to reveal themselves. The mushers themselves are so bulky in their clothes, you cannot tell men from women, let alone who is who. The essential loneliness, the quiet and cold, the grandiose spaces and subtle movements of the epic journeys by dog team, the meditative devotion of dog to human and human to nature simply cannot be conveyed in the narrow field of vision of that hot, noisy screen. Well, hallelujah.

I had to return.

That first trip, I spent only a few weeks here. Now I would devote months to the Quest. A whole winter, more than half a year, as it turned out. The country would change my view of adventure, the people would change my life.

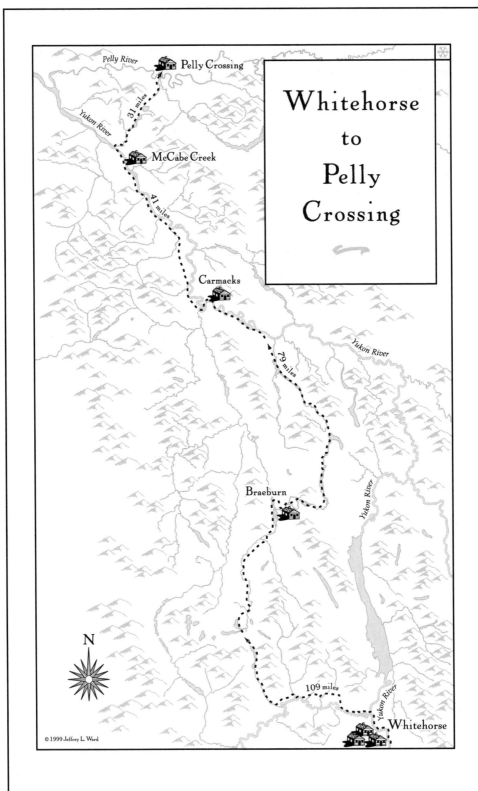

Pelly River

Pelly Crossing

31 miles

Yukon River

McCabe Creek

41 miles

Whitehorse
to
Pelly
Crossing

Carmacks

79 miles

Yukon River

Braeburn

Yukon River

N

109 miles

Yukon River

Whitehorse

© 1999 Jeffrey L. Ward

Detail of Trail from Whitehorse
to Pelly Crossing

1. Tim Mowry, *Two Rivers, Alaska*
2. Kurt Smith, *North Pole, Alaska*
3. Rick Mackey, *Nenana, Alaska*
4. Terry McMullin, *Eagle, Alaska**
5. John Nash, *Nenana, Alaska**
6. Dave Olesen, *Hoarfrost River, Northwest Territories**
7. Larry Carroll, *Willow, Alaska*
8. Aliy Zirkle, *Two Rivers, Alaska**
9. Frank Turner, *Whitehorse, Yukon*
10. Brian O'Donoghue, *Two Rivers, Alaska**
11. John Schandelmeier, *Paxson, Alaska*
12. Bruce Lee, *Denali National Park, Alaska*
13. Thomas Tetz, *Tagish, Yukon**
14. Rusty Hagan, *North Pole, Alaska**
15. Keith Kirkvold, *Fairbanks, Alaska**
16. Dave Dalton, *Fairbanks, Alaska*
17. Brian MacDougall, *Whitehorse, Yukon*
18. William Kleedehn, *Carcross, Yukon*
19. Cor Guimond, *Dawson City, Yukon*
20. Gwen Holdman, *Fox, Alaska**
21. Amy Wright, *Tok, Alaska**
22. Jerry Louden, *Two Rivers, Alaska*
23. Dan Turner, *Haines, Alaska*
24. Mike King, *Salcha, Alaska*
25. Doug Harris, *Whitehorse, Yukon*
26. Jimmy Hendrick, *Denali National Park, Alaska*
27. Paddy Santucci, *Fairbanks, Alaska*
28. Brenda Mackey, *Nenana, Alaska**
29. Tony Blanford, *Two Rivers, Alaska**
30. Walter Palkovitch, *Two Rivers, Alaska**
31. Ned Cathers, *Whitehorse, Yukon*
32. Louis Nelson, *Kotzebue, Alaska**
33. Bill Steyer, *Fairbanks, Alaska**
34. Keizo Funatsu, *Two Rivers, Alaska*
35. Andre Nadeau, *Sainte-Melanie, Quebec**
36. Dieter Dolif, *Trebel, Germany*
37. Stan Njootli, *Old Crow, Yukon**
38. Michael Hyslop, *Grizzly Valley, Yukon**

* rookie

1

"Mush-on" . . . is the dog-drivers' rendering of the French-Canadian driver's command of "marche on"—to go—hence, also the Alaskan verb "to mush," meaning to travel, in dog driving.

—James Wickersham, Old Yukon, 1938

Yukon Territory, Canada: latitude 61 degrees north—so far north that only a tiny skullcap of the planet exists above us. It is February and dark. The temperature has not risen above freezing in four months.

Dog mushers and their extended families—spouses, children, dog handlers, and dogs—now converge on the capital of the Yukon Territory. Crammed into wrinkled, coughing pickups, each with an electric cord from an oil-pan heater dangling out of the grille and each carrying a miniature plywood apartment building on the pickup bed, called a dog "box," with spaces for perhaps sixteen to twenty dogs, these teams crunch their way over the ice-covered roadways of Alaska and northern Canada. Destination: Whitehorse.

For observers, things are about to start in the world of long-distance dog mushing. For participants in the Yukon Quest, this is the culmination. All those hours, all that training, all this money. How much? So much there is nothing else.

Even by motor vehicle, travel is eerily lonely this time of year. There are only seven all-year highways in all of this part of North America, and they penetrate only a fraction of the gross topography. In summer, true enough, the Alaska-Canada Highway and its tributaries are the scene of great migrations of steel and pressed aluminum, the vacation herds. In winter you drive these same roadways for ten hours and arrive in the little truck stop village of Tok, Alaska, where the bartender asks, "See any cars out there?" Matter of fact saw four, plus one wolf and twenty-five moose. "Oh? What color wolf?" he asks.

Myself, I'm taking the easy way to the starting line. Already this year, I've covered the distance back and forth six times by car and bush plane, and during summer by canoe. Now I'm riding a charter bus with some Quest officials, a few reporters, and the veterinarians. It's a dark, fourteen-hour road trip, Fairbanks to Whitehorse, with three bottles of champagne, a tin of caviar, and a slab of smoked salmon in my satchel. Windows frost up inside the bus, the road is bouncy, the seats hard, the scene inside raucous. Among those on the bus is Stephane Deruaz, a thirty-eight-year-old veterinarian from the Jura Mountains of France. June Ryan, a specialist in the U.S. Army and a volunteer vet tech, is teaching Stephane to swear like a soldier in English. He looks proud of himself as he blurts out obscenities, the meaning of which he does not comprehend. The worse they get, the more June beams her approval, the harder we laugh, the prouder Stephane appears—like a third-grader spelling words without knowing their meaning. We're all acting like third-graders. The champagne bottle takes another round. And another. Nervous anticipation is one of the glories of any worthwhile journey.

We stop for coffee at a roadhouse just across the Canadian border, and we're yanked back to reality. The instant we step off the bus an icy wind bites any exposed flesh. There is no exhilarating brace to cold like this, just a flash burn. My thoughts go quickly to the realization that we will be without heated shelter soon. The giddy light-headed feeling of expectation collides with sober foreboding about the wilderness we're soon to enter. A sign says the temperature once fell to 83 below at this roadhouse.

In the end, all of us bus riders will be tired, stiff, and hungover on arrival, de rigueur it seems. What fun would it be to begin this thing in tip-top shape, anyway? Bring on the agonies.

The Quest is the toughest race in the world, according to its slogan. Few would dispute this claim, although from time to time nervous organizers worry among themselves whether to tone down their language for fear of scaring people off. But in this era of easy hype, if you can honestly make an unqualified statement like "the toughest in the world," could you possibly resist? Surely, any musher who ever completed the thousand-mile epic wouldn't relinquish the title. Are you kidding? The toughest race in the world! Just getting to the finish line without succumbing to fatigue, frostbite, or self-doubt; completing the trek without getting whipped by your own mistakes or knocked down by bad luck or being kicked in the teeth by nature; advancing around the clock for two weeks against extremes of weather and terrain without fouling that rare bond of trust you have cultivated with your animals—that's the essential goal of most who attempt the Quest. When you sign up for the journey, you flaunt your daring. You proclaim your own physical toughness and mental durability, you assert mastery of bush craft. But mushing is unique: you also must acknowledge reciprocal dependence between yourself and these dogs for survival down the lonely storm-swept trail. Neither of you will make it alone.

Along with the mushers, a traveling road show of volunteer race officials will be hopscotching from checkpoint to checkpoint, spreading out down the length of the trail: a race marshal, three judges, eleven veterinarians, an assortment of vet techs, a timer, a handful of logistics facilitators, and me—all of us sharing the ordeal of perpetual motion, cold, the sleepless thousand-yard stare, the rank smell of the trail, the stomach adrift from too much coffee and boiled moose meat. I know people who, thirty years later, can recall with clarity the agony of pulling all-nighters in college. The Quest will provide serious postgraduate work on the subject.

My happy-go-lucky plan to enlist once again as a vet assistant and shovel the dog yards, stick thermometers up dog butts, and otherwise try to make myself marginally useful has been dashed. I've been demoted. Down to the bottom of the volunteer ladder. I am now the Yukon Quest press liaison. The flack. Mouthpiece. Enforcer. My primary responsibility will be to manage the large contingent of reporters and photographers arriving from Germany, all expenses paid by a new race sponsor, the Frankfurt tire company Fulda. The press corps will now number more than fifty, when it used to be just a half dozen or so locals. All the old-timers up here are worried silly about the impact of this kind of press on the traditions of the race. They look to me for answers. I tell them I'm worried silly too.

Remember, don't ask what they can do for you but what you can do for them. . . .

Fateful advice.

I am issued a huge overparka, bright yellow—the color of a daffodil, the size of a grain elevator. This, so people can spot me easily. They can. They chortle and call me Big Bird to my face. God knows what they call me behind my back.

"I'm getting ready to get nervous now," says Aliy Zirkle, a brawny, handsome twenty-eight-year-old former college track-and-field hammer thrower and a sometime wilderness biologist. She is one of four women running the Quest this year, all rookies. Aliy lives and trains in the outskirts of Fairbanks, in the mushing community of Two Rivers— the densest concentration of mushers, sled dogs, winter trails, and expertise in the world. She is known for her oversize smile and for her swagger, the kind that strong, sexy women develop after a few years in the bush, where they are outnumbered ten to one by men who forgot what their mothers taught them about manners or combing their hair before dinner.

Parked in downtown Whitehorse amid a lineup of other pickups, Aliy is pulling restless, squirming dogs out of her dog box, hugging and encouraging them one by one, chaining them to the one-ton flatbed truck she shares with another Two Rivers musher, Jerry Louden, a shy but accomplished woodsman who, when not driving dogs, wheels a road grader and snowplow for the Alaska Department of Transportation. Aliy is striking and chatty, Jerry lumbering and mutely reserved. Between them is an age difference of eighteen years, a shared devotion to the remote outdoors, and a jointly managed kennel. When they travel together, salacious gossip is whispered behind them. I don't ask; I am fond of them both. And right now, they are facing serious matters, not gossip: which dogs to take and which to leave behind? Aliy and Jerry have spent months training and conditioning dogs. They have traveled more than one thousand miles behind their teams since summer. But only at this last moment are they making the final decisions about the last two dogs in the kennel: which of them goes in whose team? It is morning on race day.

Race day. The sun peekaboos through rolling hilltop clouds; temperature: zero. Everyone bundles up as if it's colder because of a cheek-reddening wind out of the north. Yukoners still calibrate and discuss that combination of temperature and breeze called windchill, as do Americans in the Lower 48. By that measure, it's something like 25 below. The local radio describes conditions as "potentially dangerous." As a rule, Alaskans do not calculate windchill, feeling no need to over-dramatize matters. If there is a breeze, zip up your parka. Meanwhile, clouds trundle low and leaden across half the sky, but distant hills up the trail are lit bright with the canted rays of a sun that never reaches high above the horizon. It seems almost inviting out there.

Am I losing my mind to say such a thing?

In a few days, I will break free from the crew of officials and mush a dog team myself along some of the loneliest miles of the Quest trail. We'll see how inviting it is. Perhaps the fascination I feel for the sun-licked hills in the distance is the same the rabbit has for headlights. Whatever it is, I cannot explain it.

In town, sawhorses and survey tape block off several streets of central Whitehorse. A population of twenty-two thousand lives in this orderly, functional clapboard community on the left bank of the Yukon—70 percent of the residents of the entire territory. The next biggest "town" up here is rollicking Dawson City, with less than one-tenth as many people. The Quest is just about the biggest winter event to hit either, and today hundreds of Yukoners in heavy boots and pillowy parkas come to watch mushers stage their dogs and finish packing their sled bags. There is knowing fascination in the eyes of these onlookers. The townsfolk understand what lies in the wild out there, what a person requires by way of skill and luck to survive in the vastness beyond the city limits.

Not only are there ten more teams than last year, but the field of thirty-eight is the strongest in recent memory, with fifteen mushers likely to vie for the top ten. Any of a half dozen are thought worthy of a victory. The purse is $30,000 for the first to reach Fairbanks. Prize money ranges downward to $1,500 for the fifteenth finisher. I'm only partly interested in the Quest as competition, however. That's a sentiment shared by most of the people I've met—including many mushers themselves. If it costs $20,000 to prepare for the journey, and that counts only the direct expense of dog food, equipment, and the like and does not include losses that a musher sustains for forgoing a real year-round, income-producing career, and furthermore, if only the first- and second-place finishers win more than $20,000 in prize money—well then, surely there is more to long-distance dog driving than paying the bills. I suspect the right word is *adventure*. Although, as any musher will tell you, a winter wilderness endeavor like this, intense and complicated, is not easily summed up in a single word, even an elegant one like *adventure*.

"My goal? Really, I just want to see if I can do it. I think it's going to be damn, flipping hard. I want to see," says Aliy. "Sometimes I think it will be fun, but the truth is, I don't have any idea."

As a youngster, she made up stories about herself. Wild stories. It became habit. Then one day she was grown and she was on an airplane and someone asked where she had come from, where she lived, and what she did. She told the truth. It made her smile: Aliy's real life was a stranger story by far than those she once invented for herself.

Her German-American father had run a shoe factory. When Aliy was young the family moved from New Hampshire to Puerto Rico, following the migration of the footwear industry from New England to the Caribbean. Next came high school in St. Louis. "A mess, suburbia after hippieville and surfdom," she recalls. Later, she pursued a biology degree at the University of Pennsylvania. Halfway through, she interrupted her studies. She saw a magazine ad seeking help for a bird survey in King Salmon, Alaska, a coastal fishing town. Pay was three dollars a day. She stayed six months. Then she signed on for another bird survey, in Australia. Back to Penn: biology, track and field, summers working construction, weekends as a waitress. After graduation, she hiked the Appalachian Trail.

Alaska, as sometimes happens, gripped her hardest and wouldn't let go. In 1992 she moved to Bettles, population 45, an Interior Alaskan village north of the Arctic Circle. No road reaches Bettles. She was a summer seasonal biologist for the U.S. Fish and Wildlife Service at the huge but little known Kanuti Wildlife Refuge, a vast breeding ground for North American waterfowl. She stayed on for winter. Her first sled dog was a present from a villager. He was an old trapline leader called Skunk. She took him for a walk and decided to let him run free. That proved a mistake. For ten days, the loose dog tormented Bettles and ruined Christmas for the villagers, raiding the local stockpile of holiday ham and turkey.

Aliy spent days setting live traps, which the dog outsmarted one by one. She paid out hundreds of dollars in damages. Finally, Skunk found a trap he couldn't fool.

"When I saw him in there I walked up and I said, 'Okay, if you growl at me I'm going to have to shoot you.'" Aliy recalls, "But he wagged his tail. So I had to keep him. He's in my dog yard now, he's my pet."

By chance the region around Bettles, lowlands south of the Brooks Range, is some of the best and most historic dog country in the Far North. Old-time breeders insist that almost every good dog carries blood from just a few native villages scattered along three hundred miles of the Koyukuk River downstream from Bettles: Allakaket, Hughes, Huslia, and Koyukuk itself. Naturally, as Aliy traveled the region and expressed interest in dogs, she picked up other people's rejects and some pups. She rescued a few more when the river flooded and villagers fled in panic, leaving dogs behind. Their owners let Aliy keep what she wanted from those she saved.

She did her duties for the government, then took time off to run her team, explore, trap, and camp out in the vast emptiness of the Alaska

Interior. As she tells it, she learned the subtleties of mushing from an old lead dog that was also given to her, a dog now dead.

One spring night, she mushed into the Brooks Range, the northern-most mountains in America. She looked up and the sky served a daz-zling delight for her. Night after night, the sky blazed. She returned and saw *Time* magazine, with a cover story about Comet Hale-Bopp. How surprising. The whole world was fascinated by something she figured only she had paid any attention to. She had been so far removed as to believe in the uniqueness of her encounter with the heavens, impossi-bly far from what others know as "reality," and the thought filled her with pleasure. Out here it is still possible to have experiences unscript-ed by science and the media. Once in a while, it is even possible to reawaken ancient feelings that one might actually discover something, a sensation that sustained the curious mind through millions of years of evolutionary history.

"I can't explain why I like it out there other than it's challenging," Aliy says. "It's about freedom, where you can grasp at life a little more. You want a hamburger? Go shoot a moose, don't go to Safeway. That's a cop-out."

She's not posing, either. I've been in her tiny cabin, where three wolf pelts dangle from a nail on the wall. One afternoon, she sorts through them. Which will it be for the fur ruff on the hood of her new mushing parka: silver, black, or brindle? She chooses the silver because the fur is especially plush. She cuts the skin and sews it to her coat by hand. Despite the marvels of modern fabric and gear, the guard hairs of cer-tain northern furbearers—wolf and wolverine prime among them—are the most reliable cold-weather protection known for exposed skin around the eyes. The guard hairs shield against incoming wind and resist freezing into a blob from moist, outgoing breath. What is unspeakable Outside is lifesaving here.

Aliy looks like this: thick flaxen hair to her shoulders, dimples, and big, shiny matched teeth behind a contagious smile. She has a girl's small nose and a roustabout's square jaw. She owns two skirts and one dress. She is six feet tall with broad shoulders and doesn't feel the need for high heels. Most people wouldn't recognize her dressed like that anyway. Her hands are like Vise-Grips. When she speaks of others the quality she judges first is not success but toughness. Ten days before the Quest she brings her dogs to a veterinarian for a required prerace inspection. Two dogs erupt in a fight, and as she yanks them apart, I see she is nipped on the hand. I ask, How bad is the wound? She glowers and stuffs her bleeding hand into her 38-inch-waist jeans.

"Let's see, what else is there?" she laughs. "Cookies? I made some cookies once. Did I mention the cookie part?"

Two years ago she moved from the bush in Bettles to the woodsy Fairbanks suburb of Two Rivers. Well, it is a suburb in concept anyway. Two Rivers is a collection of cabins on dirt roads in the hills north of town, an area where trail dogs probably outnumber people five or ten to one. The want ads in the local newspaper, the *Fairbanks Daily News–Miner*, have a special category, No. 102 Dog Mushing. At the local convenience store, Skip's Cache, I stopped for a six-pack once and the cashier gave me the current road conditions: caution, the last motorist through reported a cow moose grazing on the shoulder about a mile ahead.

Here Aliy established Northwind kennels with Louden. Last year, as an unknown rookie in the Quest, Louden impressed everyone with his sixth-place finish. This year, with thirty-eight dogs in their yard, both Jerry and Aliy have entered. To bring in money, Aliy went back to waitressing and working part-time construction. In her spare time she went beaver trapping to stock some high-fat trail meat for dog snacks. She also dissected the carcass of a beef calf that had been a local teenager's 4-H project. In exchange for her report on the cause of death ("I am a biologist, you know") Aliy kept the meat for dog food. Her family thinks her life is terrific; her dad sent her a 40-below sleeping bag for the race and her grandparents paid her $800 entry fee.

Do you know where your daughter is tonight? Yes, out among the wolves and the stars at 20 below, with the sky dancing smoky green: the otherworldly light show of the aurora borealis. Athabascans say the aurora lights the trail to heaven. Why not? What better home for God than up in those shivering firmaments of pure energy? This father's daughter is at the doorstep of a cathedral that few can even imagine. Where is yours?

*   *   *

Because snow never melts in the perpetual freeze of a Yukon winter, it cannot be merely plowed off streets. Soon all the buildings in Whitehorse would be buried in snow berms. So snow must be scooped up and trucked away after each storm. Except this weekend, when the work crews of Whitehorse labor all Saturday night hauling tons of it back into town, enough to cover the streets along a dozen blocks with a foot of squeaky hardpack. The intersection of Main Street and First Avenue, in front of the train depot, serves as the starting line. The Quest route follows First Avenue north for a third of a mile, and then drops onto the jumble ice of the Yukon River.

The great river hugs Whitehorse as a mother would hold a child, tucked in the curl of her arm. At street level, the town seems an ordinary enough place: a small winter community with a short string of traffic lights, a shopping district, bank, general store, one-hour photo finishers, fudge "shoppe," parking enforcement. Fifteen feet down the bank of the Yukon, however, the raw chaos of blue-white ice stands as forbidding and as untamed as it has been since the time of mastodons. From here the unbroken Yukon runs north, then west into the wildest part of the continent. I walk down the riverbank from the center of town to take a close-up look at the Yukon's frozen surface. Not a single footprint breaks the crust of snow; nobody has ventured here. My senses are cast loose not so much by how different the world looks only a stone's arc from "civilization," but how different it feels. Here be dragons.

By 10:00 A.M. the first dog truck lumbers into the staging area on the river's edge. Then others. They disgorge their wriggling, howling loads. Spectators wander down, sipping hot mugs of coffee, children in tow, everyone heavy-footed in winter regalia, faces turned from the wind. By noon, the scene will be a melee: each team lining out pairs of overexcited dogs, sleds at the end of ganglines, the Cordura sled bags stuffed with some three hundred pounds of specialized gear and assorted bags of dog food. At the last minute, heaps of supplies are still being sorted and packed, then unpacked to answer the recurrent question: Where did I put . . . ?

Dogs are howling, now stirred into a pack frenzy by the call of the impending hunt. A flush of positive ions lifts mushers, too. No more preparations or abstract worries. To those who know the sensation, there is nothing that tops this marvelous surrender to fatalism. It is the same thrill sky divers enjoy as they take the first step out of the airplane, the same one rafters feel after scouting a big rapid and then pushing out onto the slick-water tongue that leads into the maelstrom. No turning back.

For no reason other than contagious excitement, I'm hurrying through the staging area, walking in circles.

Here's Rusty Hagan. I'm happy to see his rough-toothed grin. Last time we talked, he wasn't smiling. He confided that he was having nightmares about breaking through the ice of the Yukon River with his dog team. He could not shake the horrifying vision of looking up and seeing the hole through which he and the dogs had plunged to their impending deaths. "I just don't know what to make of it," he said.

But now he's looking better. He drops an armload of dog harnesses to come say hello. Rusty and his wife, Lenora, are the chattiest couple in mushing. Each believes the other wastes too much time at it. Usually, it's amusing to watch them. Today I can hardly bear the interruptions I cause by just walking near. Thankfully, he mentions nothing about the recurring phantasms of his own drowning.

Rusty is a deeply weathered, mussed-hair man of forty-six, the son of a recluse. Back home, in the oddly named community of North Pole, Alaska, a satellite of Fairbanks, Rusty showed me a sepia photograph of an even more rugged-looking man on the back of a burro. The man had a spade beard to his waist, ancient boots, and a dusty Western hat. The picture was taken last year: Dad prospecting in Central America.

The Hagan family grew up in the mountains east of Los Angeles in a cabin five miles from the nearest dirt road. Rusty is the only person I know to go from a rustic log cabin to a suburban stucco home by moving from Southern California to the interior of Alaska. In between, he was a New Mexico logger. Now a backyard inventor, he designs and builds, among other things, training carousels for dogs.

These iron merry-go-rounds, thirty-seven feet in diameter, have eight spokes, with a doghouse fixed on the end of each one. In his back yard, there are three demonstration carousels. Rusty releases a hydraulic brake from his garage. There is a mechanical groan and a hiss that brings the dogs leaping out of their houses. They are affixed by neck chains to the spokes of the carousel. At first, there is a bit of confusion on the ground as some dogs aim clockwise and others pull opposite. Then they reach consensus on which way they want to run this time. Seven pull, and one straggler rides in his house. The other carousels come similarly to life. Forty-seven revolutions equals one mile. Rusty looks at his clipboard and reports that in the last six months, in preparation for the Quest, his dogs have logged 1,657 miles, or 77,879 revolutions . . . 77,880 . . . 81 . . . 82. That is supposed to keep them conditioned—once they get over dizziness, which doesn't take too long, Rusty says. For trail training, he has run the most promising of his dogs another 570 miles pulling a sled.

"I like my dog yard," he says, smiling abstractedly. "I like just watchin' 'em."

Locally, this kind of remark and the true believer's look in Rusty's eye is diagnosed as dog fever, a long-term affliction that both attacks one's wallet and good sense and compels a person to dress, day and night, in huge, white-rubber, military-surplus arctic bunny boots, scuffed and patched with duct tape, and ratty, threadbare brown canvas Carhartt overalls. These, it seems, are not clothes of necessity but a uniform of distinction among those infected with the fever. This explains why it's not a universal compliment to remark about someone: looks like a dog musher.

Like many mushers, Rusty allows one dog at a time to come into his house—"the dog of the day." It is a practical way to maintain a personal connection to his animals, like pet owners do, and not be overrun by dogs.

Rusty, his wife, and their two kids arrived in Alaska in the bitter winter of 1989. He was jobless and it was 60 below, hunkering-down weather. He took work blowing snow off the roofs of buildings. Soon, he got his first ride in a dog sled. Before the end of winter, he had five dogs. The Yukon Quest is the culmination of all the years since. Mushing has become his career—breeding dogs, training them, training himself. He wants to prove the value of his carousels, and of the other mushing equipment he makes in his garage. He has no intention of racing out there. Just finishing. And conquering the demons of his nightmares. He must finish. Anything less would reflect badly on his own view of himself and his vocation.

"I'll make a lot of mistakes," he concedes. "I always do."

I feel a cold shiver. Mistakes in this wilderness are dangerous, sometimes deadly so. But it was the Scottish poet and adventurer Alexander Smith who made sense of such endeavors as this. "Everything," he said, "is sweetened by risk."

For contrast, I walk over to where Paddy Santucci is methodically preparing his outfit. Unlike Rusty, Paddy does not break his concentration and offers only a nod. During his rigorous training, he was as generous as anyone with his time and knowledge and we spent memorable days together in the frigid bush. But Paddy is always all business. He is here not just to finish but to compete with the front-runners.

"If you come to a race, bring a race team," he says over and over, by way of a mantra.

I met Paddy a year earlier. He was not mushing but traveling checkpoint to checkpoint along the Quest trail as dog handler for another musher. Paddy had a fierce joy about him. He never took off his greasy tent-sized anorak parka, he never slept, I never saw him eat; he moved among the dogs with command, and people were drawn to him, but he always seemed apart. He had a bulge of tobacco under his lip and rarely smiled, but when he did he lit up a room. He seemed to embody the character of the Far North: thirty-seven years old, an accomplished mountaineer with one heroic rescue to his credit on Denali (a.k.a. Mount McKinley), a hunter, a bush pilot, a construction worker, a dog driver. He doesn't readily mention that he has a degree in physics from the University of California at Davis. His wife, Gina, is a nurse. For fun she goes to Hawaii and hunts wild boars with dogs and knives. Paddy is smallish but stringy hard, with sharp features, a predator's eyes, and shoulder-length hair. He is clean-shaven now because his beard once froze solid and scarred his face with frostbite. He speaks seldom and never, it seems, just to hear the sound of his own gravelly voice.

Now he strings out his gangline and hooks it to the new sled that a friend made for him of steam-bent hardwood, the joints lashed together with sinew to provide flex over rough ice. After months of training, he knows his equipment and supplies as well as he knows the contours of his own face. But he packs with slow, obsessive caution: the bags of food, the sheet-metal alcohol cooker, fuel for the cooker, medicine and balms for the dogs, food pans, ax, snowshoes, matches, maps, batteries and bulbs for his headlamp, dry clothes. . . .

The clock approaches 1:00 P.M. On the hour, the first musher will come catapulting from the starting chute, passing under a wooden arch neatly displaying logos and banners from sponsors. Teams will follow every two minutes until 2:14 P.M., when the last musher will careen out of town just as the evening sun begins to drop in the frigid sky. Already, the echo of an announcer's voice vibrates down the street. Radio carries the sounds live throughout the Yukon and in Fairbanks. The foreign press, in look-alike parkas of bright red, swarm the scene and transform the Quest into a daily news story in Europe.

Regrettably, what most of the Outside world has come to know about the start of a dog race is conducted by the Iditarod. For the benefit of TV cameras and local businesses, that race "starts" each March in downtown Anchorage. But this is ceremonial only, and lacks the crackling energy of authenticity. Mistakes don't count. The teams merely lope along on parade with guest passengers riding in the sled bags, then stop and are loaded back on trucks. The mushers drive north up the highway to the small community of Wasilla or to Willow, or wherever the snow and ice are deemed adequate, and prepare for the actual start the following day.

In Whitehorse there is no such ceremony. This is the real thing. Spectators were directed out of the staging area an hour ago. Hysteria is rising in the dogs. Seldom do creatures from the bush see anything like the hundreds of other dogs and people surrounding them now. Howls and screams ascend in waves. The solid feel of the harness straps over their shoulders has them leaping against the anchored gang-line. Sleds rattle and slam, ropes crack. Dogs screech and grunt. They claw the empty air in front of them with paws clad in "booties" of fleece or nylon, which will protect their pads against the abrasion of crystalline snow.

Humans learn with experience, or should anyway, to anthropomor-phize dogs cautiously. But what is spreading through these teams seems an unmistakable contagion: a lust to run. Nobody tries to impose calm. This pure animal desire is an attribute to be cherished and culti-vated. "Easy boy" is not in the vocabulary.

Quest rules permit up to fourteen dogs to a team, and most mushers harness all they are allowed. More dogs, generally speaking, mean more power, but also more work for the musher in their care and feed-ing, and more dog food to carry.

The ideal, always impossible, is to match dogs of equal speed and endurance, all with mellow temperament and zeal for the trail, dogs with leathery feet and unfailing appetites, dogs with the savvy to know that rest stops are for resting not goofing around, dogs that don't fight and don't have to be neutered, so they can command breeding fees later.

As important as these qualities is the intangible called "head," which is really a combination of guts and drive: the fortitude to run twelve or fourteen hours of every twenty-four for two consecutive weeks, the grit to pull up mountain passes when the eyes cannot penetrate into the swirling blizzard of snow and the ears hear nothing but the shriek of the wind. Great dogs, those with "head," can be counted on in the worst of conditions to inspire the entire team, including, foremost, the musher.

No matter what the individual qualities of the dogs, transforming them into a working dog team demands a natural hand and skills that take years to accumulate. Some people apprentice for months before they even realize how much there is to understand. Establishing abso-lute trust between animal species, sharing leadership man-to-dog and dog-to-man for the purpose of mutual survival, is no longer common in developed societies.

A few mushers come to the start with thirteen or maybe only twelve dogs, preferring to begin the journey without laggards even at the expense of power. Others will bet the odds that a weaker dog will get stronger. Or a musher may yield to sentimentality and bring a questionable dog, a young one, a favorite, knowing that if the animal falters it can be "dropped" at any of seven checkpoints or at six other designated points on the trail. These dogs remain in the care of race veterinarians until they can be returned to the musher or dog handler. There is no penalty for leaving a dog behind, but no fresh animals can be added to the team. Rules require that a musher have at least six dogs in harness to finish the race. To keep track of all these dogs, the Quest relies on technology. All the animals are "chipped," or injected under the skin with a microchip the size of a fat grain of rice, so they can be scanned with a handheld meter and electronically identified.

The launch of a fresh dog team is boisterous, savage, furious, always on the edge of control—sometimes this side of the edge, sometimes the other.

Tim Mowry is first into the chute, having drawn the No. 1 starting position at the prerace banquet. Nine volunteers, heels digging into the snow, huffing and puffing, work to hold back his lunging dogs.

A farm boy from Vermont and New York, the thirty-four-year-old Mowry is a minority among serious mushers. That is, he has a full-time job, as outdoor editor for the *Fairbanks Daily News–Miner*. So consuming is dog mushing that salary work with regular hours is a distinct disadvantage, depriving one of training time. Nonetheless, Mowry is a game competitor, having run two Iditarods and six previous Yukon Quests. Long-distance mushing now provides him with the same absorbing escape that, say, passionate golf or fly-fishing does for others, and he approaches the trail exuberantly.

"Mushing is a lot like dairy farming. You have the same routines every day. There are animals you have to care for. They have names. It's a team and you're the coach," he says, with the deadpan of someone who has kept dozens of dogs kenneled in his front yard for so many years it now seems everyday normal to buy dog food by the container load.

Mowry is hoping for that right combination of dogs and trail experience to move his team into the front ranks of contenders. So far his best finish has been sixth. Right now he brings his dogs to the chute, stops, and lumbers forward sixty feet to the front of his team. A final word of encouragement to his dogs is part of the starting ritual. He walks back down the double line, roughing the fur of each dog and saying a few words. Amid the many distractions of people and rival teams, he is trying to bring his dogs back into focus. Individually, they stop surging and screaming in his presence. Their eyes leave the trail ahead only to meet Mowry's. From the announcer: *Thirty seconds.* As Mowry moves through the team, the dogs resume their howling and lunging. Volunteers hang on with everything they've got to keep Mowry and his outfit in position. *Ten seconds.* The screaming pitch of the dogs has the crowd's attention.

Mowry steps back to his sled, puts one foot on a runner, and grips the handlebar. *Eight, seven . . .* With the other foot, he kicks his toe into the snow for leverage to push and break the sled free. *Six, five . . .* Mushers do not say "mush." *Four, three . . .* Maybe a whistle or "Hike!" but usually something easygoing, like "Okay, guys," or perhaps a wriggle of the handlebar. *Two, one, GO!*

Volunteers release the team. Mowry slingshots down First Avenue, into the confusion of colors, noise, and motion of spectators lining both sides of the road. As the team shoulders forward, the howls of his dogs cease, so abruptly as to be startling. They move in silence. A good-luck cheer from the crowd rolls down the street with the team. Mowry smiles and acknowledges his moment. Eight thousand miles of sled dog racing under his belt, going on nine. Sliding down the snow with him is every Hawaiian vacation he may have daydreamed of, or that new house instead of a trapper's cabin. In other words, these dogs and this race are everything.

At the edge of the crowd I retreat, embarrassed, into the fur ruff of my parka, where I fight wet eyes. I attribute this emotion to my being an Outsider, but then I see other people sobbing openly. It isn't from sadness, although there is some of that. On average, two dogs will die in each race. It is because the dogs are innocent, and beautiful and noble, and their pursuit makes all the sense in the world, to them. And the trail ahead is so forbidding and so awfully long. So frightful as it aims toward the sun-kissed hills on the frozen horizon.

Everything is happening fast now. As soon as one team is released, another moves to the ready, dragging a squad of straining, skidding, red-faced volunteers.

Last year's champion, Rick Mackey, of Nenana, Alaska, leaves third. Skinny, slump shouldered, graying, Mackey is the favorite of all those who are middle-aged and indulgent. He is forty-four, a two-pack-a-day smoker, and has won both the Iditarod and the Quest, only the third person to do so. His father, Dick, also won the Iditarod, and Rick's nineteen-year-old daughter, Brenda, will be following him down the Quest trail later this afternoon, the youngest musher entered. This will be Rick's twenty-first one-thousand-mile dog race. That's cumulatively ten months of nonstop long-distance racing, to say nothing of all that time training. All those cold, solitary nights with numb fingers and all those hungry dogs to feed, and those aching dog feet to massage, and only these dogs for conversation; and all that time with ice in the beard and snot icicles dangling from his nostrils, with sleep crawling up the spine, gripping the brain stem, and squeezing down while he fights to stay awake. Lumbering around in those heavy, stinky boots and all those bulky clothes, riding the sled runners through those vast and quiet spaces, across frozen rivers and under starry skies, sometimes against violent Arctic storms. This is neither a job nor a pastime nor an adventure, but all three. A way of life.

Seventh to leave Whitehorse is Alaskan Larry Carroll. Pink-faced, with a physique like a bear's, he's smiling this time. Last year, the poor man started the Quest with a fever and flu. He recovered after three days. Then he felt so damn strong he grabbed an ax to chop up a block of frozen dog food and sank the ax blade into the bone of his knee. A veterinarian sewed him up. I watched him walk stiff-legged out to his sled, take two aspirin, load up, and push on. If he thought about quitting, or even sitting down and resting, he kept it to himself.

In a few minutes, Aliy Zirkle comes fishtailing out of the chute, starting eighth, flashing her oversize smile and delivering big sweeping waves to the crowd. Then Frank Turner, a local from Whitehorse and the only man crazy enough to have entered all fifteen Quests. "Grandma" they call him because of his screechy voice and busybody approach to other mushers. His head resembles an oversize peanut in shape, but Turner is the most photogenic of them all, thanks to the perfection of his ice-encrusted, exhausted grimaces. He won the Quest in record time in 1995: ten days, sixteen hours, and ten minutes. And he remains the favorite of the Canadians.

Then John Schandelmeier, a rural Alaska fur trapper and fisherman, the most authentic modern-day mountain man I know. I would call him an adventurer, a great one, but life in the wild with nature is perfectly normal for John and he does not see it as I do. "Adventure is when something goes wrong," he says. "Do you understand what I'm saying? My point is to go out and *not* have an adventure."

A two-time winner of the Quest, Schandelmeier entered this year at the last minute and only, he says, because the commercial fishing season was lousy and "these dogs need to pay their own way now." He was short a few dogs and tells everyone he had to harness up a wild coyote that he caught in a trap. He also called on friends to loan him back some farm-club dogs he had "given away." Still, he leaves the starting line with only thirteen. The core of the team are dogs he mushes through deep snow and awful conditions all winter long, setting and maintaining his fur traps. It is a beautifully responsive team, and it's hard to imagine anything that could slow him down. Perhaps no other musher has achieved Schandelmeier's calm, atavistic partnership with his trail dogs.

Right behind him is Bruce Lee, a summer tour-bus guide in Alaska's Denali National Park. Bruce spent four years rebuilding a dog team after a tainted medical inoculation virtually wiped out his previous kennel. This race marks his return to long-distance mushing; he'd finished second in the 1991 Quest, only five minutes behind the winner. Five minutes behind after eleven days. That's less time than it takes to pull down a pair of snow bibs and take a crap alongside the trail. It's been driving Bruce nuts ever since.

Now it's Rusty Hagan's turn down First Avenue. His jaunty main lead dog, with a black coat, brindle mask, and blue eyes, is named Kid. Kid has no earthly idea of what he is embarking on. Then Dave Dalton, a clean-cut Fairbanks cab driver who once faced a painful choice: the dogs or me, his wife decreed. Eighteenth to start: Yukoner William Kleedehn, who races with a prosthetic leg and is justifiably famous, even feared, for his stamina. Kleedehn must surely be a throwback to the past century, when hard-bitten characters with all variety of spoken accents, limps, and quirks roamed this country looking for gold but settling for whiskey and adventure.

Rough country attracts its share of rough characters, and the roughest I know is Cor Guimond, a forty-seven-year-old fur trapper who lives in the Yukon bush country near the Alaska border, a place accessible only by dog team in winter and riverboat in summer. Even his smile is menacing, and his thick, blunt fingers wrap around a beer bottle like so many cased sausages. Drinking with him in a Dawson City saloon one night, I was handed a written message: "Where should we send the body?" Friends of mine across the room were inquiring, figuring I wouldn't survive the experience. Today, Cor is the nineteenth to leave. He is fresh-shaven and his sled looks shiny new as he mushes down First Avenue, and at first I hardly recognize him.

Right behind Cor is the sweetest person in the race, Gwen Holdman, a smiley, pink-faced, blond tennis player just out of college who lives on a hilltop north of Fairbanks, in a cabin she shares with a boyfriend and most of her thirty dogs. At twenty-five, she is a rookie, and these days rookies must prove themselves in a qualifying race before entering the Quest. Holdman completed a two-hundred-mile Alaska race earlier this winter, but experts rolled their eyes because she carried so much food and equipment for her dogs. She now has race judges here worried because her sled is surely the heaviest in Whitehorse. Heavy means slow. And slowness and inexperience are likely to put her way behind in the journey, perhaps too far behind in the event of trouble, or a storm. She smiles and looks out into the wilderness as if to suggest, Better to have too much in the sled than not enough. Besides, she picked blueberries all summer and baked $3,000 worth of blueberry pies to help finance this trip. She'll travel her way, thanks—slow, cautious, aiming to finish without straining her team. Happy dogs all the way. A camping-trip strategy, it's called. That itself is an outsized dream.

Every two minutes, another string of bouncing, light-footed dogs comes coursing down the street, pulling a musher and a whole array of hopes and dreads. Some of these mushers have become my friends in recent months, and others I'm counting on knowing better down the trail. I don't suppose I'll ever know them well enough to understand fully why they give up so much of themselves for this strange, wild endeavor. But I can begin to frame an explanation for my own fascination: I find myself nostalgic for authentic experience. I'll disagree with John Schandelmeier. Adventure isn't only when something goes wrong; it's when *something* is sure to happen. The greater the intensity of that "something," the more sublime the adventure. Risk and reward grow on the same stalk—isn't that what the proverb says?

After two blocks, the crowd thins and all but vanishes. Then the trail veers to the right, drops over the riverbank and onto the ice of the Yukon River. A Technicolor landscape becomes instantly black and white: snow, trees, ice, wind-scoured rock. Quiet descends. The musher's ear adjusts to the hush of runners gliding across the snow, the thump-rattle of the sled over rough ice, and the faint pneumatic wheeze of breath inside the hood of the parka. Within moments they have attained the nineteenth century, a world substantively unchanged since mail carriers, missionaries, and prospectors drove dogs, camped, and boiled their coffee along these same frigid trails, according to the unbroken rhythms of the wilderness traveler.

2

In many ways the great quest was an approximation of life itself, for in its several stages it mirrored the naiveté of childhood, the enthusiasm of youth, the disillusionment of middle age, and the wisdom of maturity. Those who survived were made wise: they had taken their own measure and now understood their failings as well as their strengths. At last they realized that the Klondike experience was as much a quest for self as it was for gold.

—Pierre Berton, writing about the 1890s Klondike Gold Rush

Months in advance of the Quest I arrive in the Far North, and already winter is the consuming fact of life. The days are growing shorter by three minutes every twenty-four hours. Today we have just four hours, eleven minutes of sun. The thermometer is dropping, and the lake in front of the cabin where I am staying is frozen. Wind has blown away the snow, leaving a naked rind of glaze-blue ice. There are twenty-three restless working dogs staked in the yard and they have been training for months already. Wolves have been seen nearby, one black and the other cream colored. Their tracks, broad as a man's outstretched hand, crisscross the valley.

We have no electricity here, no TV, no phone. In the long darkness, we rely on kerosene lamplight. A woodstove radiates heat, although the old patchwork cabin is drafty still; gaps around the door collect condensation and freeze where hot air meets cold, and one of us has to put a shoulder to the door each morning to break a half-inch seal of frost. We wear fleece and heavy socks inside as well as outside. We draw water in five-gallon buckets from a hole chopped through the ice of a creek and we pull it home on a toboggan. Inside, the sagging couch and cast-off chairs are chewed by rodents, soiled by years of working men resting in their working clothes. Damp socks and gloves hang to dry on a clothesline looped beam-to-beam across the kitchen. A pad of blue foam insulation with a hole cut in it serves as the seat for the outhouse. We unroll our sleeping bags on raw boards in a loft. The cabin reeks of game meat, dog food, and the rank ammonia odor of thawing trail-dog harnesses.

By demographic standards, and no doubt by the standards of my friends Outside, the four of us here are living in conditions of impoverishment and hardship.

Which, as we think about it, calls for a good laugh and another pour of Jack Daniel's. For there are oversized potatoes cooking in the coals and a bubbling stew of creamy ptarmigan and grouse on the woodstove. Back in the shadows of the kitchen shelf, I see two bottles of bourbon in reserve. Two cords of dry firewood are bucked and stacked handy just outside. I grab parka and pac boots and venture out to pee, and the whole night sky is aflame in furious smoky-green streaks of luminescence. Spindly spruce trees between cabin and lake are cake-frosted and silhouetted in the greenish shadow-light. Air burns pure and cold in the throat. The night is utterly silent.

Impoverished?

Hardly. We envy no one, and desire nothing.

Only the rich can say that.

"It's always been my thought that money would interfere with the fun I want to have in life," says Joe May, the sixty-two-year-old sourdough who has become my friend and brought me here to Dezadeash Lake, Yukon Territory, northern Canada, a half day's drive west of Whitehorse, forty miles from the Alcan Highway truck stop of Haines Junction. Here, to a borrowed cabin in a lake valley encircled by handsome treeless wind-scoured peaks—a landscape where it is possible to get a hundred miles from a road and still be starting out. Here, where the ways of things are old and honored; where men still measure themselves by myths that lured them north.

"You want to learn about dogs? You start with a shovel," says Joe.

This is a dog camp, training ground for these hearty, utilitarian, handsome animals who have their own rightful claims to legends of the North. May is a sled dog driver, a former champion of the Iditarod race and a respected father figure in the world of dog mushing. Later this winter, he will be a race judge for the Yukon Quest. He is my guide to the country, the people, and their passion for mushing.

Joe wears big horn-rim glasses now, his teeth are discolored, he forgot to go to the barber this winter, and there is some jowl to him, but his muscles are hard and his caterpillar eyebrows bounce with energy from a life of action. A merchant marine on the Great Lakes, he divorced and came north in a Fiat half a lifetime ago and homesteaded in the interior of Alaska. His ex took the refrigerator. He didn't replace it for twenty-seven years. Right away, though, he picked up a few dogs to help him get around in winter. He drove them along a hundred-mile trapline. He would trap only marten (as in sable coats)—nasty-tempered little scavengers that died fast in the trap and suffered, he told himself, less than the more majestic creatures of the North. Then he was invited to a local sled dog race, and his trapline dogs—surprise—won. Why Christ, he thought, I can make a living this way and don't have to kill anything.

"My only regret," May says, wistfully, "is that I'm not young again."

Pass the Jack Daniel's, please.

Most of the twenty-three seemingly mismatched mongrel dogs outside once belonged to a long-ago fur-trapping neighbor of May's, and he is helping their new owner establish a training regimen for the Yukon Quest. May ran his last thousand-miler, the Quest, in 1986. He stopped in the finishing chute, built a small fire, and ceremoniously burned his snowshoes. Never again. Too grueling. It was reported that a glob of tears froze in his eyes. For a few years he went off and indulged himself with a sailboat and long-distance voyaging. But he couldn't get trail dogs out of his blood, and he's back, kicking around the kennels and wilderness trails again.

Dan Turner is the new owner of these dogs and will be mushing fourteen of the best later this winter up the Quest trail from Whitehorse to Fairbanks. The toughest overland trail in the world, we keep telling ourselves when we get lazy about chores. A quiet forty-five-year-old native of Colorado, Turner recalls how he used to talk and daydream about Alaska when he was working construction. His colleagues asked, if it was so damn great up there, why didn't he go? He loaded his tools and was on the road north in two hours. That was twenty-two years ago. Like many migrants, he scraped for jobs: a liquor-store clerk in Anchorage, taxi driver, engine-shop mechanic. Now he is, of all things, a tax assessor in the coastal Alaska town of Haines. He is rangy and good looking, six foot seven, with a trimmed mustache, and like many people up here, he still answers to the romance of the North. This will be his second try at the Quest. Two years ago he made it halfway before the trail broke his spirits.

"When I quit in Dawson City, I said I'd never get on a dog sled again. Then last year, I began having flashbacks, like Vietnam. I'd dream about the Quest. So I decided to do it again. Why? Easy: there's a lot in just being able to do it. Not just the race, but the characters, the traditions, the places. The race itself, there's nothing I've done that's been so miserable. . . . I never really realized I was in a race. Except maybe at the prestart banquet. But the rest of the time, it's between you and yourself, I guess."

To prepare these dogs for the extreme climate and agoraphobic terrain they will encounter, May and Turner established their training camp here in the remote western Yukon. With them is nineteen-year-old Will Rhodes of Crescent City, California, whose summer visit to an uncle in Haines has now stretched into winter, plans for college postponed. Rhodes, too, grew up aware of legends about Alaska and the North. After his arrival, he answered a newspaper ad in Haines from someone seeking a dog handler. Beginning in late summer, long before the snows, he started conditioning these animals by running teams on dirt roads. Instead of a sled, he had them pull a fat-tired ATV, one of those machines that resemble a motorcycle with four tires.

"The deal was, no money. Just food and experience. And the beer. The beer's been big." Rhodes grins. He has a youngster's reluctant beard and a football player's build. He also shovels up the dog shit, hauls water, helps with feeding, administers medicines. He drives the camp snowmachine, which elsewhere is called a snowmobile, to extend the training trails ever deeper into the bush, and he mushes dogs on their training runs. Yesterday a shotgun, dislodged from its ready position along the seat of the snowmachine, whipped around and hit him in the back with enough force to splinter the stock. A quick student in the ways of the North, he is treating himself with canine liniment and Budweiser.

The hookup is chaotic: sled dogs are bred for strength and endurance but, more than that, for heart, for enthusiasm. So they scream at the sight of an armload of harnesses, bloodcurdling desperate howls. They lunge and spin on their chains. They dance on the roofs of their unpainted, straw-filled doghouses. Don't forget me, you bastard, they say—or the canine equivalent.

The dogs were fed earlier with a broth of hot water and chopped raw meat—perhaps freezer-burned beef at fifteen dollars for a twenty-five-pound block or the trimmings from a moose. Later, they will have a snack, a piece of frozen whitefish. Then for dinner, a bouillabaisse of salmon, beaver, chicken skins, horse meat, and kibble. A greedy appetite is one of the best qualities in a trail dog: a fifty-pound dog will need to consume ten thousand calories each day during the Quest, more if it's really cold.

For now, the sled is pulled from last night's snow, shaken clean, and aimed in the starting direction. To hold things in place during preparations, a snow hook is affixed to something solid. The double-jawed, fourteen-inch stainless steel hook, attached by stout rope to the frame of the sled, is the parking brake for a dog team. When dogs are fresh and in a fury to bolt, the hook must be gripped to something very solid, the trunk of an eight-inch-diameter tree, say, or the bumper of a ton-and-a-half pickup left in gear. Later, when the dogs settle into work, it will be enough to stomp the hook into hard-pack snow to keep them in place.

Today, Joe May is running ten paired dogs, not quite a full fourteen-dog race team. A second sled is tied behind his on a six-foot polypropy-lene rope. I will ride the double. From the front sled, a fifty-foot cable gangline is unrolled. Harnesses are unbundled and spread on the snow.

The scene is now complete hysteria, with howling dogs throwing themselves against their chains. To be heard, May must roar out the lineup of dogs for today's run: Piggy, Big Dan, Linus, Solo. . . . What? Huh?

Harnessing dogs is a task something between rodeo and diaper changing. You grab a collar with a tight-fisted grip, unclip the dog from its chain, and raise its powerful front legs off the ground. People who underestimate the brute-muscle force of these lunging, thrusting creatures have been surprised to pull away with broken fingers. Trying to move a dog with all four feet on the ground permits it the advantage of traction, and you are likely to find yourself dragging on your face. But when you hold the front feet aloft, the dog hops and jerks forward, in an awkward dance across the slippery packed snow of the dog yard. First come the lead dogs, positioned where they are supposed to remain in place and keep the gangline taut.

Straddling a squirming, half-berserk dog, you wrestle its head into the harness and then one front foot and the other. A loop at the back of each harness is clipped to an individual tugline that vees off the main gangline. Eventually, each pair of dogs will be clipped collar-to-collar with foot-long necklines to keep everybody aligned in the same direction.

Behind the lead dogs will be the swing dogs—their job is to "swing" the team around corners and prevent everyone from turning at once, as in a flanking movement. Next, the team is filled out with the pullers, the "team dogs"—organized by who will not quarrel with whom, or who might keep their partner motivated, or for any of a dozen other reasons. At the end are the last pair, the wheel dogs, bruisers who must absorb the jerk and sway of the heavy sled right behind them.

At first, because of the screams of the dogs, you may miss another sound: the murmured, reassuring words of dog driver to dog: *Easy, good girl, that's it, ready?* Many good mushers spend much of the day communicating with their animals, by sound or touch. That way dogs come to know the voice or the tics, body language, and moods of one person who stands as God.

Whatever the routine, mushers stick with it and try not to vary their

pattern. "Personally I don't talk to my dogs much," Aliy Zirkle told me
once. "So if I do, they say, Wow, what's up? If I say, Gee did you see that
sunrise, they say, Who is sunrise? We don't know sunrise. Who the hell
is sunrise?"

Even with two people, hookup and untangling takes a half hour.
And now, impossible as seems, the dogs are even more frantic—those
left behind and those in harness. The howls are incessant, the rising primordial delirium of the pack readying to move. The gangline cracks
and stretches tight with every lunge. The two tied-down sleds shudder
from the strain.

Standing on the runners of the forward sled, Joe May nods, one of
his bushy eyebrows arching. I wait on the second sled for slack and
yank the snow hook free from the pickup bumper. Joe barks the command "Okay," but it's unnecessary. The dogs felt the release and we're
already catapulting forward, zero to twenty in a single leap. Howls
cease. We whip-snake up the trail in silence. Except for my voice
to myself: Wasn't it Gus Grissom who said, Please, God, don't let me
fuck up?

These first moments with a fresh team are the most exhilarating.
And the most dangerous. Even though each sled, in addition to a snow
hook, has a hinged brake, which drives two steel chisels into the snow
with pressure from a boot, plus a drag brake made from an eighteen-
inch section of snowmachine tread that rides between the runners and
creates friction when you apply weight, we could no more stop these
animals now than we could teach them to eat with knife, fork, and finger bowl. You want your dogs to go, not stop. *Whoa* is a command usually overlooked in training. So each day, and after each stop, the dogs
must be allowed to burn through that first release of adrenaline, a crazy
rush that passes through the team in a seeming contagion of emotions,
at least as we humans figure it: competition, exhilaration, fear, and who
knows what else. Hang on. Or, as dog drivers say, don't ever let go.

I had this conversation earlier with Joe May:

How do you steer a sled?

"I don't know."

What do you mean you don't know?

"I can't tell you how to ride a bicycle, either."

I have mushed dogs alone before, including big teams, but I still cannot entirely grasp the physics of maneuvering a sled down a winding, hilly, lopsided trail with trees whizzing by. At any given time some dogs are going uphill, others down. On S-turns, some dogs can be going *haw* while others are already headed *gee,* the old mule-skinner terms for left and right. I know that you lean into some corners and away from others. You can gain advantage by pulling the sled up on one runner and torquing the handlebar. Sometimes it seems natural, and other times mystifying. I know you never put on the brake when you're cornering around a tree or it will pull you right into it. But if you're skidding right for a tree anyway, what do you do then?

Training for the Quest this winter, popular musher Peter Zimmerman, a Swiss living in the Yukon, was worried about losing his team. Sometimes no matter how tight you hang on, it's not tight enough. So he lashed himself to his sled with a rope, figuring he would rather be dragged behind the sled than separated from it. He flew out of his dog yard behind a furiously fresh team, and was whip-snaked into a tree. In a hospital bed four months later, he still could not move his arms or legs.

Uphill, we dismount and run-push behind the sleds, jumping on the runners for the elevator ride down. And right now, this particular downhill is uncommonly steep and, oh, a ninety-degree right turn awaits us at the bottom. I was just relishing the manly feel of ice growing in my beard and marveling at the ice frosting on the spruce and aspen that hug the trail, sometimes merging overhead into a branch canopy and sometimes opening up so I can see the bare, faceted faces of the mountains beyond. I was enjoying the pleasant glow of exertion, and the soft satisfying glide of runners over the hardpack snow, and the tugging, bouncy-alive feel of the gangline ahead, the low-slung, deceptively easy-footed cadence of dogs shouldering forward. And now this impossible turn at the bottom of a steep hill. I ride the drag until the last second to try to control our speed, and then I torque my weight to pull the front of the sled around the corner. Harder, with all my might. Oh . . .

I'm somersaulting into the brush now; I can feel snow down the neck of my parka as I tumble along. Over on the trail, the sled is on its side, ricocheting against trees like crack-the-whip.

Using brake and snow hook, May works the team to a stop at the next rise. When I come lumbering and huffing up, I am greeted by dogs looking over their shoulders, tongues dangling loosely, puffing little clouds of vapor, quizzical expressions on their hairy, frosted faces. I right my sled, brush dry powder snow off myself, and acknowledge my duty with the camp dishes tonight, the penalty for coming off a sled. And quit staring at me, you wide-eyed, whiskery beasts. Don't you know, Gus Grissom fucked up on his first space flight too?

At this point in training, we are making only a twelve-mile run, and I will become separated from my sled three more times, each occasion on a corner that calls for some shift of weight or twist that I cannot fathom. Dishes all the rest of the week. The most difficult maneuver proves to be turning our chain gang around in the thick, spindly forest at the halfway mark. From a stop, the command is *Come haw*, a 180-degree turn that doubles the dogs back down the left side of the narrow trail. We try to yank our sleds around into position but are not quite fast enough as the dogs break into a lope. May's sled comes leaping across the bumper or brush bow of my own and he is knocked down. When the towrope tightens I'm spun off my feet too. The two of us are dragging behind tipped-over sleds, plowing up snow, holding on for life. May is barking profanities. I'm muttering the only words left in my vocabulary, Oh shit. Eventually, the whole strung-out apparatus grinds to a stop. May rises, encrusted head to toe in snow and spruce needles, grinning, his long gray hair frozen into a stand-up fan like Don King's. "See, nothing to it." Behind him, those bristly, maniacal faces once again looking back impatiently.

Right the sleds, jump back on the runners, push up the hills, hang on coming down, duck the overhanging branches, lean into the corners . . . or was it lean out?

At this point, I ask myself if it is enough to say that the rough, twisty, windblown, three-foot-wide trail chopped through the wilderness for the Yukon Quest covers just about the same distance as from New York to Daytona Beach.

3

There were some who longed only for gold, but there were
those others who scarcely realized that the land with its endless fascinations was the siren who held them here. . . .
Here, surely, was God's domain, and one proffered reverent
thanks for a glimpse of a quiet paradise.

—Peggy Rouch Dodson, *The Girl in the Gold Camp*

Bordering the Yukon to the West is Alaska. For some absurd reason
related to the assertion of sovereignty, a twenty-five-foot-wide
and perfectly straight clear-cut was once chopped hundreds of miles
through wilderness to designate the boundary here between the U.S.
and Canada. For what benefit, no one seems to know. Apart from the
color of the flag and the color of the money, cultural values remain
much the same on both sides of the clear-cut. People who live with two
dozen dogs but have no running water or electricity or full-time jobs
are not automatically thought insane, or even unusual. They might, in
fact, be admired, emulated—the kind of good folks who rarely have to
buy their own beer in the event they ever come to town.

By the standards elsewhere, it is an obvious sign of psychopathic
weirdness to live alone in a small junk-filled cabin without a steady job,
consumed by a single obsession. Consider Unabomber Theodore
Kaczynski. Some accounts of Kaczynski's life seem to suggest that

authorities should have known that anyone who lived as he did would be inherently dangerous. Perhaps he should have been locked up before he killed. People in Alaska and the Yukon are uncomfortable with the implication. If you rounded up all the strange, obsessive people here who live in junky cabins—well, there would be many fewer people to visit during the long nights, that's for sure.

Besides, Kaczynski used to ride his bicycle into town, which means (a) he lived near a road and (b) he was in the proximity of other people, and up here that would classify him as a suburban, not a rural, resident at all.

For the next stage in I traveled to Alaska my own at training Paddy Santucci's invitation.

Unlike Dan Turner, who just wants to finish the Quest, Paddy is serious about competing. There is an intensity about him, and I think I can detect the same intensity in his dog team. I asked if he would explain the process of preparing for a long-distance journey and talk about the culture of the dog musher. He agreed to show me what he could.

Paddy came to Alaska on his twenty-fourth birthday thirteen years ago, the culmination of a boyhood dream. Alaska, the outdoors, the mountains—these were always his goals. His family had started in Azusa, California, outside Los Angeles, and then moved north to Portola, northwest of Reno, when Paddy needed more room to roam. At sixteen he got his pilot's license so he could range farther. Ten years ago he started mushing for the same reason. He liked to wander from the city lights of his home outside Fairbanks to the remote Athabascan villages of the interior. Dogs were an intimate, quiet, and traditional mode of winter mobility—originating with the Eskimos, their teams splayed out in fans to traverse the shapeless topography of the Arctic coast, and then modified to teams hitched in-line for the forest and river trails used by the missionaries, mail drivers, and gold miners. Perfect for a twentieth-century loner.

I met Paddy last year. He had twice before run the Quest, finishing seventeenth and then ninth, but he was following the 1997 race as dog handler for Mark May, Joe May's veterinarian son and an accomplished musher. Paddy and I talked along the way, although, to be honest about it, he is not much of a talker.

I'll be racing next time, he mentioned.

I'll catch up with you, I said.

Somewhere there is a telephone message machine and sometimes Paddy checks in. Weeks in advance, we agree to meet. A half hour early, he arrives at the appointed rendezvous in Fairbanks, with his dog handler friend John Boyce, an itinerant professor of economics who now teaches in New Zealand. In locker boxes built into the bed of Paddy's crew-cab pickup are seventeen dogs. On top is a sled. We will add a trailer and two snowmachines. Destination: by road to Manley Hot Springs. And then overland to Tanana, an Indian village at the confluence of the Yukon and Tanana Rivers, right in the center of Alaska, sixty-five miles from any kind of a road. Among mushers, Tanana is another of those places synonymous with dogs. The brood stock for many good teams originated in this village, where sled dogs and racing go back generations. It was here that the U.S. Army once maintained a vast dog yard. It was here that Fred Jordan introduced the sleek saluki into the mongrelized lineage of the husky, hound, malamute, retriever mix of the Tanana village dog. The resulting animals, small-hammed and with gracefully arching backs, have proved to be some of the fastest sprint racers in the world, traveling a nine-mile course at average speeds of twenty-two miles per hour. Such dogs have no place in long-distance mushing, but they are exciting to watch.

To reach the jump-off spot of Manley Hot Springs, we drive up the oil-company haul road toward Prudhoe Bay. Partway there, we join in a convoy behind another friend, Peter Moore, who is the state Department of Transportation worker in charge of plowing the treacherous passes we must travel. After driving seventy-five miles north, we turn left into high hills onto an icy, windblown, single-lane road, toward Manley, population sixty-five. After another seventy-five miles, we arrive in darkness at 4:00 P.M. Paddy stakes out and feeds his dogs. He has brought seventeen and hopes that among them are fourteen that he can drive a heartbeat faster than anyone else's fourteen.

In summer, Manley Hot Springs is the end of the road for occasional tourists. In winter, it is a no-frills outpost for both natives and whites. Yellowish lights glow here and there in the darkness, marking cabins among the trees. The snow-packed roads are crossed with the tracks of snowmachines. The quiet is sometimes broken as dog teams begin singing to one another, a round-robin of melodious, snout-to-the-sky howling that begins without warning and passes from dog yard to dog yard through the neighborhood.

That night, at Manley's one tavern, I introduce myself to Susan Thomas. I ask, What do you do here?

"I'm a mail-order bride," she says, beaming.

Until two months ago, Thomas, a plump woman with an attractive smile, was an office manager at a dental clinic in Belvedere, Tennessee. She answered an ad in the magazine *Alaska Man,* a lonely-hearts publication that owes its existence to the gender imbalance in the Alaska bush, where men sometimes outnumber women ten to one. She received no answer. She wrote a second letter. He called on August 12.

"Between then and October third, I sold my house, sold my car, sold everything I owned, quit my job, and came here. The best decision of my life." She now lives without running water but has joined the town's crafts guild, and is getting used to the quiet. She couldn't sleep for the first two weeks because of the stillness. She is learning how to can food. Her first chore was canning the meat of a bear. Tonight, her new husband is behind her, shooting pool and listening shyly.

"Oh," she confides, "we're not officially married yet. But we will be in about six months."

Long before sunup, we have unchained Paddy's dogs and inserted them back into the truck, driven to the edge of town, unloaded and restaked them, attached harnesses, rolled out the sled and gangline, and hooked them up. Our commotion has riled up about half the dogs in the village, so we've no doubt awakened everyone.

Now the seventeen insanely shrieking dogs are rocking the big pickup back and forth, pulling on the bumper, then pulling harder. Something is about to move, or break. Paddy releases the snow hook and catapults, silently, into the darkness of the trail, his high-powered headlamp barely able to penetrate the ninety feet to his lead dogs. He vanishes.

It is 20 below and windless. Ahead, in the low country and along the river bottoms, where the cold air collects in sumps, it will drop to 30 below. Down there, your breath clouds up in front of you and you find yourself walking through ice crystals of your own making. A rind of hoarfrost builds quickly in your beard, and in the fur ruff of your parka. These are the temperatures where Interior Alaskans begin to talk seriously about the cold and its cruel compounding toll: it now takes longer to do a chore because you are numb and slow, and consequently you are exposed longer. Dogs and humans both dehydrate quickly—you feel like you are being freeze-dried—and it is essential to gag down prodigious amounts of liquid, which means building fires to thaw water. That requires stopping, but when stopped you lose the warmth of exertion. At 30-below, mushers will begin to put fleece jackets on their more sensitive dogs. Males are affixed with pile jockstraps, "peter heaters," to guard against frostbite.

For a serious competitor like Paddy, this trek is a sophisticated part of the conditioning of his team. By breaking their regular training routine, penning them in the truck and bouncing them along roads, exposing them to strange trails, altering their mealtimes, running them for long distances with minimum rest, he will come as close as possible to duplicating the circumstances that await them when the voice of the Yukon Quest starting announcer echoes down First Avenue in Whitehorse.

Three hours behind Paddy, we follow on snowmachines. John Boyce on one; I'm on the other. Dog breeder and former racer Fred Jordan, a native of Tanana, has agreed to be our guide—although he is such a notorious speed freak on his souped-up "snow go," as the machines are called among Interior natives, we seldom see anything but his tracks or, sometimes, a faint cloud of atomized snow crystals suspended in the still air long after he has rooster-tailed by. From Manley Hot Springs, our route leads north and west into the heart of the great Interior of Alaska; a landscape of only modest vertical drama when compared to the galactic expanse of the horizontal. The first fifteen miles down a seasonal mining trail are no more rugged than a lumpy one-rut road. Then the trail narrows, barely shoulder wide in places, and veers left and downhill and we encounter, in succession, the three topographies that will occupy our imaginations and our exertions the rest of the day:

the twisty, hilly, snow-frosted forests of stunted spruce and willow; the maddeningly dimpled meadows of tundra tussocks; and, lastly, the long-frozen sections of lake, slough, and river. We drop fifteen feet down vertical stream banks and wrestle our way up the other side. We jounce and skid along sidehills, sometimes slipping off the trail, having to dismount and hoist ourselves back on. Overhanging willows poke at our faces and shower us with spindrift. Protruding logs grab out at steering skis and at our numbed feet. Tussocks slow us to a crawl; we jerk and bounce along like fleas creeping over pimples. And then we tense for the furious, screeching, full-throttle runs across the river and lake ice, blinded from the fine snow crystals churned up by Jordan in the lead but unable to slow down for fear of encountering a weak spot in the surface that would send us into frigid water below. No matter how cold, ice remains alive—with springs and currents underneath eating away at the bottom, with changing water levels opening gaps between the ice and the water beneath, with wind blowing against the surface mass and pushing open cracks, which may now be covered with snow and hence invisible. Paddy has called Fred Jordan "the finest woodsman I know." Paddy also reminded me that once, during a previous Quest, Jordan's lead dogs broke through the ice of the Yukon River, a bit of bad luck that has sent other mushers and their teams to death.

Sixty-three miles down the trail, Paddy is feeding and resting his dogs, awaiting us. Together, we cross the vast Yukon River, the continent's last great waterway to be explored, the highway of the Far North, the storied pathway to the Gold Rush. We are a few hundred miles downriver from the route of the Quest, but the scene is similar: half the Yukon is frozen glassy smooth; the other half is a maze of knife-sharp ice blocks with a rough trail chopped through them by ax and chain saw. I blink and notice my eyelids are beginning to freeze; I blink again and my right eye will not open. It is at least ten degrees colder down here on the river surface than up on the bank only a few feet higher. But we are almost there. We navigate the last of the trail and I arrive half-blind in the village of Tanana, less than a hundred miles south of the Arctic Circle. Within a few hours, my cheeks and nose will swell and turn chalk white, then fiery red. Surface frostbite. I have no feeling in my feet, and when I take off my black rubber "bunny" boots my socks are sheathed in ice. Altogether, a rookie arrival. I will feel better later, though, when I hear one of the locals mention he had cold feet today too.

Tanana has a population of three hundred or so, a mix of Athabascan natives and whites. For the most part, people here lead subsistence lives. Fishwheels along the banks of the Yukon throw out tons of salmon and whitefish during the summer. In autumn, the seemingly boundless expanse of spruce and tundra, known locally as the Yukon Flats, yields moose and caribou for meat. And in winter, trappers seek the fur of lynx, wolf, beaver, fox, wolverine, and marten. Transportation of supplies, via river barges in summer and bush airlines the rest of the year, is a major enterprise. And so are dogs. Insulated by distance and united by the culture of the wilderness, the village has been fundamentally unchanged in character and ethos for a century—except, importantly, for the arrival of television, which has deadened social interaction here the same as it has in most places in the world. Adults recall the first winter after TV came. The New Year's Eve dance was delayed until everyone could finish watching the movie *Raging Bull*.

We bunk at the lofted log cabin of Pat Moore, a white who came here as a boy when his father got a job at a now closed FAA tracking station. He is married to a native, Lorraine, who is the town's postmaster. They have two children, Courtney and Thomas, plus sixty-five sprint dogs. The living room of their one-and-a-half-story log home is like a hotel lobby, with a constant stream of people in and out—kids wandering through after school, a trapper dropping by from the bush, a few people over to say hi to Paddy, a village elder or two who heard about some strangers in town, the local state trooper hiding out from his girlfriend for reasons he does not specify, and an assortment of others whose intentions seem mainly to warm their hands around the stove and see if anything interesting is happening. As the day ends, pools of meltwater spread across the entryway under rows of heavy boots and heaps of parkas hanging from nails driven into log walls. A large wire-mesh screen, hung by wire over the woodstove, is piled with drying gloves and socks. For dinner we have thick, gamy moose chili with slices of cheddar. The Moores must haul their water from a spigot in town, and it's for washing only, too bitter to drink. So we choose instead from cases of soda pop and beer, airfreighted in.

I would be lying if I did not confess to being exhausted this night. But this seems an everyday part of the mushing culture—resisting sleep. Maybe it is a habit that comes from the trail, where rest is for losers. Or it might stem simply from the fear of missing something. Sometime late in the night while I'm feeling warm, leaden, drowsy, Pat Moore leaps into his parka and leads us around the side of his house to a building that is his dog shop, smelling of liniment, sour fish, thawing harnesses, and the smoke from a small, puffing woodstove. He taps a baby keg of his home-brewed Scotch ale—a beautifully wrought and well-aged beer with a preposterously high alcohol content. We drink from Kerr jars. Good ale, we agree. The shop fills with people, the haze of cigar and cigarette smoke, and the murmur of conversation—most of it about dogs, training dogs, the pain in the ass of having dogs, the equipment of dogs, the latest race results, which dog has a bum foot, who has puppies, how a naturally fermented whitefish aids digestion in a nervous dog, which medicines work, the nuances of sled design . . .

Sam, the old full-bearded refugee from California, has found a miniature cattle-prod and is busy jamming it into his shoulder. *Zzzit.* His head jerks to the side and his boots lift off the floor from the voltage. Keeps the soreness out of the muscles, he explains. *Zzzit.* Paddy shows me the scars on his ropy arms from where he broke up a dog fight. There is Darwin, drunk already, trying to focus his eyes, trying to keep from falling down while looking for a stool on which to sit. Best damn snow-go mechanic in the village.

I talk to Ken, the trapper, carpenter, and handyman, who came here in 1972 out of high school in Sacramento. Upriver that summer, he and a friend gathered some empty fifty-five-gallon drums, lashed up a few logs, and built a raft. They put Ken's old pickup camper shell on it and floated downstream for two weeks to get here.

"That first winter, I never had enough money to leave. Same the second winter. Then, by the time I made enough to leave, I liked it here."

He went down to Fairbanks once in three years and it scared him:

too big and bustling. He has a rotten tooth. I ask him where he will go to get it fixed.

"I'll go to the toolbox and get a pair of pliers when it gets bad."

Later on, when I think back on this night, I remember John, one of the village elders, who did not drink or smoke and whose quiet, contented dignity made me feel loud and coarse. I remember going outside to pee and seeing the thermometer at 28 below. Then, at some point, I stop remembering.

It is morning. There is commotion in the dog yard. Pat Moore's hired assistant Soren Lund, an eighteen-year-old musher from Denmark, is hooking up a sprint team for a training run. Come along, he says.

"Get him to sign a release," jokes Moore, spitting tobacco juice into a cup he carries around with him.

I climb into the sled "basket," which is roughly like reclining in the pouch of an oversized slingshot. No place for a grown man recovering from a bout of Scotch-ale poisoning. If trail dogs are strong, sprint dogs are only fast. Their screaming howls during hookup feel like needles into my brain. Soren pulls the snow hook from its solid anchor. We hurl out of the yard, the dogs a blur of fur and feet, the sled whip-snaking behind. A quick right turn and then a ninety-degree left onto a long, icy straightaway.

We do not get to the straightaway. The sled skids through the second turn like a car in a four-wheel drift with the dogs lunging on the gangline for more speed. Now almost sideways, the sled encounters some imperfection in the ice and we are flipping over. It happens so instantaneously, I cannot raise my hand from the side of the basket to cushion the fall. My forehead smashes into the ice. I think to myself, Jesus, that was a hard one. I am aware of myself clinging to the overturned sled careening down the ice. *Never let go.* A loose team will crash and tangle; perhaps half the dogs will be injured, and some will die. But in their absolute trust, dogs make no allowance for human mishap, and these are still digging for more speed. Then I begin to worry because somewhere bouncing along with me on the end of a rope is that evil snow hook. Sharp, dangerous—where is it? Later I will see that it has entered my parka, ripped through the front at midchest, and emerged at my throat, slicing my neck gaiter in two but sparing my neck some-how. I am aware that Soren long ago fell off the sled. I am facedown, holding on, grinding over the trail at twenty-five miles an hour. Then the snow hook is in my hand and I jam its points into the ice and, with a two-handed push-up, bear down with all my weight. The gouges in the ice run for more than a hundred feet before the dogs are drawn to a halt. They look back curiously.

Soren comes puffing up. "What the fuck happened?" he demands.

As if I should know, puffing back.

Curtis Sommer, the village nurse, thaws my forehead so it bleeds clean. "Your skull is very white," he observes. Then he sews me up. The bill: thirty-five dollars, which includes a handful of aspirin. Liisa Penrose, general manager of Apocalypse Design cold-weather outfit-ters in Fairbanks, sees to the sewing up of my parka. "Aw, it was almost brand-new too," she laments. Maybe because I didn't let go of his dogs, Pat Moore gives me a patch to sew onto my hat: TANANA DOG MUSH-ERS ASSN. By the way, Pat, where is that release I'm supposed to sign? Later, when I board a bush plane for the trip back to Fairbanks, a young mother turns her child's head from the sight of my bloodied face. Eventually I become purple with bruises down my legs and across my chest. I have banged loose the edge of my left retina and I will see strange flashing crescents of light in that eye for months, whether it's open or closed. My frostbitten nose and cheeks will scab and peel away in chunks.

Winter is not half over yet. I tell myself that when I get to Fairbanks I absolutely must buy a warmer pair of boots.

The easygoing feel of the days begins to dissolve after New Year's.

Training grows intense. More miles on the trail each day, more wor-ries about dogs, about late-season injuries, accidents, illness, worries about some dog's loss of heart or failure of "head." More worries about money, about the cost of premium meat and fat and dried kibble, which is consumed in greater quantities with the lengthening miles of training and the deepening cold. Mushers share a nearly universal preoccupa-tion with procuring still more dogs in order to replace those that have shown themselves to be weakest in the team, or slowest or most prone to injury. Because there will always be a weakest and a slowest and a most injury-prone dog among any fourteen, this is an endless process, a perpetual yearning, a constant source of frustration, and it accounts for the fact that everyone's kennel seems to grow larger each year.

Weather, as always, is cause for anxiety. South and west of Fairbanks, a two-hundred-mile qualifying race is cut short by half because of a sudden buildup of high pressure in the atmosphere. That brings to a halt all polar air circulation, and temperatures plunge to 50 below for almost a week. The Quest will continue no matter what the weather, but in a preliminary event mushers generally are ruluctant to take on extremes. Despite this cold snap, the regional weather has been intermittent and the Yukon River is only partly frozen over in Canada right now. At Whitehorse, the mighty stream, although heavily loaded with small bergs, flows blue and wide still. Perhaps the start of the race will have to be rerouted.

Race officials have their own absorbing concerns. For the second consecutive year, the German tire company Fulda, a subsidiary of America's Goodyear, has signed on as the largest single sponsor of the Quest, part of a marketing campaign to sell a European tire called the Yukon. Never before has a foreign company made itself the dominant backer of a North American mushing spectacle, and never in the decade-and-a-half history of the Quest has any sponsor demanded a profile like the one Fulda insists upon. In the eyes of the executives from Frankfurt, the Quest was a commodity for sale, so they bought it, and cheap, and affixed their logo on everything and almost everyone that might end up in a photograph. As for the locals, well, they best be grateful or stand out of the way. Side contracts were prepared so that potential critics would be silenced by the gift of a flashy Fulda-logo parka or some other mushing equipment. For the most part, the hard-headed marketing executives found it easy to buy in and silence any criticism from the small-town construction workers, shopkeepers, bush pilots, civic boosters, and dog mushers whose part-time, volunteer efforts keep the race running each year.

To my eyes, Fulda became a metaphor. This was not the first time up here that tantalizing promises of riches made people act gooney. This was not the first time that the value of money clashed with the other values of the Far North. I had come up on the one hundredth anniversary of the great, awful, fabulous, colorful Klondike Gold Rush. And I found that some things never change.

At the start of winter, Fulda's sponsorship had created warring camps of the two separate Yukon Quest boards of directors, Alaska's and the Yukon's. There had always been rivalry across the border, but nothing as bad as this. At one point in autumn, the Alaskans pulled out of the race entirely, threatening to establish their own alternative sled dog endurance contest, noting that the Fulda sponsorship contract with the Quest was entirely the doing of the Canadians, who had never before fetched a big-money sponsor and were eager to do so. Fulda, for its part, showed little interest in the Alaska half of the race. It was selling a tire called the Yukon, not the Alaska. The Americans complained that Fulda's domineering attitude was antithetical to the traditions of the Quest and was muscling out the small feed stores, fuel companies, and other hometown businesses that had previously sponsored mushers. The Alaska directors were soon replaced with a more compliant group, which agreed to continue the race. Friction, though, remained acute until midwinter, when even the Canadians finally had a bellyful of demands to turn Whitehorse into a theatrical set for a long-running Fulda commercial. The new sponsor seemed to succeed at what had never been possible—drawing the two Quest boards together. The clincher occurred in mid-January when a Fulda spokeswoman addressed a luncheon of Whitehorse civic leaders. There was no sweet talk, no expressions of understanding about local sensibilities. Instead, she said point-blank that Fulda's sponsorship was not charity, and that the company would "demand service" for its money. Those people who might object to the over four hundred corporate banners placed around town were told to imagine they were twenty-dollar bills.

Fulda sales director Bernd J. Hoffmann was, at least for North American tastes, amazingly forthright when he said this in a Fulda promotional book: "Image transfer, those are the magic words. The dogs of the Yukon Quest must be tough and have endurance, and be fast and reliable. All characteristics that tires should possess. Strong, quiet, environmentally friendly—the list goes on. Dogs on four paws and cars on four wheels . . ."

Fulda's glossy coffee-table promotional book further declared that among multinational retailers "the smart ones have long realized that through sponsoring you can take your target group unawares in a so-called 'non-commercial' situation. The consumer is reached during his active and passive leisure time and therefore accepts sponsoring as an integral part of his free time activities."

Said Fulda, "If anyone should still wonder what the logical connection is between a dog race and a manufacturer of automobile tires, then this person is actually beyond help. We are pretty quick to come to this conclusion."

By the terms of the Fulda contact, race officials were bound to "not publicly comment on Fulda, its products or services in a negative manner." For its part, Fulda agreed to take the reputation and prestige of the event "into serious consideration."

Nothing like trying to tell a Yukoner or an Alaskan that he cannot speak his mind.

Meanwhile, amid all this rising activity hardly anyone noticed a subtle but important milestone: we were starting, at last, to gain precious seconds of daylight. It would be months, however, before we would feel the first faint warmth from the fires of the sun.

North of Fairbanks, in an area called Two Rivers, a spur road cuts into forested hills. Because these hills reach a few hundred feet above the valley and because warm air rises, the temperature is several degrees higher up here all winter: 5 below in the hills when it's 20 below down in Fairbanks. On both sides of the road, cabins push into the forest. And deeper still, a spider web of winter pathways spreads over the hills, the most extensive network of dog mushing trails and the densest concentration of trail dogs in the world.

Here, where hand-lettered road signs advise of sled dog crossings, Aliy Zirkle maintains a small loft-cabin, and the Northwind kennels she shares with Jerry Louden. She has fifteen dogs, Jerry also has fifteen, and they jointly own another eight. Today, in the canted gray light of midday, the two of them are packing their food drops for the Yukon Quest. I'm helping.

Heaps of frozen meat, sawed into blocks and packaged in uniform bags, are piled in front of the cabin: chicken, lamb, horse, turkey, beef, beaver, fish, and a commercial high-energy mix that combines horse, turkey skins, fat, lamb, beef, egg, oil, liver, and chicken. Dog food. Bags of dry kibble are piled on the porch along with plastic bags of frozen fat, which can be melted and added to meals according to the temperature. That is, calories can be increased to offset the cold without significantly altering the volume of the meals. During an ordinary Quest day, a fifty-pound dog needs the caloric equivalent of twenty double cheeseburgers, and more if the temperature drops.

Stacked in another pile are woven plastic fifty-gallon feed bags. Each has a name written in permanent-marking ink, Zirkle or Louden, as well as the designation of one of the Quest's seven trail checkpoints. These bags will be packed with the dog food, extra dog booties, spare batteries for headlamps, replacement plastic strips for sled runners, and maybe a pair or two of dry socks. They will be sealed and taken to a warehouse in Fairbanks, where volunteers will sort and transport them ahead to the checkpoints. According to the rules, mushers will resupply from these bags and nothing else while on the trail. The idea is to replicate the actual conditions of travel during the Gold Rush era, when mushers could rely, at least most of the time, on established way stops to restock their larders.

On one wall inside Aliy's tiny cabin hang detailed topographical maps of the Quest route. On another wall, handwritten charts show what food and equipment should be packed for shipment to each of the designated checkpoints, calculated by just how long it is likely to take her to travel each section of trail, how much food and replacement equipment she thinks she will need, what she can afford, and how much it will weigh in the sled. Consider something simple, like batteries for the headlamps mushers wear strapped over their hats: lithium D-cells cost ten times as much as alkalines but last three times as long. But alkalines signal when they are getting weak, whereas lithiums burn and then quit suddenly. Which to take for which section of trail?

Even though she is a rookie, Aliy has already earned a no-frills reputation. At a two-hundred-mile qualifying race earlier this winter on her home trails of Two Rivers, she came to the starting line carrying the lightest load in her sled of any Quest first-timer. Experts regarded this as a sign of her confidence and bushcraft.

"I couldn't think of anything else to carry," she said with a shrug. She finished second.

Now Aliy stands on her porch wearing an oversize fur hat and holding a clipboard. Jerry Louden and I grab the empty bags for the first designated checkpoint, Carmacks, a small Athabascan Indian village 188 trail miles from Whitehorse. Then, from notes on her clipboard, Aliy calls out the mix of food: two drys, one chicken, two fats, and so on. Thirty-eight pairs of dog eyes watch our every move. The smell of food, even frozen, has everybody in the dog yard riveted.

The exertion, compounded by the cold, seems doubly tiring. Feed bags mount up, with three or sometimes four for each team at each checkpoint. I am tempted to ask what Aliy will be packing to eat herself for the 1,023 miles, but I know I'll be accused of having my priorities wrong. It's the dogs who will be doing the work and who are the chief concern. I keep quiet, looking forward to a nap or to at least sitting down. Not Aliy. When we're through here, she will add a layer of clothing and take her team for a twenty-mile run into the spruce forests of Two Rivers, and then she'll switch into city clothes for the evening shift as a waitress at a pricey Fairbanks inn, where she will serve wine, escargot, and scampi to families out celebrating. Tomorrow she will begin the day at home by feeding thirty-eight dogs, giving each one just enough attention to keep it connected to her. She'll shovel shit out of the frozen dog yard and run her team another twenty-five miles, feed the whole yard again, and pull another shift at the inn. She has trail clothes to sort, repair, and pack. Gear too. Her sled is new, sleek, modern, and constructed of aluminum, and she is still making adjustments to it.

It is cold outside and dark and there is a race ahead.

For most of our evolutionary history, two million years—or four million years, you decide—we humans lived by the rhythms of nature, in proximity to the wild and according to the seasons. These were the forces that shaped us, our instincts, and our urges. That is, nature itself is the pattern for human nature. We were bred this way as surely as the Chihuahua was bred for the lap or the leopard for the lunge.

As I spent time with and grew closer to Joe May, Paddy Santucci, and Aliy Zirkle, I found myself fascinated with a modern dichotomy. The lives of people like this are different, extreme, unfathomable—at least as my friends Outside might see it, those who can more quickly define success than satisfaction. Joe and Paddy and Aliy, by contrast, live close to nature and the seasons and thus closer to the essence of human nature. They exist more like humans were evolved to live. They connect us to who we really are.

4

This is the Law of the Yukon, that only the Strong shall thrive;
That surely the Weak shall perish, and only the Fit survive.

—Robert Service, "The Law of the Yukon," 1907

They make no sound rounding the bend, a double string of dogs, tongues flying, ears bobbing like windshield wipers, torsos long and angling into the snow-packed turn, muscling forward, sleek, their striding movements transmitted along the twitching, high-tension gangline. Behind them flies a mounted sled, flexing as its driver torques the handlebar and then jumps off and lopes heavy-footed alongside to shove the weight through the skidding apex of the corner. Halfway around, the sled rises up on a single runner as if to topple over. The musher grunts and hauls back with his own weight to keep it upright. Then a slip and the person stumbles, hanging on to the sled, lumbering in bulky clothes so as not to lose his footing and be dragged. The narrow beam of the headlamp strapped over the musher's fur hat has been illuminating the scene, but now everything goes dim in the moon shadows as the beam of light stabs aimlessly into the sky and then swirls crazily into the trees. With another grunt and a mumbled profanity, the musher madly pedals his oversized boot-clad feet to regain balance. Then he steps aboard the runners again. The light beam bobs and steadies, and again points ahead. Then, emitting the heavy-breathing puffing of exertion, the whole contraption passes by—moving as a single living, jiggling, purposeful being. In the dry, absolutely still cold, the scene is rendered in dazzling sharpness. There is nothing by way of density in the air to dampen sight or sound. Ahead the trail tops a small rise, and drops into another corner through a cluster of spruce . . . run, slide, push, huff, grunt. Somewhere under a rind of ice, beneath overlapping neck gaiters shielding mouth and nose, is the face of this deep-breathing musher. If we could see the face in the light of its own headlamp, it would already be showing fatigue.

By now the confused excitement of the hook-up and launch has steadied gyroscopically into pure forward motion. Time becomes measured by the passage of distance, glossy intervals, leaving you unconcerned whether it's day or night; you, the musher, are stuffed in the cocoon of your vestments, your body its own survival furnace, with all sounds muffled by heavy insulation, your vision reduced by the frosty guard hairs of a fur ruff pulled around the face. In the vastness of space, reality closes in tight. The mind relaxes, trancelike, filtering out ordinary stimuli, allowing muscle reflexes to bypass consciousness. Some mushers enhance the otherworldly feel by playing wild track music—music unrelated to the scene—on a Walkman. Earphones are sometimes sewn into their hats.

Then the pop-flash of internal warning lights, a split-second pause in metabolism before adrenaline hits the plunger. Maybe an angry moose is advancing up the trail. Or weak ice cracking underfoot. Or the lurch-crash of your sled into a tree.

Less than 100 miles down the trail, Paddy Santucci misses a corner. The trail turns to the right. His best lead dogs, Spaz and Coal, are not out front. He's taking it easy on them, letting the two run back in the pack. Being in lead is stressful for a dog, and there's no use burning up the best now. So Paddy relies on dogs with lesser skills—trail leaders, as they're called—to follow the route, which at this point appears obvious and well marked. For a while they do. Then a mistake. At the turn, the leaders proceed on a snow path leading straight ahead. Paddy may have allowed his concentration to drift. Or maybe the slanting bars of moonlight played tricks on his vision. The direct illumination of a seven-eighths moon reflecting off crystal-cold snow is plenty bright to read a book by. But unfriendly pools of blue-black shadows lurk in the trees. Driving into a stand of spruce is like entering a movie theater from the midday sun.

Somewhere in this play of light and shadow, Paddy Santucci is snapped back to reality by the violent crunch of his rig against a tree. One of his dogs is injured. Linus, a lanky black bruiser and one of the strongest pullers in the team was running in the wheel position, next to the sled, and apparently took the blow directly. The dog has been torn out of his collar and flung back over the sled, landing with Paddy. Such was the force of the collision. Jesus, God.

The musher's survival instincts take over. Linus is shaken, but how badly is hard to tell. Trail dogs can be fantastically tough, but no less than household pets, they tremble with fear and pain. The remainder of the team must be checked and reassured. Paddy must muscle his sled around, and inspect and untangle the equipment. Shit. A setback way before there should have been one.

Onward. Linus is now riding in the sled bag, not pulling.

Less than a half hour ahead, the trail crosses a two-lane highway—one of only fifteen times that Quest mushers will encounter even the remotest road. Here there is a patchwork gray linoleum and fake-wood-paneled roadhouse with a leaky fifty-five-gallon-drum wood-stove and six cramped Formica tables for customers. At times tonight, sixty-five will squeeze in. Braeburn Roadhouse. Mile 109 on the Yukon Quest trail. Famous for Steve Watson's twelve-inch cinnamon buns and his one-and-a-half-pound hamburgers, the biggest in the Yukon. Veterinarians set up here to give passing teams a first once-over. Linus is not fit to continue, they determine. The dog is passing dark red blood in his urine. But he is also up on all four feet and eating. He will survive just fine. His Quest, however, is over.

Paddy is now down to thirteen dogs. Of more concern is the toll the accident could take on his confidence. Two years ago, when he last raced in the Quest, Paddy watched helplessly as a dog died in harness.

The dog faltered and was dead before Paddy could stop the team and run forward. The horror of that experience was worsened when race officials, in the exhaustion of the final days of the race, seemed to imply that Paddy had pushed his team too hard and was to blame. A necropsy on the carcass exonerated Paddy. The death was not his fault, not the result of detectable overexertion. But Paddy worries about his standing with Quest officials. At this highly visible level, the sport of mushing has little tolerance for those who would put its image at risk by endangering dogs. Eleven veterinarians will follow the race and check the dogs nearly a dozen times each along the trail, making perhaps six thousand physical exams in total. As for the mushers, the only available doctor along the trail is Dieter Dolif, a German physician who is a competitor. He will be lagging behind, so if you get sick or injured and want a doctor's attention, be prepared to put on the brakes. Most of us will rely instead on veterinarians, the same as the dogs, for medical emergencies.

Paddy appears to be holding himself together, looking ahead and not dwelling on his accident.

"I'm sorry I had to drop him. Linus, he's stronger than some of the others," Paddy says in his hoarse, soft voice. He ends the thought there and shifts to an upcoming worry, the inexperience of his team.

"Some of these young dogs, they run all right but they don't rest. They don't eat. They screw around. They don't get down to business," he says, talking half to himself. "They'll either get with the program . . ." He does not finish the thought.

Like many experienced mushers, Paddy had planned to pass right through Braeburn without stopping. For one thing, there are people and other teams and noise and lights here—distractions that make it hard for dogs to settle down and rest. For their sake, it's better to carry on and camp somewhere quiet in the woods. But a musher must weigh his personal interests, too, and stopping at places like this, where there is shelter, warm water, and a heated stove, becomes almost impossibly difficult to resist. Temperatures have not yet plunged into the bitter range of 40 below. Yet it remains inhumanly and ceaselessly cold, dark, and lonely along the trail—a fact you can see in the drawn, variegated faces of thawing mushers. The chance just to heat one's hands and shed the weight of a heavy parka, to share some human company with people who understand, grab some sheltered sleep, dry your underlayers, now sweaty and dank from exertion—these are temptations enough to undo many a race plan.

In these matters of warm cabins and trail hospitality, race rules emerge straight from Gold Rush days: mushers can stay at cabins as long as they are open to any passerby. Food and hot water may be accepted, or purchased, as long as the terms are the same for anyone. So the way stops at roadhouses and cabins, public and private, become essential experiences in the adventure, very much in keeping with the traditions of the Far North. For local holdouts in this faraway bush, the same today as one hundred years ago, the visits of mushers provide the only social mixing of midwinter.

Last year, when he was not racing, Paddy Santucci arrived at Braeburn cabin with $300 in his pocket, of which he spent $180 on beer that first all-nighter. His boozy antics are recalled while he fills his thermos bottle with hot Tang.

"Terrible to have drinking partners with memories," Santucci mutters, as he leaves the warm lodge to hook up his dogs.

This much is now apparent: the Quest is not comprehensible as a one-thousand-mile race. It is thirty-eight simultaneous one-thousand-mile races, each one occurring in a discrete bubble of space. In the slanting light of day, on the unobstructed ice of the great river, this bubble can extend in a line-of-sight radius of a mile or more around each dog team. In darkness, the space shrinks to only ninety feet in any direction, the distance a halogen headlamp penetrates the darkness. Paddy Santucci's ordeal, for instance, occurred in isolation from anything else happening on the trail. The musher whose sled runner catches a tree and is ripped from its stanchions has an entirely different account of trail conditions than do others who whiz by unscathed. Thirty-eight mushers are sequestered in boundless wilderness.

Leaving Whitehorse, the mushers drive their teams north, or downriver, on the Yukon. Sometimes, a few may bunch up in a group, the

energy of the teams playing off one another and the mushers enjoying
the camaraderie. With twilight fading, the trail veers left off the main
Yukon River and onto the tributary Takhini River, then passes under a
highway bridge, where the last hardy spectators gather, and into the
wilderness. This is country celebrated by Robert Service in his poem
"The Cremation of Sam McGee":

> *On a Christmas Day we were mushing our way*
> *over the Dawson trail.*
> *Talk of your cold! Through the parka's fold it*
> *stabbed like a driven nail.*
> *If our eyes we'd close, then the lashes froze till*
> *sometimes we couldn't see;*
> *It wasn't much fun, but the only one to whimper*
> *was Sam McGee.*

From here, the trail winds up a creek bed, over a small hill, and
down through another drainage, across some small frozen lakes, and
into dense spruce forest. The route will be traversed chiefly in darkness, with most mushers taking two long breaks along the way and a
few brief stops to give their teams a snack. The competitors will briefly
reenter "civilization" here at Braeburn.

Rusty Hagan almost doesn't make it. Just a few miles from
Whitehorse, where the trail veers away from the road, his dogs are surprised by the sight of a cluster of spectators. Instead of continuing
straight, they charge happily up the riverbank and into the crowd, tails
wagging. No big deal.

Hagan dismounts, grabs his leaders by the neckline, and begins to
turn the team around. But a tangle develops in the middle of the team,
and Thunder, a team dog, becomes entangled in the lines. She is chok-
ing. She struggles violently. The whole team bunches itself in a snarling
knot. Hagan senses from Thunder's desperate lunges that the dog is in
serious trouble. He also knows that when a frenzy develops in a pack,
teeth flash, and often a wounded or struggling animal, even one who
is part of the team, is the target of attack. He has no alternative except

to plunge into the mass of snapping jaws to wrestle dogs and loosen the knot from Thunder's neck.

The dog is freed and stands, dazed and gasping. Hagan doesn't notice the trembling of his hands.

Frank Turner, the pint-sized, black-bearded veteran of all fifteen Quests—the only person who can make such a claim, or admission— also has a rough time of it. He tips over his sled and drags behind it for a while, then struggles to stop his team when it seems they are headed dangerously close to a spot on the Takhini River where the ice has opened up and deadly water is visible.

Frank's wife, Ann, expresses no apparent worry. "He can make things look a lot harder than they are," she says gaily.

Ann saves her expressions of sympathy for the only female in Frank's dog team, two-and-a-half-year-old Tatchun, a dog one-third smaller than the thirteen males. "That's my dog. That's my baby! Now he's got her in the lead with the big boys." Is she speaking with pride or alarm? It's hard to tell.

At the Braeburn Roadhouse, Frank rests over a mug of coffee, his eyes already showing some of the vacant sag that makes him a favorite with photographers. He does not seem concerned about his bumpy ride here, though. The open hole in the river, he says, "caught me by surprise. But otherwise, it was wonderful."

He is looking at his wrists. On one, he is wearing a $24.99 plastic digital watch that he recently bought for the race. On the other, he's wearing a $3,000 mechanical watch with a blue leather band that he is testing for a German watch company. It's supposed to be good to 45 below. Frank is marveling that, after 109 miles, both watches remain in agreement.

"Look, it says the same thing." He points to his dime-store digital. Turner is a smart competitor and says nothing critical of the sponsors, but I sense that he is wondering why someone would pay $2,975.01 more for one watch than for another that does the same thing. Maybe it will endure longer.

The watch company has distributed these cold-weather timepieces to five of the better-known mushers in the Quest. The first to cross the finish line gets to keep the watch. The others will have done the promotional field-testing for the manufacturer. Among the journalists who have come across the Atlantic to "cover" the Quest is one who writes for a German wristwatch magazine. He tells me the secret to the watch is that it runs without lubricants, which could become gummed up in the cold. The same as an electronic watch? I ask. Precisely, he says.

Just how does a writer "cover" the Quest anyway?

In my case, certainly not without lubricants, even at the risk of gumming things up. This is, after all, a celebration of the Gold Rush era. And there are traditions besides adventure to be upheld, as, for instance, was suggested by a 1898 Gold Rush headline from the *San Francisco Examiner:* FIRST BOATS FROM ST. MICHAEL EXPECTED TO CARRY LARGE QUANTITIES OF WHISKY TO CAMPS IN THE FAR NORTH . . . IT IS EXPECTED THE FIRST BOATS WILL BRING LITTLE BUT WHISKY AND MAIL.

Indeed.

Almost a week prior to the race, I set up operations in Whitehorse with the race organizers. Mine is the unhappy task of attempting to accredit, break in, condition, acclimate, sensitize, educate, and police the strangest press corps ever assembled to commercially exploit an event about which they know little. It is presumed by Quest officials that I know at least something about the press and about mushing. Or, more to the point, that I at least care about the fragile wilderness nature of an event like the Quest and how it could be diminished by thoughtless media hordes. The German tire company Fulda has paid for the transoceanic transportation and cold-weather outfitting for an entire press corps. All these journalists are hungry for "news" and, apparently, wholly beholden to Fulda. The TV sporting press, like EuroSport, regards the Quest as something of an outback Formula One kind of competition, and its members arrive in Whitehorse with the odd supposition that viewers in Europe actually care who among thirty-eight people they don't know is ahead at any given moment in a remote event they can barely comprehend, presented to them primarily so they will see hundreds of images of a tire-company logo and hear the word *Yukon.* The others in the foreign press contingent include a scattering of

automotive writers, travel writers, the wristwatch man, some general-
ist feature writers and photographers, and one of Germany's better-
known television weathermen, who will be giving nightly forecasts
from the trail.

Thank God for whiskey, I say.

In their private moments, a few of the European reporters who have
become my friends complain, but only halfheartedly, about being
under Fulda's thumb. A public-relations executive from the company,
for instance, works out of the same hired van where broadcast
reporters edit and transmit their reports each day. He watches the editing of their reports carefully. Negative images that might be in conflict
with Fulda's marketing campaign are resisted—not so much by threat
or demand as by mutual "understanding," my friends explain. Fulda
pays for this junket; the home-country press pays the company back by
keeping the story to Fulda's liking.

To my eye, the essential fascination of any exotic place is its people
and culture. Over the years, I have worked at home and abroad with
British, French, Italian, German, South African, and Latin American
journalists, and we shared this premise. So I am unprepared for the dis-
regard of this press corps for matters of local culture. When I suggest a
story to the press—say, about the life of native Athabascans along the
trail—I receive a shrug. Later, they say. Right now, man, there is a *race*
to cover. It takes me a while, but finally I realize the difference. These
are sports reporters; the Quest is purely a sporting event. Asking some
of these journalists to consider the local culture is like asking a photographer at the Miss America pageant to give up his front-row seat and
step outside to take pictures of protesters. They stroll the streets of
Whitehorse in clusters, like at a Grand Prix circuit, all in their matching
red parkas festooned with Fulda logos. In appearance, they match the
three hundred European tire dealers Fulda also brought over to see the
start of the race and spend a few days in Whitehorse living it up. The
entire German contingent was transported in a chartered jet repainted
with Fulda's name on the fuselage. Quest officials complain under their
breath that the tire company spent more for this flying logo than on
direct sponsorship of the race.

Virtually all such comments are whispered, however, if voiced at all.

Any company that brings this many free-spending Europeans to the remote Yukon in midwinter can behave as it pleases, thank you.

I think of all the communities that want to be part of the tourist boom, and of all those that are. All those that smile even when they don't like it, just as Whitehorse smiles when its street signs are covered with banners advertising a tire not even sold on this continent, when a corporate flag is hoisted alongside the flag of Canada. I follow behind a camera crew as it roams downtown, interviewing residents for a Fulda promotional video. The question the crew wants answered is not about local customs or life but this: What do you think of Fulda? Great, wonderful, thanks for coming. That's what the locals dutifully say to the red parkas, the red army. A few minutes later, I lean over and ask a gray-haired woman, Is that how you really feel?

Oh God, no, she replies. "Have you ever seen such arrogance? I wish they'd just go."

Inconsequential thoughts. Who cares, really? The Europeans are filling up the pubs and buying the T-shirts. They've booked every room for miles. Whitehorse can have its street signs and flagpoles back soon enough. And the folks of the Far North can go back to freely speaking their minds. Hurrah for the deutsche mark. What's the harm?

At this moment, I am endeavoring to suggest how one "covers" a spread-out, lonely event like the Quest. For me, the unpaid job as press liaison grants insider's rights. I hope from this vantage I can see more, or at least be in a position to gather up more by word of mouth. And I'll have expert guidance in trying to filter out the chronic, and colorful, bullshit for which mushers are renowned. In turn, perhaps I can do right by sharing with my press colleagues what I have learned of the Quest's traditions. I hope the press will better understand the Quest's connection to history, to the communities of the Far North, as well as to raw adventure. Either that, or at least let's hope the reporters won't screw up, get in the way, accidentally step on a dog, crash a snowmachine into a team on a hairpin corner, fire a photographic flash in some musher's face out on the trail, or forget to share the largesse of Fulda's expense account.

For the first half of the Quest, I'm driving a loaner car and will be keeping pace with the mushers via the road. The colorfully named Klondike and Top of the World Highways, virtually deserted this time of year except for now-and-again trucks, will get me five hundred miles, to Dawson City, north and northwest of Whitehorse. Along the way, I will intersect the trail at only four places: Braeburn Roadhouse, two small Indian villages, and a distant cabin. There will be no bed on which to sleep, little time for sleep anyway, and no shower; my stomach will be soured by a diet of cigarettes, coffee, and greasy game meat.

For some of the Quest rookies, the first leg of the trail is daunting.

Brenda Mackey had family footsteps to follow. It was a miserable exercise.

For one thing, she lost her way for a while between Whitehorse and Braeburn. When she tried to turn around, she wedged her sled in the trees and had to unpack her ax and chop her way out. Fighting lack of sleep, she also let go of her dog team and could have been in serious trouble except another musher was only a short way ahead of her and brought them to heel. Somewhere, she lost her knife.

The petite rookie's one-line comment beat her to Braeburn.

"I think next year I'm going to college."

In mushing, the Mackey clan is like none other. Brenda's dad, Rick, won the Quest last year and the Iditarod in 1983. He is a favorite again this time, even though his much celebrated lead dog, Leon, has been retired. The patriarch of the family, Grandpa Dick Mackey, the 1978 Iditarod champion, is following the first half of the Quest in a motor home. Brenda is just a year past the minimum entry age of eighteen and this is her first epic race. Together, they are long-distance dog mushing's first dynasty.

After an hour's rest in the warmth of Braeburn, Brenda is decidedly more cheerful, and college isn't sounding so appealing after all.

"Next year, I'll probably be stupid and say, Gee, I'd like to do this again," she remarks.

Misery of a different kind drops Aliy Zirkle to her knees on the opening section of trail.

Before the race, a friend had handed her a tarot card. "It was the fool;

it was right on," she says. "I went into this not knowing shit from shinola, except that it would be the toughest thing in my life."

Yes, but did she have to be violently sick too? Her kennel partner, Jerry Louden, reaches Braeburn just before dawn on the second day of the Quest and pauses long enough to report that Aliy is struggling behind him, sick and vomiting. Louden is levelheaded, painfully quiet, and as tough as they come, so his concern is not taken lightly. Race officials and Aliy's friends begin looking at their watches.

Out on the trail, Aliy resigns herself to the flu. She's holding on, riding the runners, and periodically throwing up. The greasy sweat that flushes across the face when you're vomiting freezes and chills her. She relies on her dogs to stay on the trail and keep out of trouble. In the shadow light of the big moon, Aliy tries to assume a trancelike state of mind, pushing aside thoughts of the 950 miles ahead of her, the cold, the dog food that needs to be cooked, the steep summits ahead, all of it. But there is no reliable "off" switch to the brooding part of the brain, so sometimes she must let her self-image for toughness wrestle with her self-pity until her stomach turns over and she can enjoy that momentary, quick-fire return of equilibrium that arrives after a fresh purge.

Finally, she can go no farther. She stops her team, cinches down the hood of her parka, and passes out on top of her sled bag. It is one of those hallucinogenic fevered sleeps with the muscles tight and achy, with bouts of shivers made interminably worse by the subzero temperature surrounding her. But it is rest. And even though she is falling behind, the rest is good for her dogs too. That thought consoles her.

She awakens still weak but resumes the trail. Then George begins to give her problems. A floppy-eared team dog, white with brown ears and mask and with a flash of pink on his muzzle, George was born into the tough life of the native village dog. Aliy first introduced him to me as a "trot-along kind of guy," a stable, athletic dog with no history of quitting. A screecher, he helps excite the whole team whenever he is put into harness fresh. He is not fresh now, though, and is "necklining." That is, he has quit pulling. You can see it because there is slack in the tugline at the trailing end of his harness, and the short neckline that keeps him close to his partner is taut—the rest of the team is pulling him. This is a danger sign. Perhaps George is also ill or has injured himself in some way not readily apparent. Or maybe he just lost his "head" for the trail. She unhooks the dog and packs him inside the sled bag so only his head is exposed. He will ride the rest of the way to Braeburn.

"I think he had a mental breakdown. And I didn't want to argue with him," Aliy explains.

The morning sun throws a pink blush over the snow as she arrives at Braeburn, still queasy but hiding it. The temperature is already above zero, signaling the onset of a day that is on the warm side of perfect. There is no spectator crowd, just mushers, dog handlers, veterinarians, and a few officials. She flashes her brilliant smile as if a million people were watching. If points were allotted for style, Aliy would be among race leaders right now.

After a four-hour rest, Aliy heads up the trail, leaving George behind. She also drops Skinny, who is coughing enough to worry her. They are two of fifteen dogs dropped at Braeburn. Both might perk up if brought along, but the seventy-nine-mile section of trail ahead winds through a valley where mushers must cross a chain of a dozen elongated lakes, en route to rejoining the Yukon River. In between, the trail crawls up steep banks, threads through rough forest, and then drops back onto the surface of the next lake. Like canoeists, mushers call these portages. They require scrambling up banks and marshaling intense concentration though the wooded sections—no place to burden the team with an unwilling or sick member.

The loss is not critical because the other dogs in Aliy's team are running well. Foremost among them is Flood, a brindle male with a vanilla-colored face and comedic ears that stand at half-mast, the tips drooping limply forward, ears that quiver at the slightest movement and that beat steady, like metronomes, when he runs. As any pet owner knows, one of the responsibilities of a dog, even a serious working dog, is to be amusing. Flood is also the team's main leader, Aliy's pacesetter, and the brains of the outfit—a dog given his name after being rescued from an abandoned native village when the Koyukuk River jumped its banks in 1994.

"He's taught me so much. Now he kind of reads my mind. He's my most important dog. It's me and him. We're going to see if we can do it. I have that much faith in him," says Aliy.

Kronk is another leader, a village dog, plain brown. He doesn't teach, but he reliably invites instructions. What now, boss? Rubia is an alternate leader who often runs in the slot behind the two front dogs, swing position. She has a strawberry-blond coat with a pink nose and weighs just forty-one pounds, noticeably less than the males around her. She is a spirited dog; Aliy calls her the team spark plug on account of her heart and drive.

She is paired with various team dogs; they are Stasha, a fine-boned animal whose stamina worries Aliy, and Stasha's eighteen-month-old offspring, Roger. Martin is another of the dogs that Aliy considers most worrisome. Plink is a last-minute addition to the team, replacing a dog that became sick at the starting line. Missy is another late starter. Chip, with yellow eyebrows interrupting his black face, is a powerhouse: "He goes and goes." And then there's shy, nervous, black-coated Cisco. "It's kinda sad," says Aliy. "She'd enjoy life a lot more if she wasn't so spooky."

Just in front of her sled are the wheel dogs, Twister, a lanky brindle-colored dog with the blood of sprint dogs in him, and Prince, another blond with a liver-pink nose, who is tough and fast "and too smart for his own good," as Aliy puts it.

Lead dogs, swing dogs, team dogs, wheel dogs: for now, they are your family as well as your drivetrain—a long-fanged, well-muscled, interdependent and temperamental family.

Traveling long distances, dogs run and rest in about equal measure. As with money in a bank, you take out of a team only what you put in. Under normal conditions, a team may travel for two hours. Then the dogs are stopped and given a snack, perhaps a chunk of frozen white-fish the size of a baseball, or a piece of salmon that had been intentionally allowed to sour before freezing. After another two hours on the trail, the dogs will rest for four hours, scraping themselves nests in the snowpack.

There is little rest for the musher. At the four-hour stop Aliy first has another twelve snacks to hand out. She strips booties off forty-eight feet. From her sled bag, she unpacks and assembles an aluminum alcohol stove. She stuffs a handful of spun insulation into the fuel pan to act as a wick for the alcohol (mushers once used rolls of toilet paper). She gathers heaps of snow to melt in her five-gallon cook pot. While the water heats, she rubs each dog foot with liniment and checks for swelling, soreness, chafing. Tender wrists need to be massaged with a penetrating balm and wrapped in neoprene to prevent swelling. She has praise for each dog; each dog gets its moment. A belly scratch or a rub on the withers for Flood and Kronk and Rubia and Twister and Prince and Stasha and Roger and Martin and Plink and Missy and Chip and Cisco.

Woozy, battling waves of nausea, she feels herself stagger and droop. No, she tells herself. A musher must exude leadership and confidence above all, for the team must never doubt that the greatest and only thing in all the world is to be a sled dog and to be out here right now, in Aliy's company, running around the clock, hell-bent in the dead of winter.

Maintaining this spirit in the animals is one of the magic tricks of mushing. It occurs mostly beyond what the eye can perceive or the ear hear. As children, we are taught to behave as if we're not scared around dogs, but we also are taught that dogs will be able to look inside us and "sense" whether we are being honest or if we're really afraid after all. As any observant pet owner can attest, dogs can. There are no words that humans can utter to make dogs, even willing ones, rise and run and pull with heart for days on end.

So just how does the dog driver drive? Surely some of the skill is conveyed in a musher's tone of voice, the patterns of movement. It's also a consequence of the musher's understanding of dogs, of the dynamics of rivalry and competition within the members of a team, and of the team's expectations for itself. It is, in short, a question of leadership. Any military commander can leap from a foxhole and yell *Charge!*, but only some are followed. Ultimately, the qualities of leadership are as mysterious as the colored dust on a butterfly's wings, or the crystalline shape of a snowflake. The slightest chink in attitude can spread through a dog team and destroy its will to pull as thoroughly as a crack can ruin a wineglass. Conversely, a single inspired dog can goad everyone else into action. Skillful mushers are considered "doggy."

Into the cook pot, now nearly boiling, Aliy adds frozen meat and kibble. This mixture must steep for a half hour. Then the dog food is ladled into twelve pans. When temperatures plummet, a second batch of broth may have to be cooked to keep the team hydrated. Because she is still fighting bouts of nausea, Aliy passes on her own dinner. She is carrying three things: cookies, prepackaged crackers with peanut butter, and some Ziploc bags of precooked stew, or something like it, that a friend prepared for her. The sealed plastic bags are meant to be dropped in the dog water and thawed.

Among the musher's many fears is oversleeping. To crawl into a puffy sleeping bag is to risk being comfortable, which leads to inevitable deep, satisfying, unbearably wonderful sleep—while other mushers are on the move. So if Aliy can claim an hour or even two out of this rest, she will lie down on the Cordura cloth of her sled bag in her trail clothes, shivering and dozing uncomfortably until rousted by the cold. The best mushers are known for their small sleeping bags and their large alarm clocks.

Three hours into the stop, Aliy rises, almost drunkenly as she battles against her body's insistent argument to remain asleep. There is more snow to melt, another batch of dog food to cook, forty-eight fresh booties to fit, wrists to unwrap, the sled to pack. . . . And Aliy must change her own socks because her bunny boots, insulated by rubber, felt, and air, do not allow for the evaporation of moisture. She can feel her feet sloshing in their own sweat. She must also find new batteries for her headlamp and load them into the power pack that she wears inside her clothes, close to her body, to keep the batteries warm. Frozen batteries give off virtually no power. The battery pack couples to the headlamp via an insulated wire.

The team stirs. George is no longer among them to raise excitement with his screeching. Maybe Rubia will howl and get them psyched.

Okay, guys, let's go.

The dogs shoulder forward. Aliy pushes to help. Wind hits exposed skin, the inside of the nose hardens with a glaze of frost, ice beards begin to form on hairy dog faces, eyes sting and blink as Aliy looks for trail markers ahead and studies the gaits of her twelve remaining dogs, one by one. Her headlamp throws a narrow beam into the wild, while the moon casts a white sparkling glow over the lake ahead and the hills beyond.

So the cycle continues, unceasing, through the short days and long, violet nights.

When I was young and growing up in the West, the greatest pleasure in our family was to get in the car and go. Sometimes we had a destination and other times not. Joy was derived from movement. And, oddly enough, it gave us all a sense of accomplishment. What did we do? We went for a drive. Out there on the road, I learned, no one bothered you. Yet you had not succumbed to idleness. You had, in fact, done something. Forward motion almost always meets the test of worthwhile activity. For these same reasons, I still enjoy getting in the car or even folding myself into an undersize airline seat. When I am traveling I never feel I should be doing something else. I always feel I am on the verge.

Over the years, naturally, I was influenced by an assortment of writers. Most of them, as it turns out, reinforced my belief that the journey is itself a meaningful end, because it is the fountainhead of adventure: Conrad and Hemingway, London and Saint-Exupéry, Jack Kerouac and Bruce Chatwin, Redmond O'Hanlon and Edward Abbey. For a while, I wrote a column about travel books. I found that most worthwhile books fit the category. Love and war and religion, to name three of humankind's preoccupations, are serious journeys all. The late Bruce Chatwin, once described as the British writer most would-be writers in the United Kingdom wished to emulate, argued that humans by nature were nomads. He believed that our urge to wander was coiled deep and unmistakably in the DNA. As much as I admire Chatwin, I think he is but partly correct. Only some of us are nomads. In each generation, there are those who are content to stay in one place and those with an itch under their feet. Over the ages, this accounts for the fact that people did not band together and roam in circles from place to place. Some people have always stayed put while others wandered. That way, we've gradually spread out and filled in all the empty spaces on our planet. Upon arrival in a new place, some set up homes while others moved on.

One of the last places on our planet to be explored and filled in was the western edge of North America. Those who wandered here from the East, to the Pacific rim of the continent, were the most restless humans ever: self-selected over thousands of generations to wander. They ran out of space and hit the seashore at temperate latitudes, turned right and headed north until they came to the end of the line, to those places we know as Alaska and the Yukon.

A pioneering Jesuit missionary in Alaska, William Judge, said the early settlers here were "men running away from civilization as it advanced westward, until now they have no farther to go and so have to stop."

From here, every human who wanders, at least on the surface of the planet, will be headed backward to somewhere already settled.

Who did these ancestral wanderers meet in the Far North? A population of natives, two families of them: the Eskimos of the coast and the Athabascan Indians of the Interior. We can only postulate about the ancestors of these peoples, but it would seem that they, too, were among the restless in their originating part of the world, and that during the Ice Age they crossed the great Bering Sea land bridge to push east into the unknown and reconcile humankind to the extremes of cold and latitude.

Exactly when the dog entered the culture of the Far North is more open to speculation. Perhaps it was domesticated from the short-faced wolf some 10,000 years ago in the Ukraine and Siberia. Or maybe the occurrence was wholly apart from all the other evolutionary friendships, born of dependency, between the forebears of man and the ancestors of the wolf, relationships between hunting companions that may go back 500,000 years. DNA analysis of bones found around ancient campfires elsewhere on the globe suggests the first dog evolved as a distinct animal from the wolf at least 135,000 years ago. There are no signs so old of the dog in the high latitudes. In fact, hard evidence goes back only 1,000 years to indicate that seminomadic Eskimos of the Arctic used dogs as draught animals. At the same time, it appears that while Athabascans employed dogs as hunting partners, they did not develop the dog sled until introduced to it by Russian and Canadian fur trappers in the nineteenth century.

Soon after that, all hell would break loose for man and dog alike.

5

They are like crazy people. All the time do they go on, and on.
Why do they go on? I do not know. Only do they go on. What
are they after? I do not know. . . . But I ask questions no more.
I, too, go on and on, because I am strong on the trail.

—Jack London

The first feverish reports from the Far North reached San Francisco in the summer of 1897. When the steamship *Excelsior* docked, sunburned passengers staggered off, dragging carpet bags and grips too heavy to carry. Gold! By the sackful. Two days later, the SS *Portland* docked in Seattle. Newspapermen hired a tugboat and intercepted the ship on her way into port. They found more riches and raced back. Extras were printed and ready when she tied up. GOLD! GOLD! GOLD! screamed the headlines.

During the next year, the Klondike grew into a national mania. Perhaps one hundred thousand people would join the chase, risking everything for passage to the territories of Alaska and the Yukon. Men—and it was mostly men who were drawn north—ascended in social standing just by declaring their intentions to travel to the Klondike and scoop untold riches from the bottom of the streambeds. *Argonauts* they were called, after the sailors of Greek mythology who sought the Golden Fleece. In the departure port towns of Seattle and San Francisco, they wore buttons proclaiming, YES I'M GOING THIS

SPRING. They had their photographs taken in extravagant Klondike costumes against painted backgrounds of snow and mountains. Their faces were cocky, their poses swaggering, their thumbs tugging at the armholes in their fancy vests. At least for a while, they measured their prosperity in the currency of hope. Among them was Jack London. He was twenty-two and he stayed just one winter. Suffering from scurvy, he returned home with $4.50 in gold dust. The good ground had been staked long before he and most of the others even left home.

Ah, but the tales. London had given up writing, but now he tried anew. This time, his stories endured. They tell us most of what we know about this country in winter, its wild cold and danger, the dependence of humans on dogs, and the outsized dimensions that men and women assume when they step over the line between civilization and frontier. In varying parts, London both captured and created these myths, and his writing conveyed them through the generations.

In the 1890s, North America suffered two financial panics and a four-year depression. The U.S. Supreme Court approved the "separate but equal" terms for racial apartheid. The Indian wars came to a bloody end at Wounded Knee, South Dakota, with the killing of twenty-nine soldiers and two hundred or so Indian men, women, and children. The fires of the Industrial Revolution drew families off the farms. Waves of European immigrants washed up from across the Atlantic. For growing millions, there was no longer such a thing as fresh air or bountiful vistas, only city squalor and factory labor. The most celebrated men of the time were those who hoarded the nation's wealth in extravagant fortunes. Coxey's army of the unemployed marched on Washington. Jacob Riis published *How the Other Half Lives,* an exposé of urban slums. The term *social Darwinism* became popular, describing an order in which the fittest—or should we say, the most rapacious—survive. As if to prove the theory, confidence men and snake-oil swindlers became an everyday part of life. Burlesque shows featured helpless maidens in the clutches of tenement landlords, a real enough slice of life.

This is what history myopically calls the Gay Nineties, the Gilded Age.

So the great Klondike Gold Rush of 1898 provided a distraction from the drudgery and the doubts that came as a consequence of rapid economic and technological change. A poke of gold could vault any man into a mansion with satin sheets, and going to get it meant honest adventure. Think of it! Adventure, freedom—what healthy man could resist? But the trouble was, by the time most Argonauts struggled their way to Dawson City they were too late for gold. All the creeks were sectioned, bottom to top, into lawful five-hundred-foot claims. Yes, six of the streams happened to be the richest ground, inch for inch, ever found. But just as in the factories back home, most people ended up doing the backbreaking work for those few who held ownership. There would be few mansions for the latecomers. Maybe it was no accident that Jack London eventually became a muddleheaded socialist and, for many years, the most popular American author in the former Communist bloc.

Although the Gold Rush was a socially explosive event, it lasted only a few short years. And unlike the 1849 stampede to California, the Klondike did not foreshadow permanent settlement. Within two years of the California strike, the state was admitted into the union. Within five years, San Francisco had grown into the West's most storied city. By contrast, the Yukon, 30 percent larger in area than California, remains but a Canadian territory over a hundred years after the Klondike discovery. Its current population is but 32,600, perhaps just a third its Gold Rush high, smaller even than some California subdivisions. There are barely eleven hundred miles of paved road in the territory, and Yukoners even today are outnumbered almost ten to one by caribou. According to the government census, the Yukon has only one city, three towns, four villages, and two hamlets.

Why the difference in lasting outcome between California and the Klondike? No doubt the twin difficulties of climate and geography in the Far North. And surely, these account for the strange fact that in rural reaches of the Yukon, and Alaska too, there are fewer inhabitants today than at any time since whites began to settle the Far North, and significantly fewer in the cities and bush wilderness than at the height of the Gold Rush. Back then, miners' campfires in the canyons glowed and made the valleys appear like the "Inferno itself," as one account

described it. A dog musher or river paddler could rely on finding a
public roadhouse every thirty miles or so along major trails, one day's
travel from the last. Today, that would be true only on highways. In the
remainder of the bush now there are Indian villages and some remnant
trappers, miners, and social holdouts, but few public services.

Today's travelers must be self-sufficient, although they can usually
expect a hot pot of coffee, a hunk of boiled moose meat, or sleeping
space on the floor if they happen upon the cabin of a bush rat.
According to the customs of the North, unoccupied cabins remain open
for the benefit of travelers.

"Good day and welcome," reads a sign inside one unoccupied
Yukon cabin I found on a dog trail ten miles from a road. "If you chose
to inter [*sic*] Please: (1) Fix any thing that needs fixing (2) Clean up what
ever needs cleaning (3) Replace it if you take it. That includes wood and
lamp oil."

An Outsider might wonder at this collectivism among some of the
continent's most defiantly independent people. But such a doubter
would be forgetting the difficulty of travel at these latitudes and the
small margins of error for survival.

Even war, that consuming human pastime, can be overwhelmed
here. If asked whether North America was invaded by the enemy during World War II, most people would reply no. Actually, the Japanese
captured and held the Alaskan islands of Attu and Kiska early in the
conflict. Some six hundred Americans died recapturing these islands,
and the conditions were so miserable and impossible that the combat-
ants chose never to fight here again.

Jack London conveyed the difficulties of high-latitude survival most
unforgettably in his short story "To Build a Fire." This tale coinciden-
tally occurs just about where the Yukon Quest mushers are on the trail
right now—along the Yukon River, south of Dawson City by a couple
of days. A single winter traveler, accompanied by a lone dog, breaks
through the thin ice skin over a hidden spring and soaks his feet. He
struggles against the cold to make a fire and dry out. But he makes a
mistake: he places his kindling under a spruce tree, and the accumulated snow held in the branches cascades down and smothers his fire. By

now his hands are too numb to build another. He strikes all seventy of his matches in a final, futile try. Then he feels the numbness spread up his legs and arms; as the story closes, he "drowsed off into what seemed to him the most comfortable and satisfying sleep he had ever known."

Bad luck and a single mistake: the cold forgives nothing.

Variations on the story have echoed for a century. Robert Service's poem "The Cremation of Sam McGee" tells of a sourdough's last request to have his body burned rather than face the "awful dread of the icy grave."

My friend Joe May, the old dog musher and Iditarod champion, remembers a time he broke through the ice in a creek one winter when he was trapping south of Mount McKinley in Alaska. His matches were in his pocket. They became soaked and were useless. In the cold, his mood alternated between despair and euphoria. He drove his dog team the rest of the day and all night to reach a cabin where a fellow trapper had a fire going. Joe thawed his feet in buckets of warm water. Pieces of seven toes turned black and sloughed off.

"This is dangerous country," says Joe.

Sharp tools, wild animals, and fire. And more dangerous still, as I will hear again and again, is the lack of fire when you need it.

The Yukon River region had been yielding lesser quantities of gold for several years before the great strike.

In 1896, Circle City, located on the Yukon River, downstream in Alaska, had a music hall, two theaters, eight dance halls, twenty-eight saloons, and a library. The smallest coin in use was the silver dollar. Gold also was found at a Yukon tributary called Fortymile, near the U.S.-Canada border. By the early 1890s, the town of Fortymile had an opera house, a cigar factory, and saloons with Chippendale chairs. Men formed Shakespeare clubs to give readings. One miner known as Old Maiden carried fifty pounds of old newspapers with him, explaining they were "handy to refer to when you get into an argument."

Today, Circle is no longer a city but a wilderness outpost with a small restaurant, a trailer-hotel with four rooms, a schoolhouse for native children, and a seasonal general store. It can be reached at the end of a gravel road, although you're as likely to see a bush plane as a car outside the restaurant. Fortymile is abandoned except for a wilderness caretaker, its buildings rotting and sinking into the permafrost and its mining equipment great heaps of rust. It can be reached only by river or airplane.

The trail of the Yukon Quest intersects both camps after passing through Dawson City. To those familiar with history, they serve less as reminders of the wealth once extracted here than of something that seems even more remarkable: the prevailing code of brotherhood among the hermit-prospectors who roamed this country in the years preceeding the great Klondike rush. This code had nothing to do with the lingering stereotype of the lawless, greedy free-for-all mining camp. It seems there was just enough gold in circulation during those days to make life agreeable but still interdependent for these men who chose to live four thousand miles from the outfitting port of Seattle. But there was not so much gold, yet, to attract the avaricious and ruthless. Social Darwinism was still a year or two away.

According to the pre-Klondike lore, when a man paid for his whiskey he would place his poke on the bar and turn his back to show his trust that the bartender would measure out proper payment. Credit was extended to all, and even the town drunks were provided employment as "swampers" in the saloons. Most important, anyone who struck gold was expected to share the news and hold back nothing. Government and justice were the responsibility of citizens. Disputes and accusations of wrongdoing were settled at community miners' meetings. Both sides presented a case, whether a breech of promise or something more serious. Anyone could ask questions. Miners then voted and the verdict of the majority was final. There was no appeal.

James Wickersham, who arrived a few years later as the first U.S. judge for the region, recalled in his memoir *Old Yukon* the story of one such community gathering: "A young woman appeals to the miners at one of the camps to compel a dance hall fiddler to marry her and pay hospital and other bills resulting from her surrender in reliance upon his promise and his subsequent repudiation of it. A miners' meeting was called at which the miners from the nearby creeks appeared in numbers. . . . The trial was prompt. The plaintiff told her story and the defendant was heard in ominous silence."

The verdict was unanimous. The fiddler was ordered to pay the woman's medical bills plus $500 "and marry her as he promised to do, and that he have until five o'clock this afternoon to obey this order; and Resolved, further, that this meeting do now adjourn until five o'clock." According to Wickersham, the judgment was satisfied on time, whereupon the miners retired to the saloon to congratulate the newlyweds.

A decade later, Wickersham used his powers to impose the first tax on the Alaska side of the border: a fee on saloons to finance the construction of a courthouse. Modern jurisprudence had arrived. Wickersham administered it. But he never lost his sense of wonder for the simple elegance of citizen justice. Looking back, he wrote about the shotgun wedding, "It would have taken my court two years, with many pleadings, hearings and arguments, instead of two hours, to give judgment, which in all probability would have been reversed on some technicality!"

The big strike occurred on August 16, 1896.

Within two years the hermit-miners who had settled the region were overrun, their customs trampled in the greed of the stampede. Arthur T. Walden, who hauled freight by dog sled before, during, and after the Gold Rush, described the demise of the pioneer code in his charming memoir *A Dog Puncher on the Yukon*. At the time, he was working out of Circle City, traveling the same remote trails as today's Quest mushers. "After the gold rush of '98," he wrote, "conditions here and elsewhere in the Yukon changed. Civilization, with its religion, laws, disorder, stealing, education, murder, social life, commercial vice, comforts, and broken pledges crept in; justice cost money and disease raged. But before '98 life and property were safe."

Credit for the Klondike discovery goes to a jowly, sleepy-eyed American named George Washington Carmack. At the time he was traveling and working with two Tagish Indian friends, Skookum Jim and Tagish Charlie. A racist remark turned their luck.

The story is told most vividly by Canadian historian Pierre Berton in

his book *Klondike Fever*. It seems Carmack, Jim, and Charlie were standing at the mouth of the Klondike River, where it spills into the Yukon—
the future site of Dawson City. Here, they received news of a gold find
upstream in a creek now known as Gold Bottom Creek. Remember, this
was still the era when news of strikes was, by tradition, passed along
to everyone. George inquired if there was room left for other claims. A
man said yes there was, but not for any damn Indians. Carmack, the
son of a prospector in the California rush of '49, said to himself, "Never
mind. . . . This is big country. We'll go find a creek of our own."

Carmack, Jim, and Charlie ended up on Rabbit Creek. A first test
with the pan yielded a quarter ounce of "color." The three staked
claims—one five-hundred-foot section of the river for Jim and one for
Charlie. Carmack claimed a thousand-foot double stake as the discoverer, although the two Indians later disputed his right to a greater
share.

Within five days, the valley was a frenzy of men and gold lust.
Within two weeks, the stream was renamed Bonanza and every inch of
the canyon, rimrock to rimrock, was legally claimed.

It took word of the strike five months to spread the 325 miles to
Circle City. It would be two years before hapless Argonauts arrived
from Outside, looking to load their packs, quick, with all the gold they
could carry so they could hurry home, wealthy and suntanned, before
winter.

By one account, $60 million was spent outfitting and transporting
people to the Gold Rush in 1898. Newspapers across the continent carried ads for Klondike mining syndicates. Berton reports that these
organizations were backed by $165 million in capital. But the Klondike
had been oversold. Its gold production that year was $10 million.

Contemporary readers will not be surprised to find the press guilty of
hyping the Klondike Gold Rush. This, after all, was the heyday of ruthless press barons and their sensationalist "yellow" journalism.
Countless thousands of men, with overblown hopes and an underap-
preciation of hardship, were lured from their families. Many suffered
horribly and nearly starved in a land that could not support them, surprised by conditions unlike anything they had imagined. Seattle's

Mayor W. D. Wood was at a meeting in San Francisco when the rush began. He booked passage direct to Alaska without returning home. Streetcars on the West Coast stopped running when their drivers rushed for ships; businesses scraped for workers. Even newsmen caught the fever. The *Seattle Times* lost most of its reporters.

William Randolph Hearst, for one, was to blame. When the ship *Excelsior* docked in San Francisco, Hearst's local *Examiner* misjudged how the strike would ignite the popular imagination and gave the story only a few lines, while competing papers went wild over the scene of bags of gold being unloaded. Hearst's *New York Journal* carried no story at all, while a competitor told the fascinating scene in detail. No man to accept second place on a tale that promised to drive people to madness, Hearst dispatched expeditions to the Klondike and vowed he would not be beat again. His papers flogged it like an old mule. One of his reporters was a writer of national standing, Joaquin Miller, the so-called poet of California's Sierra Nevada Gold Rush.

Miller was fifty-six when he left for the Klondike late in the summer of 1897; he stayed just a year. His stories fueled the nation's gold lust. He openly exhorted men to drop their workaday lives and come north. He wrote about riches for the taking. He underplayed hardships. Shameless and irresponsible, his critics said. But in truth, Miller captured the very essence of the Klondike—what it was then in the human imagination and what it remains now: a sublime escape to adventure.

On his approach to Skagway on a boat up the Inside Passage, Miller filed this initial dispatch with a description of the landscape: "To the right snow and clouds, and clouds and snow, lighted up the bleak steeps and peaks and blazed as the sun battled for supremacy as in some majestic dream; awful, fearful, as not of earth. One needs to coin new words, words that are brighter, bigger, keener than common words, to describe even a single day in Alaska."

Later, on the awful and deadly Chilkoot Pass that led to Whitehorse, Miller waxed lyrical: "Right in the pass and within ten feet of the snow-bank that has not perished perhaps for a thousand years, I picked and ate a little strawberry, and as I rested and roamed about a bit, looking down into the brightly blue lakes that feed the headwaters of the Yukon, I gathered a little sunflower, a wild hyacinth, and a wild pea

blossom for my buttonhole. This is not only a big land, but a big heart-
ed land, a grand land, a savage land of savage contrasts, a land that is
grand and glorious even in its savagery."

What man working a textile loom in a darkened city factory with no
hope of bettering himself could resist the lure of the quest? Photographs of that era show pride, freedom, and braggadocio on the faces
of the men who collected in Seattle and San Francisco to await passage
north. To paraphrase Jack London from another of his books, the eyes
of these men showed spirits uplifted with the knowledge that one of
the great moments of living was upon them, when the tide of life was
about to surge up in flood.

Sure, they were foolhardy. But they were no longer held in captivity.
Their blood tingled with anticipation for the sights and encounters to
come. They had read the novels of Jules Verne and the pulp cowboy
tales of the Wild West. Now it was their chance to go forth into the fantastic. They were not the least reluctant to test themselves in the wildest
lands on the continent for the chance to walk tall among rich men all
the rest of their lives. And while they waited their turn to go, they stood
with their feet on a saloon's brass rail, dressed up in the silly garb of
what they thought an Argonaut should wear; they drank steam beer in
the middle of the afternoon and let their dreams soar, because they
were on their own and bound for adventure. And if someone could
have told them that photographs of their return would show faces that
had aged five years in one, with the cockiness knocked right out of
them and their eyes staring vacant—well, I wonder how many would
have slunk back to the factory bench?

Few, I would guess. Maybe none. I can almost hear them now, up all
night, pacing the boardinghouse floor in Seattle, tugging the handlebars of their big mustaches, waiting for their ships, talking over every
scrap of news from the North. My God, man, did you hear? A boy
panned $278 in fine gold just from the sawdust on the floor at the North
Saloon in Dawson City. That was gold what sifted out of men's pokes,
and that's a fact.

In many ways, the Gold Rush lived up to the worst stereotypes.
Dawson City, a ragged tent encampment on a gravel spit where the

Yukon and Klondike converged, was home to the world's greatest concentration of wealthy people living in abject squalor. In a swamp of mud and mosquitoes, real estate along the streets went for $5,000 a linear foot. For the sake of winning a bet, a man made his way down main street grotesquely jumping from the carcass of one dead horse to the next and then to a dead dog, never once touching ground.

Many found it easier to get gold from the pockets of miners than from creeks. And the deserving—no surprise—were not always rewarded.

"The story of the Klondike is remarkable for the fact that in an extraordinary number of cases the industrious and sober prospector profited little from the goldfields. . . . It was perhaps coincidental that Horatio Alger, Jr., should die when the great stampede reached its climax, but it is certainly true that many Klondike success stories made mincemeat out of his accepted formula," wrote historian Berton.

Some of the women of the Klondike were prostitutes, some were opportunistic widows and would-be brides, and others were spouses who refused to be left home. Dance-hall girls made a hundred dollars a show and could choose their consorts according to the yield of their claims.

Occasionally, however, someone rose above the stereotype. There was, for instance, a Mrs. Wills in Dawson. By herself she could not work the claim she had obtained for her invalid husband. So she baked bread for a dollar a loaf until she could afford the $250 for a single box of starch. With that she built a laundry, which earned enough money so she could hire men to work her claim. Later, she was offered $250,000 for the mine and turned it down.

The Argonauts surely found time to race sled dogs for the fun of it. But the first race to be recorded in history and lore was for real.

This was the race for a mining claim on Bonanza Creek early that first winter after the strike. It turned out to be a morality play fit for Hollywood. At the time, the law required that miners work their claims or lose them after sixty days. One such five-hundred-foot section on the upper part of Bonanza had been abandoned by its original claimant and was due to come open at midnight one day in early November. To stake a claim, a miner had to post a notice at the site and then register it at a government recorder's office, which happened to be fifty miles away.

Naturally many would-be miners coveted the section. After all, other claims on this creek had yielded pans of gold already and work had only begun. Fearing trouble, constables were dispatched to the scene. Miners milled around in the cold lantern light as midnight before the fateful day approached. They took stock of one another, weighed their chances. Most decided it was hopeless. But two men with fast dog teams pounded rival claim stakes exactly at midnight and sped into the darkness toward Fortymile and the recorder's office.

Jack London wrote of their epic dog race, and so did others. Everyone tells of how one team passed the other on the trail, and was then passed itself. Neck and neck, they arrived in town. The musher who happened to know the location of the recorder's office held back at the last minute, turned, and beat his rival to the threshold by a second, screaming out his claim. But the finish was so close and tempers so heated that a Mountie was summoned. He advised the men to split the claim, which they did. It proved to be one of the few on Bonanza that was worthless.

Before the rush was over, Alaska and the Yukon would be the scene of thousands of these encounters, where people and dogs, wonder and adventure, greed and cruelty all seemed larger in scale for the grandeur of the background.

These were legends to live up to.

6

The more one gets to know of men,
the more one values dogs.

—Anonymous

I am feeling tired already. Could I say "dog tired"? And through tired eyes, I see telltales of creeping exhaustion in those around me.

This is day three of the Yukon Quest and the leaders have passed through the community of Carmacks, named, of course, after the discoverer of Bonanza Creek's gold. An Indian village with a population of about 480, Carmacks hugs the bank of the Yukon River northwest of Whitehorse. There is one motel, one bar, and one six-table restaurant to serve summer tourists. Now, in winter, most residents and seemingly all the village children crowd into the government-built community center that the Quest uses as its way stop. Aside from deaths, divorces, and romance, the passing of the Quest is just about the only break from winter routine that people here can expect. Some years, villagers assemble a chili kitchen as a community fund-raiser, but I see no signs of anything but a two-gallon coffee percolator this time.

Like many native settlements, particularly those where alcohol is allowed, Carmacks appears numb to the joy of life. When I retreat inside the community center to warm myself, I am reminded of an airport at some remote outpost where the plane has been weathered out for days now and everyone is reduced to lassitude. Those few villagers who have been given official standing as race checkers or timers assume the air of petty tyrants. The sounds are the shuffling of heavy-booted feet, the squeak of folding chairs, coughs, snores. The children's smiles seem uncommonly bright, especially by comparison to the blank expressions of the adult villagers and to the vacant, pained looks of the passing mushers. The children have drawn fanciful crayon posters of each dog team. They root for favorites. The adults root for nothing, although perhaps down deep they root for spring. For now, they are dulled by the dark and cold, and maybe by booze. There are few jobs for the northern Indians in winter, and they live in a state of semi-hibernation, also known as welfare.

Carmacks is the first official checkpoint of the race. There is a mandatory two-hour layover here for all mushers. This is to allow the veterinarians time to inspect every dog. Logic might suggest that well-conditioned sled dogs start strong and wear down incrementally as the race goes on. This is not necessarily true. The first checkpoint is often an unsettling sight: a half dozen or more quivering, forlorn dogs in veterinary triage. A few are hooked to IVs to restore hydration. The first couple of hundred miles tend to weed out the unsound dogs. Many of the remaining animals hit a rhythm and get stronger as the miles pass, or so it seems. Maybe that's not the case. Maybe they hold their own better than the humans they are dragging behind them. Maybe they just look stronger because the mushers will get weaker so much faster. The fact is, not much science has been devoted to the physiology or psychology of long-distance sled dogs.

In any event, while dogs have been working more vigorously than humans in this Quest, they also have rested better. So far, I have slept twice in three days, both times in the front seat of my borrowed compact car. I got two hours at Braeburn and two hours here in Carmacks. This second time, I awoke very stiff in the 20-below cold. There are knots in my muscles and my ankle squeaks. Some of the mushers are complaining that the midday highs, reaching to 10 above, were too warm for their dogs. For me the days have been lovely. But the nights are cold even when I'm bundled in everything I've got, and I feel my body arguing with me constantly, urging me to sleep.

Medical studies for the U.S. Army suggest that, in fact, I am receiving adequate sleep to function. I should be just fine at physical tasks, like movement, although my cognitive abilities are already supposed to be slipping. In other words, with so little sleep, I won't be shooting or thinking very straight unless I slow way down. My body obliges naturally. I don't feel I have a choice in the matter. A couple of times, I feel my brain drifting away.

The standings at this point are meaningless. But like everyone else, I stare groggily at the acetate leader board. The first to arrive last night was Terry McMullin, a sixty-three-year-old Quest rookie. He is a former schoolteacher who lives in Eagle, Alaska, a village located several days up the trail. I don't suppose Terry wants to be first at this point in his first race. Almost certainly this is a sign that he is pushing too hard too early. Otherwise why wouldn't more experienced mushers be here with him? Why would history show, again and again, that these "rabbits" who break the pace fade long before Fairbanks? Surely Terry's game plan calls for him to keep his dogs from burning out. But rookie game plans are easy to draw up; they are harder to follow. McMullin seemed surprised to find himself in front. Maybe the cold has fogged his thinking. It has mine, and I have only myself to take care of—and an occasional Fulda press group. I don't have to feed fourteen dependent dogs and find my way down two hundred miles of icy trail through the heart of absolutely nowhere.

McMullin is a burly, good-looking man in a weather-beaten way. He has a thick head of silver hair, an easy smile, and is the oldest guy in the race, so he automatically has his share of fans. But I also happen to know about the small, cliquish community at Eagle, Alaska. I've visited in summer and winter, and one doesn't need to be there long before catching the echoes of small-town, cabin-fever gossips. So I also know that McMullin has plenty of detractors, too. They say he has been stingy with his hospitality and help in the bush. That's a harsh verdict in this country. I doubt if he'll be a contender. The experts expect he will not even finish.

A half hour behind McMullin is Louis Nelson, a fifty-four-year-old Eskimo from Kotzebue, Alaska. (A word about the word *Eskimo*. In Alaska, it is not considered a pejorative and is widely used among Eskimos and nonnatives alike. Attempts to discourage its use are met with resistance among Eskimos themselves. On the other hand, Canadians, both native and non, have the opposite view and the term is not favored.) Nelson is one of only two natives in the race. Most people in the mushing community are sorry there are so few. But years ago the snowmachine displaced the working dog in most native villages, and building up and maintaining large kennels is now beyond the financial means of most natives.

Natives who do race are encumbered by a stereotype, for which, I fear, there is at least some justification. Natives are said to be tough on dogs. Some are. I've seen it in races, and I've seen it in villages. I've also heard some explanations: native economies in the bush tend to be hand-to-mouth, except in the oil-rich borough of Alaska's North Slope. A dog that cannot earn its keep is a burden that a native musher may not be able to afford. And if he can afford it, he might wonder why the hell he should. Why not just kill that old dog that can't run anymore, or the pup with a bum paw?

Cultural crosscurrents make this a squeamish subject. As with all things cultural, one must rely on generalizations for which there are enough exceptions to allow for argument. Still, there is a generalization that is hard to deny: many Indians and Eskimos who live in the bush— and I say "many" when I believe it's almost all of them—either lead subsistence lives as hunter-gatherers or are not far removed from the culture that does. From this world view, animals are regarded differently than they are in Los Angeles, say, or Toronto or Bonn. In some ways, the animal holds a loftier place in native life because the animal is the cornerstone of survival. The food chain is not an abstraction. Animals serve humans with food, and sometimes with labor. Animals also compete with man for survival. A native village will hire lobbyists and fight all the way to Washington, D.C., or Ottawa to save the caribou from the incursion of white developments, all the while killing and eating caribou, and shooting any wolf or grizzly bear that may be competing for the same dinner. The native beholds this life cycle as "natural" and may

ask, Why does it make sense to kill more caribou to feed dogs that have
no usefulness? A twenty-year-old vegetarian in New York City, on the
other hand, may not give a thought to saving habitat for the caribou and
wolves to roam through, but objects vigorously to killing a single one
because animals, like people, are living beings endowed with individual rights. Killing a dog is even worse, because dogs are creatures bred
by humans for the purposes of companionship and draft labor. How
can you kill something for which you are responsible?

Unfortunately, Louis Nelson's arrival in Carmacks gives doubters a
reason to wag their tongues. His team is exhausted. Seconds after he
stops, the duty veterinarian unclips one collapsed dog and rushes it
inside for treatment. A camera crew records the scene. The dog is
reported to be dehydrated and suffering from muscle collapse. Other
animals in the team seem wobbly. In this, his first thousand-miler,
Nelson looks a little disoriented himself.

Matt Hall, the burly head vet from Alaska, cautiously observes, "I
think most of us agree, they're running a little faster than they should.
But who knows, maybe they're planning on long rests here."

Race officials have worried expressions on their faces. But they do
not, at least in my presence, say anything to Nelson, a thin, hard-faced
man who seems to keep his distance from the others. As it turns out, he
will spend exactly twelve hours resting here and will drop three dogs.

Worrisome reports are coming in from the trail. Stretches of open water,
called leads, are sighted. Those who passed at night are spared the terror. They do not see much of it at all. But those who follow in daylight
are appalled at the steady erosion of one section of sidehill trail. Each
musher who passes skids half-sideways along the slope and pushes the
trail further downhill. By the time stragglers come through, the pathway is only twenty feet from running water and who knows how much
closer to thin ice.

Back here somewhere in the field is Rusty Hagan, and I feel my
stomach tighten as I think about his nightmares.

In November 1993, one of the most likable mushers in Canada, one-
time Quest champion Bruce Johnson, was training for the 1994 race.

His team had ventured across a Yukon lake when the thin ice began to bow underneath them. Johnson's dread can only be imagined. Suddenly, the whole surface broke through, opening a lead almost a hundred feet long. From signs along the edges of the hole, Johnson apparently waged a struggle to pull himself out of the water. But in the few seconds before the cold took his strength, he could not find ice solid enough to support his weight. Johnson and his team perished, and the memory haunts the Quest to this day.

Several other Quest mushers have experienced the terror as part of their team plunged through the ice over deep water. In 1989, Fred Jordan won the sportsmanship trophy for stopping after his leaders went into a lead. Although wet and freezing, desperately yearning for a fire, he chopped down small trees to mark the danger for those who followed. In 1994, Alaskan Peter Butteri fished his lead dogs out of a hole in the Yukon River, all the while hearing the ice cracking under his feet and fearing he would crash down into the deadly current. This year Butteri's wife, Amy Wright, is running back in the pack, and reports of dangerous ice leave him on the edge of panic.

For some reason, I begin to amuse myself with a preposterous thought. Back beyond these hills and icy rivers is a "real" world of prime ministers, presidents, chancellors, stock markets, traffic lights, high fashion, movie premieres, and gourmet lattes. No matter how much of our lives we have spent there, and how acutely we have been tethered to the teeming rhythms of that world, it is now merely an abstraction. Beyond reach. It no longer touches us. For some who have been up here longer than I have, surely this reality is also beyond comprehension. Leaving Whitehorse, I could receive two radio stations, the local Canadian Broadcasting Corporation affiliate and AM 570, Gwich'In radio, on which natives in scattered villages of the Far North tell stories for one hour a day in their hoarse whisper voices. Those stations no longer penetrate the wilderness beyond Carmacks. Like the mushers, I am now connected to the electronic age only through audiocassettes.

Sing it, Emmylou. And sing it again.

Beyond Carmacks, the trail follows the Yukon River north and west forty-one miles to McCabe Creek. The race leaders are en route to McCabe before many of the other mushers check in to Carmacks, and I hurry along to meet them. In contrast to Carmacks, McCabe Creek is one of the most pleasant way stops of the Quest: a creekside homestead of log and frame cabins belonging to sourdough Jerry Kruse and his extended family. In the summer, Kruse operates a river barge and delivers freight to the mining camps that still dot the region. In the winter, he hunts and traps. And every February, since the Quest began, his family assembles here for what amounts to an annual reunion and party. Some of his ten kids have scattered elsewhere. Half came back this year to chop wood and bake fresh bread rolls and cook big tubs of McCabe Creek memorable moose barley soup. For a family like this, hosting the Quest is, I imagine, like a nineteenth-century farm family welcoming the traveling circus.

"We've met a lot of good people," Kruse says enthusiastically. "That first year, I remember there were fifty-three people in my living room. Now we clean out the wood shop. It's like a spring break. It's about having fun."

Mushers look forward to the stop too, for the opportunity to gather together away from the glare of race officials and timers and, yes, usually away from the press. Most will warm up here, eat, perhaps sleep for a couple of hours—and collect in the old bare-floored wood shop to sip coffee and trade bull. There is a worktable with benches in the middle of the shop that is reserved for mushers alone. The rest of us stand apart, or collapse on the floor. We have peeled off our parkas and fleece shirts but it still seems broiling hot in here. I pull out a thermometer: 60 degrees. Outside, spread across the acre-and-a-half snowfield between the main house and the shop, dog teams are lined out like semis at an interstate truck stop. Cook pots are bubbling, and the steam they release infuses the brittle-clean Arctic air with the ripe odors of boiling fish and raw meat.

Social respites like this are brief but essential to the character and joy of the Quest. Just like the old mail drivers, dogsled freighters, and prospectors, today's mushers spend most of winter alone, and the very idea of returning to friends and comfort softens those last hard miles of the trail.

This year, these last miles to McCabe are uncommonly difficult. Until now, the toughest aspect of the trail, aside from cold and distance, has been thin, crusty snow. Leaving Carmacks, the snow is progressively more abundant and pliant. But about thirty miles up the trail, as the teams drop from the riverbank back to the Yukon itself, Quest mushers encounter the first of the ugly obstacles about which they have been warned: jumble ice. The last eleven-mile stretch leading to McCabe is a lumpy, twisty, and dangerous labyrinth of sharp-cornered, uneven, unmovable, and unforgiving blocks of ice, some as big as railcars, all hard as tile and sharp enough to cut flesh. Conditions are not always this way. In some winters, the river freezes smooth and mushers worry about winds that blow away the snow and leave behind just a glazed, tractionless surface. Other years, like now, when temperatures are more fitful, the river freezes, breaks apart, and freezes again. Slabs of ice form and tear loose to float downstream. Eventually, the whole mess collects and freezes tight in jagged, random ice jams that can extend for miles. No safe passage is possible. A rough trail must be chopped with ax and chain saw ahead of the mushers. Through such an entanglement, a person or a single dog might carefully pick its footing. But when hooked together into a team, the lunge of one dog can whip-snake another into a bone-crunching protrusion; a pulse at one end of the gangline can fling the other end into a crevasse. A successful passage requires concentration, hard physical labor, and luck.

About eight miles before McCabe, Jerry Louden's spirits sink. He is a tall, iron-hard man who doesn't flinch. If he has any weakness at all, it's his difficulty staying focused when exhausted. He's run the Iditarod and he finished sixth in last year's Quest, but he still lacks enough thousands of trail miles to work through his run-rest cycles automatically in the fog of sleeplessness. For sheer toughness and strength, however, Louden has few equals. His teeth clamped shut, his face drawn fiercely, his breath coming in grunts and huffs, he wrestles his heavy sled through the confusion of obstacles that come not just every so often but constantly—the middle of his team invisible behind one shelf of protruding ice and his lead dogs already clambering over another further ahead. His determination, however, is not enough.

Smash! His lead dog, Maria, scrambling for purchase on an uneven slab of ice, pulls forward just as the gangline snaps tight. She is flung sideways into a block of ice and damages her shoulder. Damn. Scotty, one of the team dogs, is favoring his shoulder. Perhaps he stepped in a crevasse or banged into an overhang of ice. Damn. Then Taiga quits. Head problems. When a dog succumbs to fear, it's as apparent as one who has pulled a muscle. When a strong, confident dog holds back, its tail drops and curls between its legs, and it hunches its head back into its shoulders like a hunting dog that cannot stand the sound of a shotgun anymore. Damn, damn.

Louden arrives at McCabe slump-shouldered and quieter than usual, if that is possible. He feeds his team and himself and departs after a four-and-a-half-hour rest, his big size-fourteen bunny boots clomping through the snow as he pushes off. His team is now down to eleven dogs. Damn. All the big hills are still ahead, as well as 790 more miles.

Aliy Zirkle is still weak from the flu. Her dog Plink, who was a last-minute stand-in, is also having problems. He's not been pulling. Aliy drops him.

Paddy Santucci is unhappy with himself again. On the trail, he decided to swap leaders, giving a break to those who had been out front for a long time. Lead dogs feel extra pressure. They cannot, even for a second, break concentration or ease back in the harness. As he starts the rotation, Paddy unclips a leader named Mischief. In his fatigue, he forgets to reclip him to the gangline.

Paddy looks up and Mischief is loping into the woods. Aw, for fuck's sake. Paddy lumbers in pursuit. Even tired, a sled dog knows how to play. But this game is getting the team nowhere. After a half hour, a frustrated Santucci switches tactics. He gives up the chase and lies down under a spruce. Mischief, sensing the fun is over, comes and sits with him. The dog is reclipped back to the gangline. Almost forty-five minutes have lapsed. Victories have been decided by much less.

It's still early, mushers tell themselves. Stay calm.

For some, there may not be enough time to recover.

The inevitability of defeat looms for the musher who has become my closest friend and soul mate. Jimmy Hendrick is a wild man in the mold of Hunter S. Thompson, a social rebel whose antics are so far off the register and whose character is so singular that you want to applaud for the fact that such people still exist. Indeed, many people do applaud. If mushing is a culture of shy reserve, Jimmy is a saloon comic, boisterously loud, spontaneous, profane. You just know that men exactly like him enlivened the old gold camps a hundred years ago. He has a bushy thatch of strawberry-blond hair and a soup-strainer mustache. He moves in loose-jointed gangly bolts of energy. He goes from scowl to leer in a millisecond, laughing with a growl. Nearly everything amuses him.

Jimmy is an old hand at the Quest and he knows, better than most, when luck runs out. He scratched in 1994, a bitterly frigid year when temperatures averaged 40 below. His knee was fractured before the race and he limped to the starting line with a brace and a grimace. Several hundred miles down the trail, the brace constricted the flow of blood. Fluid pooled in his leg and foot and froze. He ended up with gangrene. "It's been like that all along—one disgusting failure after another." Haaahaaa.

This time, Jimmy is in fine condition but his dogs are not. They're ill. He's falling back and they aren't rallying.

Just two days before the start of the race, a shiver of panic spread through the contestants. A canine virus called corona had been diagnosed after the deaths of two puppies in Whitehorse dog yards. That meant local dog teams had been exposed. These animals had shared the practice trails with the Quest teams, so now everyone was exposed. The flulike Corona is not typically fatal to adult dogs, but Canadian veterinarian Marina Alpeza determined that many teams had not been vaccinated against it. It's too late, anyhow, for preventive measures.

Hendrick's team, which he has spent more than half a year assembling and conditioning, seems to be one of the unlucky ones. Corona induces uncontrollable diarrhea in dogs, weakening them rapidly. Jimmy has been traveling the trail on a runny carpet of dog scat, another year's dream and every dime he has now squirting out of his team. This cannot continue, he knows.

The Hendrick legend began on a river far from the Yukon. Back then he was a boatman on the Colorado River in the Grand Canyon—128 commercial trips, always making the white-water runs that others cheated, always redlined with exuberance for the wonder of it all.

When guiding Outside became unbearably bureaucratic and rule-bound and the rivers too familiar, Hendrick came to Alaska looking for new streams. The following year, 1989, his eye was caught by something else: the spectacle of people driving dogs for epic distances through the northern wilderness—going without sleep for days, without any reasonable chance of help, against weather and darkness, human and dogs alone.

"Jimmy isn't easily impressed. And that impressed him," says his partner and companion, Julie Boselli, a thirty-eight-year-old guide, businesswoman, mountaineer, musher, and beauty.

The couple now runs Too-Loo-Uk River Guides in the summer, along with the Patagonia retail store outside Denali National Park, near their three-room log cabin, which has neither electricity nor running water. In the winter, they train and race dogs in the cold flicker-light of the north. Why? How the fuck do I know, Hendrick says. I could be in Arizona where it's warm. I've been in this nine years and I'm not in the top three. How the fuck do I know? Haaahaaa.

These days, young men and women wait in line for the chance just to row a baggage boat on big-river trips without pay, gaining experience toward a license and possible seasonal employment. When Hendrick started in 1971 after a hitch in the Marines, it was different. Companies were popping up everywhere. Boatmen jobs went to the daring, the fun, and the footloose. "Coming from the regimented world of the military, it was unbelievable—people were just partying, having fun, having sex, smoking marijuana." In 1975, he was on one river or another, or en route, for the entire year. His first bout of skin cancer came in 1980, and he has battled it since.

With dogs, he started as a handler for others and began to collect their cast-offs. By 1991, living off the returns of rental property he purchased after a summer working on the *Exxon Valdez* oil spill cleanup, Hendrick had assembled a team of also-rans. He thought he would run the Quest once, just to see the trail. His goal was that shared by most rookies: finish. He remembers the more experienced musher who told him, You'll never get over the mountains with those dogs. You'll never make it.

"Who the fuck are you, I thought. . . . And when I passed that guy by in Eagle it was my first victory." At that point, the doubter was kind enough to mention that Hendrick was racing with his canvas sled bag attached backward in the basket of his sled. Oops.

Hendrick stumbled to the finish line that year. Seeing the trail once, however, wasn't enough. He ran the next five races and finished three, but never better than thirteenth. His total prize take of $4,200 is less than the cost of a good lead dog. Perhaps his flaw is only that he cannot push his team as hard as others can. He has always been tenderhearted with his dogs. The Humane Society team, he calls them. "I saw too many Bambi movies, I guess."

Why keep coming back?

"Why? . . . Why, goddamn, that's a hard question. I guess I sort of enjoy it. At least when it's over. There are some sections of the trail that blow me away. And, shit, there are some fantastic highs."

His face blotchy red from the cold, Hendrick arrives at McCabe Creek at almost midnight. He feeds and rests his dogs. The team curls up in the snow and Hendrick drifts in and out of uneasy sleep in the wood shop after almost everyone else has passed through. The coffeepot has gone cold.

I'm not going to scratch here, Hendrick remarks. I'm going to Pelly and scratch like a man. Haahaa.

By contrast, the leaders are advancing relentlessly.

At this stage, it is more important how the teams look than where they are in the pack. Rick Mackey, last year's winner, and John Schandelmeier, himself a two-time champion, might fool you into thinking they are on a camping expedition, if you didn't know better. Their work is automatic, their cadence effortless. They have no injured dogs, no corona virus, no harrowing stories from the trail. Fatigue fits them comfortably, like an old suit of clothes.

Watching them is like being at one of those dinner parties where the host cooks for fourteen, keeps the guests entertained, and has the house picked up before you leave while never really looking the least hectic.

At this moment, Mackey has just fed his dogs and is going to give them two more hours of rest. He's resting too. But instead of coming inside, where it is warm, he stretches out comfortably on his sled bag in the snowfield with his dogs. He lights a cigarette and pulls his hat over his eyes. His hand slowly feeds smoke into his mouth. Then his arm droops and the cigarette dangles in his outstretched fingers and he's asleep.

Schandelmeier, who is so lean you might think he never eats, is sitting inside at the workbench, devouring a huge bowl of moose barley soup, working his spoon with hands that are gnarled like welder's gloves. He has dark hair, dark eyes, a dark mustache, and kind of a lopsided carriage that is exaggerated when he walks because his scuffed bunny boots seem about two sizes larger than a man of his compact build should have to lift. He claims to be a loner, but if you're patient he'll give you an oversize grin and talk your ear off.

Right now, John is holding forth on the two theories of assembling a good dog team. One is to have a huge kennel, which increases the odds that you can pick out fourteen good dogs for race day. "Or you can have just a few dogs—and motivate them," he says, grinning, because that, of course, is his theory. "All you have to do is convince a dog that's been running all night and is tired that it's the greatest thing in life to be out here with me."

Schandelmeier stops talking suddenly, pauses as if he's just remembered something. His eyes are fixed on a battery-powered satellite telephone that a veterinarian has set up near a window.

"What day of the week is it? . . . Oh, shit, I missed my anniversary by a day. I could have called, but my wife turns off the phone at eight P.M. I gotta think of an excuse why I was not near a phone. I'll call her on Valentine's Day."

Eyes in the room roll in surprise. John Schandelmeier, mountain man, has just confessed to harboring a cellular telephone at his house near Paxson, in east-central Alaska. It would be like John Wayne telling you he grew pink pansies in his garden.

Mackey and Schandelmeier now dominate the Quest like no one has dominated a mushing event since the heyday of Susan Butcher in the Iditarod. They set the pace. Their strategy becomes every contender's strategy. Other mushers ask themselves not, Where am I in the race? but Where is Rick? Where is John? Everyone sets out with a personal game plan, but many of them will later confess it wasn't long on the trail before they began asking, Where did John make camp? How long did Rick rest? The musher's motto has always been Drive the dogs you have, not the dogs someone else has. Many mushers have forgotten that wisdom in the excitement of the race, however, and have exhausted their teams trying to run with Rick Mackey and John Schandelmeier.

Three hours after her father awakens and advances rested and confident down the trail, baby-faced Brenda Mackey rides into McCabe Creek. She looks younger tonight than her nineteen years, which makes the agony of exhaustion all the more apparent. Before coming inside to warm up, she unpacks her sled bag, pours alcohol into the fire pan. She lights the stove, and waits. Slowly, she sags and slumps onto her side. Nothing moves except a curl of steam venting from her cooker. She is asleep in the snow.

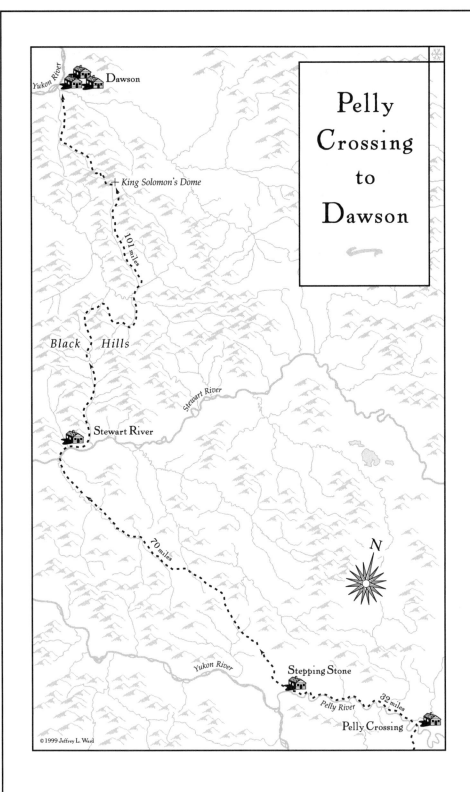

Yukon River

Dawson

King Solomon's Dome

101 miles

Black Hills

Stewart River

Stewart River

70 miles

N

Yukon River

Stepping Stone

Pelly River

32 miles

Pelly Crossing

Pelly
Crossing
to
Dawson

© 1999 Jeffrey L. Ward

Pelly Crossing to Dawson

ARRIVING AT PELLY CROSSING

1. Andre Nadeau,
    *Sainte-Melanie, Quebec**
2. Louis Nelson, *Kotzebue, Alaska**
3. Bruce Lee,
    Denali National Park, Alaska
4. Terry McMullin, *Eagle, Alaska**
5. Doug Harris, *Whitehorse, Yukon*
6. Brian MacDougall,
    Whitehorse, Yukon
7. John Schandelmeier, *Paxson, Alaska*
8. William Kleedehn, *Carcross, Yukon*
9. Rick Mackey, *Nenana, Alaska*
10. Frank Turner, *Whitehorse, Yukon*
11. Jerry Louden, *Two Rivers, Alaska*
12. Paddy Santucci, *Fairbanks, Alaska*
13. Cor Guimond, *Dawson City, Yukon*
14. Dave Olesen, *Hoarfrost River,
    Northwest Territories**
15. Keizo Funatsu, *Two Rivers, Alaska*
16. Amy Wright, *Tok, Alaska**
17. Dave Dalton, *Fairbanks, Alaska*
18. Ned Cathers, *Whitehorse, Yukon*
19. Tim Mowry, *Two Rivers, Alaska*
20. Aliy Zirkle, *Two Rivers, Alaska**

21. Mike King, *Salcha, Alaska*
22. Thomas Tetz, *Tagish, Yukon**
23. Keith Kirkvold, *Fairbanks, Alaska**
24. Larry Carroll, *Willow, Alaska*
25. Stan Njootli, *Old Crow, Yukon**
26. Jimmy Hendrick,
    Denali National Park, Alaska
27. Walter Palkovitch,
    *Two Rivers, Alaska**
28. Rusty Hagan, *North Pole, Alaska**
29. Brenda Mackey, *Nenana, Alaska**
30. John Nash, *Nenana, Alaska**
31. Brian O'Donoghue,
    *Two Rivers, Alaska**
32. Dan Turner, *Haines, Alaska*
33. Gwen Holdman, *Fox, Alaska**
34. Bill Steyer, *Fairbanks, Alaska**
35. Tony Blanford, *Two Rivers, Alaska**
36. Dieter Dolif, *Trebel, Germany*

Scratched:

Michael Hyslop, *Grizzy Valley, Yukon**
Kurt Smith, *North Pole, Alaska*
* rookie

7

Ever tried. Ever failed. No matter.
Try again. Fail again. Fail better.

—Samuel Beckett

Rookies are taken aside two days prior to the start of the Quest. Behind a closed door in a stuffy motel meeting room, they listen to the wisdom of Joe May, the mushing old-timer and race judge. The penalty for skipping this lecture is $500 under race rules, and perhaps disaster down the trail according to the rules of nature.

None of these rookies, fourteen men and four women, is a novice to sled dog racing. All qualified for the Quest by finishing at least one other race of two hundred miles or more. But, as Joe tells them, they are about to discover something new in the experience of living hell.

You will encounter something that doesn't occur in a mid-distance journey, Joe begins. Three or four days out, you and your dogs will lapse into a depression. Your team will look like it's been hit by a train. You will think there is something wrong. Naturally you will think this is your problem alone. You must realize, however, that the same thing is happening to others, physically and mentally. You must realize that in another day or so you will start to think that the dogs are getting better, or you imagine they're getting better. There is light at the end of this very dark tunnel.

Sitting indoors in shirtsleeves, on chairs in a carpeted room, with hot mugs of coffee, the mushers nod. It is not, however, a knowing nod. They merely add to their list of worries: mood crashes early in the race. Okay, nothing to dwell on now. Only the Quest veterans really know how hard the gloom can hit you. They aren't dwelling on it either, because there is never anything to do except suck up your guts and push on. Or say, Enough of this shit, then unhook the dogs and go home. No one has yet figured out a way to train for despair.

It is a short and not particularly challenging run of thirty-one miles from McCabe Creek to Pelly Crossing, another Athabascan village. Two-thirds of the route winds northwest over the jagged Yukon River. Then teams leave the river, veer right through a canyon and onto the flood plain of the Pelly River, a big west-flowing tributary of the Yukon. Pelly is another official checkpoint, a village of 285 people. For Quest mushers, it is the first big psychological Wall of the journey.

Ten below says the thermometer when I arrive this night. A haunted moon glows indistinctly up there somewhere, backlighting the sheet of clouds that has closed in overhead. Pale neon white washes over the refrigerated land. With each mile north, each day, the feeling of remoteness grows; it is no longer an abstraction but something tangible. I feel a shiver, not so much from cold as from awareness. I am far away from familiar places now, and I am advancing even deeper into the untouched. Back at Carmacks, basic services for a few tourists gave the place recognizable character; Pelly has only a gas pump and a general store. The winter road here is as empty as the wilderness around it. All the buildings have the look of government projects, but there is no mistaking the feeling that one now treads on native land. Signs posted at either end of the village warn that it is a crime to bring alcohol here. Pelly is one of many Athabascan communities that voted itself dry, and the result is apparent. Its citizens are more lively, but, unfortunately, they share with so many other natives a dearth of gainful livelihood. The crafts, music, dance, and purposeful struggle that puts flesh on the bones of a culture are either gone or only schoolhouse novelties. Without welfare, there would be no Pelly, even though the elders cling to desperate hope for the next generation. A group of sixth-graders greets me. They ask if I know Julia Roberts or Tom Cruise. No, I tell them. But I once lived in Hollywood. Really, they exclaim, in Hollywood! How is the snow there?

Where do these wonderful smiles go, I wonder? What is their place in the world?

Danny Joe remembers Pelly before 1947, when they put the road in. He was a teenager. The only transportation was dogsled. A one-time territorial legislator and former chief of this Northern Tatshoni band of Athabascans, Danny Joe shows me through the band's tribal office, its walls covered with black-and-white photographs of natives in caribou-skin parkas and fur mukluks with sleds made of willow and spruce. Teams had fewer but bigger dogs then, huge hundred-pounders, six to a team. The skin clothing is gone now. Danny Joe wears a nylon bowling jacket now. There are no dog teams here anymore either. Everyone has a snowmachine, and few people even bother to hunt because the general store sells meat in packages.

Portable spotlights illuminate the trail at the checkpoint. There is no mandatory layover here. The rules require only that mushers stop, open their sled bags, and show that they are carrying their mandatory gear: ax, sleeping bag, snowshoes, and a notebook in which the race veterinarians are keeping a running log of the team's dog inspections. I park, open the car door, and change my socks in the frigid air. When I pull off a boot, my damp sock explodes in steam.

I walk into the tiny, characterless community recreation center that serves as race headquarters. We are 260 trail miles from Whitehorse.

Inside, the experts are scratching their heads and drinking thick coffee. Naturally, they maintain, it is too early to be really racing at this stage. But one stranger might be. And rather than burning up his dogs, as would be expected, Andre Nadeau seems to be getting stronger. More than that, he is disregarding the fundamental physics of mushing. Instead of running his dogs at a fast pace and resting them 50 percent of the time, Nadeau seems to be trotting along for four hours at a clip and then resting only one. He is not a rabbit but the proverbial turtle. And he's leading.

Impossible, the experienced mushers say.

Then how can he be doing it?

No one has an answer. Andre isn't saying. A fierce-looking forty-two-year-old fireplug of a man, Nadeau is a mid-distance musher from Quebec. He speaks only French and, like many French speakers in Canada, has no time for people who are limited to English. Our French veterinarian, however, says that Nadeau isn't speaking much at all right now. He keeps to himself and hardly stays anywhere very long. We are beginning to learn that he is an irritable sort.

MYSTERY MUSHER reads the headline in today's *Fairbanks Daily News–Miner*. The paper's Quest correspondent began her daily account with this admonition: "It's a thousand-mile race, Andre. . . . Trouble is, no one can catch him to relay the message."

Nadeau arrived first in Pelly, more than two and a half hours ahead of anyone and five and a half hours ahead of John Schandelmeier, six ahead of Rick Mackey. In the past, when other mushers have bolted into the lead, the old pros of the Quest have always smiled and dismissed them. I notice the absence of smug faces now. French Canadians, from the stock of the legendary canoe voyageurs who pushed out the early Canadian frontier and established their own heroic myths, are not the kind of individuals one should take lightly. Nadeau has mentioned to someone his intention to win the Quest, and that remark now circulates feverishly.

A summer campground operator in Sainte-Melanie, Quebec, Nadeau is part of a Canadian contingent of mushers that is the strongest in Quest history. Fellow mushers from the Yukon encouraged him to come although he knew little about the Quest. His experience was all in the East, where he has dominated the Labrador 400, a race renowned for its miserable weather. He has never raced one thousand miles. No one here has ever raced against him. No one took him the least seriously. Outside mushers from Europe and the Lower 48 have swaggered into town before with high hopes, and gone home humbled.

There is another thing about Nadeau. He has the gall to be leading the Quest with Siberian huskies—a matched team of shaggy gray, white, and black dogs with great bristly tails, dogs that typify the storybook image of the northern sled dog. Mushers hereabouts, however, say that they cannot run. They call them Slowberians, and insist that they are vastly outmatched by the smaller, leaner, less hairy mongrels known as Alaskan huskies. Or so it has always been.

Only hours behind the leaders, followers face the Wall.

Dan Turner, the Alaskan tax assessor who opened his Dezadeash Lake training camp to me, is despondent. All those around him are despondent. Joe May, who helped him set up his training program, is downcast but not surprised. Joe knows Turner best. The musher's six-foot-seven frame has shrunk into the slump of a man who is beaten mentally and now on display for others to see, and to pity. Turner says little. When he attempted the Quest before, he made it halfway. It seems apparent he will not get that far now. Turner tells race officials his dogs are reluctant and that he has injured himself.

Some mushers enter the Quest purely for the love of dogs or because of the lure of the trail. Turner regards the Quest as something an Alaskan man should do. Compared to others I know, he shows no deep connection to his dogs. He does not express wonder for the trail or the winter wilderness. He has what is surely the largest sleeping bag of anyone in the race, and he worries about comfort. He wants to finish because it would be an accomplishment. The doing of it is not as important as having done it.

He takes a six-and-a-half-hour rest. It is not enough. He departs, but soon doubles back and calls it quits. There is no shame in quitting. So many others of us would not have the fortitude to try. But Turner looks like a man who judged himself harshly and is shamed. His dogs are loaded in the dog box.

Mike King hits the Wall just as hard, but lands with a snaggletooth smile. A thirty-seven-year-old biker with a Harley-Davidson patch on his sled bag and a tattoo of the Quest trail covering one-third of his back, King is an oddball character, even by Alaskan standards. He bears an unfortunate resemblance to mass murderer Charles Manson, complete with shoulder-length hair and beard. His eyes, though, are gentle, as is his demeanor. The Quest probably means more to him than to anyone here. He has devoted his life to the race. It is a loving obsession. Two years ago as a rookie, King finished seventeenth with probably the lowest budget of anyone to attempt such a feat. His cold-weather gear was hand-sewn out of blankets, remnant fleece, and a memorable old blue plastic poncho. The story is still told of his arriving in Dawson, his poncho torn and stiff and rattling in the 45-below cold. Nobody could believe his smiling face. He vowed he'd never stop until he won. Last year, King lost his heart and, some would say, his mind to a doe-eyed German woman who wanted to race too. He divided up his best dogs, let her run half of them, and was forced to scratch with a weak team. This year, with dogs bred mostly from stock he brought with him from Maine to Alaska, he pronounced himself ready for contention.

Right from the start, however, King erred. He let himself fall into a run-rest rhythm that put him on the trail in the "heat" of the afternoon, while he rested during the cold of night. Ambient air temperature may vary only 20 degrees during this period, but in the radiant afternoon sunlight, his long-haired dogs collect heat, suffer, and slow down. One of his dogs, Johnny, is so abundantly coated, he resembles a lion more than a dog, complete with mane. So his dogs are overheating and unhappy.

King, who used to work as a logger, was nearly killed in 1993 when a tree crushed him and broke two vertebrae in his back. After rehabilitation, he moved to Alaska, but he has worked only intermittently since, selling his Harley to finance his first run down the Quest trail. Since then, he has won a small following among those who admire his homespun grit. Dave Rich, the race marshal, quietly sponsors King with a few bags of dog food. I stake him gas money to get to Whitehorse. Although he has almost nothing, King gives generously, handing out chunks of the smoked salmon he carries for his personal food and happy to do it, although it's doubtful whether he has even enough for himself.

"Great, huh," he says with a smile, chewing the rich, candied fish. "All a man needs."

Bedraggled, King arrives in Pelly Crossing more than ten hours behind the leaders. He vows to change his tactics. He will run at night and rest during the day. But in his exuberance for the Quest, King has shorted himself sleep these first days, and his judgment now suffers. Inexplicably, in the high sun of midday, King changes plans. Another musher is readying to leave. King feels an irresistible pull and begins putting booties on his sleeping dogs. The temperature is 15 degrees, but it will be warmer up in the hills where the trail goes next. After just a mile, King's leaders quit and curl up in the snow. He waits with them, reclining on his sled bag, his arms crossed sullenly over his chest. Five motionless hours pass. Finally King points his team in the return direction and they happily trot back to Pelly, their hairy hides steaming in the oncoming nighttime cold. He drops out of the Quest. His dogs were just too young, he says.

"They lost their head. I didn't lose mine," he says. There is no regret on his sunburned face.

Aliy Zirkle finally seems to be over the flu and has her strength back. Once again, her grin consumes about a third of her face. She is in twentieth place, ten hours behind. But she and her dogs are so well rested as to be fresh. While her dogs eat in Pelly, she hammers at a bent spike on her brake with such exuberance that I wonder if she is going to smash it to pieces.

"On a high right now," she says. Whack.

Jimmy Hendrick straggles in, six places later. Both he and his partner, Julie Boselli, have been holding back from each other for a couple of days now. When they meet up at checkpoints and way stops, Julie does not mention that the family pet, a puppy named L.B., for Little Bastard, is missing. She fears it ran off and was taken in a wolf snare that one of Jimmy's enemies has strung in the woods north of his property. Hendrick's outspoken opposition to snaring wolves has prompted this trapper to set even more snares—awful traps that catch a wolf, or a dog, with a wire around the neck. Death is slow and brutal, as evidenced by the blood and destruction that can be found around every snare kill. "I just don't think one living being should do that to another living being," Jimmy says. So now the rednecks are after him.

For his part, Jimmy has been reluctant to tell Julie just how sick the team is. After all, Julie has a stake in their success. She gave as much to training as he did, running half the dogs herself for weeks on end, sacrificing pocketbook and all other pleasures for the trail.

"This virus is kicking my butt," he tells her now. "I'm tired, I hate this. I'm not going to finish in the money. Why can't I just scratch."

Julie is torn between affection and residual hope that maybe the worst is over. "Play another record, Jimmy. Get some sleep and then see."

Five of his dogs are still sick. Three aren't eating. They all rest. The sleep puts him back in shape for the trail, but not them. He scratches.

Brenda Mackey is facing the possibility of failure too. In another of her poignant moments, she tries to rally her dispirited team. "They're year- and year-and-a-half dogs who don't know what the heck we're doing out here," she says.

Spread out on straw beds in the snow in front of the checkpoint, the team ignores the first meal she cooks. If they won't eat, she will not push them on. Bone tired, she will try again with a different menu. Fish instead of meat. She undertakes the tedious task of cooking another round. Tentatively, the dogs stir, sniff as she ladles hunks of salmon and broth into their dented stainless steel bowls. They eat. She will continue.

"I've been as bad as them," she admits. "I think I've eaten just half a Danish. . . . College is looking better all the time."

Sitting on a filthy ice chest, sorting gear from the feed bags she packed and had shipped ahead to Pelly Crossing, Brenda looks worse than she sounds. Her eyes are puffy and red, her hands raw. Her movements are slow. She pauses as if she has forgotten what she is doing. First she buries her hands in a bag and searches to find a pair of plastic sled runners. A few minutes later, she absently packs the same runners away again.

"I'm going to be twenty in April and I sometimes feel that life is passing me by. When I'm going down the trail I have a lot of time to think. I have daydreams about school. And shorter races. At the beginning, I thought I'd run the Quest and get race experience, and come back next year and be competitive. Now I don't know. I'll probably be stupid and be here."

I had lost track of rookie Rusty Hagan, but he arrives near the end of the pack, twenty-three hours behind the leader. With the grimy patina of the long trail on him, he is the picture of—surprise—enthusiasm. Some people find the Wall in Pelly. Others find euphoria in exhaustion. Rusty seems born to be tired.

"That's one of the best runs of my life," he shouts. He has shoved out of his consciousness those nightmares about falling through the ice, or at least he's no longer talking about them.

Imagine trying to walk fourteen dogs on leashes when you're as tired as you've ever been. Then, start clipping and unclipping dogs, moving them from one leash to another. Kurt Smith, a rangy, hard-luck musher from the Fairbanks suburb of North Pole, was attempting the equivalent: rotating dogs in his team. Maybe his grip was loose, or maybe his mind wandered for an instant. A dog broke loose and dashed for the horizon. It marked the end for Smith, who had unsuccessfully attempted the Quest twice before. Luckily, a van transporting veterinarians to Pelly later finds the animal happily loping down the packed snow of the roadway. After some cajoling and a good deal of playful chasing, a vet assistant gets a hand on the dog's collar. The dog objects and sinks its fangs into her arm before it is finally brought to a leash.

Pelly has been the scene of considerable wreckage, physical and emotional. Now a larger crisis is brewing behind the scenes.

For the second year in a row, the tire-company sponsor, Fulda, has provided money to outfit each musher with free dog booties. Naturally, they bear the Fulda logo, to match the logo on the mushers' parkas and dog blankets. But also for the second year in a row, the check arrived late. Fulda did not commission the booties itself, nor did it allow mushers to buy their own and get reimbursed. Instead, the Quest organization was given the task of ordering booties in three sizes and two materials, fleece and heavy denier nylon. The only problem was, there is almost no standing Quest organization to undertake such a chore.

Rather, a vast assemblage of volunteers do what they can when they can.

The result now threatens to wreck the race.

A single team may consume fifteen hundred booties during the Quest. At a dollar apiece, that's a significant expense. For a musher with no steady income, free booties are gold. Naturally, most mushers counted on these booties in planning their race. They brought no back-up. And their dogs, accustomed to foot protection, could no more run without booties on the sandpaper-like snow and coarse ice than a marathoner could run on gravel barefooted.

Now the booties are falling apart. Checkpoint garbage cans are heaped with them, worn through after only a few miles. The allotment of fifteen hundred will not get a team to the finish line. The mushers are in an uprising. A protest is filed. Joe May mumbles that the Gold Rush Centennial Yukon Quest may be doomed.

Mushers blame Fulda, a faceless and easy target, for the poor-quality materials. Why, if Fulda's tires aren't any better than their booties . . . and so on.

All along, Fulda anticipated some controversy as a result of its involvement and tried to quash it. Its contract with the Quest specifically forbade anyone connected with the race from speaking unfavorably about the company. That grated wrong to begin with, because the right to shoot off one's mouth is prized in these reaches. Some of the mushers say they are not honor-bound to keep quiet.

Fulda's representatives are nowhere on hand to respond. But over the satellite telephones, they are said to be fuming and blaming the Quest. It's the fault of the host organizers in Whitehorse who promised to get the booties made to mushers' specifications. Race officials from Alaska share Fulda's criticism of the Canadian race officials. The Alaskans had dealt with Fulda last year on booties, and had warned the Canadians against it this time. Getting sixty thousand of anything made and shipped to Whitehorse on short notice is no small feat.

For now, race officials and volunteers say they will do what they can. Calls go out to every mushing outfitter on the continent and to companies that make booties. Surplus stocks from across the region are tapped. Mushers scrounge under the seats of their pickups. A dozen here, fifty there, booties of all colors and materials are collected. There may not be enough to finish the race, but there will be enough to keep the Quest on the trail to Dawson. Already pushed to exhaustion, the small contingent of race officials must now work around the clock.

To me, the bootie fiasco is bitter justice. I blame Fulda for exploiting one of the last big sporting events free of this kind of commercialization. I blame Quest organizers for being so greedy as to accept it. Perhaps the corporate executives don't know, but they should: muscling in on mushers to flaunt a logo is the worst kind of exploiting of the poor. These are not million-dollar sports stars with agents and lawyers to protect them. Many of them are people who exist close to desperation.

Stanley Njootli, for instance, is a forty-five-year-old musher from the Athabascan village of Old Crow in the Yukon, one of the coldest inhabited places on the globe. He is one of the two natives to enter the Quest, but his team is not prepared and he is running poorly. He tells race officials in Pelly that he should quit. But he hesitates, brokenhearted, because he has received a new logo parka from Fulda. He fears that if he scratches he will have to give back the jacket, which is the warmest garment he's ever known in a lifetime in the cold. He's advised that he can keep the jacket now that he's come this far. At that, he brightens up and scratches. What he has gained in a jacket, he has lost in pride.

Had Fulda wanted to play by the rules of the Far North, it would have given mushers parkas and then would have handed out logo patches. Here, if you don't mind, we'd like you to sew these onto your jackets. Fulda would have got its way and made friends too.

My own grudge against the European newcomers is about to reach a head for an entirely different reason.

In 1997, village elders in Pelly Crossing heard about the important men from far away who had spent so much money to sponsor the Quest, the men from Fulda. This called for a feast. Some native traditions have died away, but not this one. So the invitation to feast was issued. The fires were lit, the caribou meat roasted, the bannock fish boiled for stew, the tables set, and the food put warming on stoves. That year, the mushers came, of course, and the race officials and me. But the corporate executives and their press corps drove by and flew overhead, never even stopping for gas.

Although no one said much, the village was hurt and confused by the snub. Sure, the villagers had hoped to somehow share in this new vein of sponsorship prosperity. But the feast was more than that. There was pride involved, as well as the hospitality of the Far North.

This year, as press operative for the Quest, I vowed it would not happen again. No feast was prepared, but I promised myself I would get the foreign media to Pelly Crossing for a taste of North American native life. I arranged with the village school for camera crews to film the daily grade-school instruction in cultural heritage. For interviews, I lined up village elders, some of whom had mushed these same dog trails fifty years ago, men whose grandfathers had watched the coming of the white gold-seekers.

As a former foreign correspondent, I know that an event like the Quest cannot be portrayed apart from the culture in which it was born. I know about colorful people. I know about spoon-feeding the press good stories.

I have the village of Pelly Crossing standing ready.

Once again, Fulda and the press pass by without stopping at Pelly Crossing. This time it cannot be in ignorance. I told the TV producers and Fulda organizers they had an obligation to at least pay their respects to the elders. I went so far as to say, If you cannot spare the film will you at least pretend to roll the camera? Will you at least listen to their stories? Will you let these children meet the foreigners from a different land? Will you tell them about the snow in Germany?

Suddenly I hear of a change of heart. Over the satellite phone comes word that a few reporters are doubling back by bush plane and will arrive at midday. I reassemble the village, muttering apologies for the inconvenience.

A camera crew, one TV correspondent, and a still photographer arrive, and I explain what awaits them.

Sorry, no time for that, I'm told.

"We need pictures of mushers," they explain.

Argument does nothing. As the reporters hurry through the checkpoint, cameras rolling, villagers watch in confusion. There are no action pictures, just another pit stop with dogs sleeping, alcohol stoves cooking, mushers clomping through the snow with heavy boots and sagging eyes.

This time, there is no misunderstanding. These are but sports reporters, and only that. They have no eye for what lies beneath the race, and they are not polite enough to look. Stefan Peine, the correspondent for EuroSport, blames his editors back in Bonn. But I know that old line of bullshit backward and forward. Anonymous editors take the heat for many misdemeanors. Once again, the natives of Pelly Crossing watch as the modern world passes them by without so much as a hello.

Hudson Stuck, the Episcopal archdeacon of the Yukon, saw this future as far back as 1905, when he traveled the region as a friend of the natives. In his memoir *Ten Thousand Miles with a Dogsled,* he wrote: "The time threatens when all the world will speak two or three great languages, when all the little tongues will be extinct and all the little peoples swallowed up, when all the costume will be reduced to a dead level of blue jeans and shoddy and all strange customs abolished."

I apologize to village leaders. They turn away stoically. Inside the checkpoint, I tell race marshal Dave Rich that I'm through. I won't lift a finger to help any of these jock sniffers. I won't get in their way, but I'll give no help. As far as my relations with Rich and the other officials, however, it may be too late. Our clubby little group of race officials is no longer so friendly, and my membership seems to have been revoked. Rich just scowls. Even Joe May, who had given me so much of his time and friendship, now turns his shoulder. They were suspicious of, even hostile to the Outside press from the start. I took my volunteer responsibilities to include being policeman of the press but also press advocate. I tried to take reporters inside, to get them good stories and fancy pictures. That may have harmed me with my friends. Something has.

Why the hell did I ever let myself be cast as press handler? If anyone knows what a pack of jerks reporters can be, it's me. And this bunch, at the bidding of Fulda, takes the prize.

I am reminded of something Jimmy Stewart said in the movie *Destry Rides Again:* "I had a friend who was an opera singer who went into cement. Now he's the cornerstone of the St. Louis post office. It shows he should have stayed with what he knew." I should have stuck with shoveling dog scat. Honorable work.

Later in the race, Stefan Peine tells me that editors back home are complaining about how the dogs, at nine miles an hour, are not running fast enough. Not enough action for the cameras. What a pity.

I shoulder my sleeping bag to the Pelly Crossing schoolhouse, where the indoor gym serves as a crash pad for the Quest. I lapse into sleep to the roar of snoring. Some of it, I'm told later, comes from me.

8

In harness, they are a line of fluid energy.
They are grace and power in motion.

—Mark Derr, *Dog's Best Friend*

Nobody will believe this, Dave Dalton thinks to himself. Nobody will believe what I am seeing.

Behind him, a full moon hangs bloated over the horizon and showers light across the snow on the high hills ahead. In the sky opposite, the first flickers of northern lights emerge in faint, smoky streaks of green. As the celestial voltage rises, the green intensifies into neon and widens into a vast curtain, slowly billowing in the ionospheric winds. A tinge of translucent pink emerges on the bottom edge. Then the rarest color in all the sky materializes as the pink collects, gains density, and transforms itself into a red nebula, as if the curtain has caught fire in the cold overhead. A vast, ethereal dance of light and color spreads above him. Tonight, the aurora borealis battles the full moon to rule the Yukon sky.

In the cold dry air, shadows of craters can be seen on the face of the oversize moon, itself now greenish in the glow of the aurora. The northern lights are so vivid as to seem, at the same time, both tangibly close and mysteriously, impossibly far off.

This is a night. Dalton congratulates himself. This is part of the pay-off. This is why a man will build his life around dogs and the Yukon Quest. This is why Dave Dalton nurses no regrets that he chose dogs when his wife said them or her. This is why he drives a cab for a living, so he can be master of his own schedule and train his dogs to run as one fluid, silent line of energy under such a sky on a night like this, feeling purposeful and all alone in the wonder of the world.

His sled glides over the surface of the earth, the frost crusts on his face, his dripping nose grows a dangle of salty snotcicles, but he is part of the sky now. Dalton no more needs a headlamp to see than he needs an ice bag to keep from overheating. To say he could read by the illumination of the cosmos begs the question—just what would one read on a such a night?

This is, I believe, authentic adventure. It strikes me that authenticity is an important means for distinguishing adventure from adventurism today. So many of us have reduced the concept of adventure to just another recreation, a diversion from the otherwise ordinary ambitions of living. We go on adventures and read about them in one dimension: seeking the triumph of self. Our expectations are fixed with small tolerances for serendipity, or discovery. We know because guides and guidebooks tell us what to anticipate, what to bring, when to come, what we will see, and how long it will take. We exchange money for adventure. We are willing to sacrifice little. At the basest, people go to amusement parks and ride the roller coasters for "adventure," but if they happen to have a real one and the cars come flying off the tracks, they sue. The *New York Times Magazine* recently ran a story with a snide, but telling, headline: GOING WHERE A LOT OF OTHER DUDES WITH REALLY GREAT EQUIPMENT HAVE GONE BEFORE: THE CALL OF THE PSEUDO-WILD.

The difference between adventure and adventurism is, I think, as subtle as the difference between being a traveler and a tourist. That is to say, all the difference in the world. Tonight, on the trail of the Yukon Quest, there is no guide or guidebook, no schedule, and no amount of money that could lead the casual adventurist to this circumstance where, just this moment, the heavens open and embrace a man for his devotion to the trail.

Overhead, the curtain of the aurora has duplicated itself—two shimmering arcs of green in parallel. They slowly dim, then return even more forcefully, dancing exuberantly from one horizon to the other. They join together in a great plasmic sheet. Later, green-white rays spark across the face of the aurora.

For more than two hours, Dave Dalton glides along on a black-and-white landscape while the sky flames in color.

Yes, a wealthy adventurist can write the checks to buy the dog team and hire the personal trainers and prove that he, too, can travel the trail of the Yukon Quest. A car dealer from Fairbanks once did just that. But such a man has invested little of himself. His dividends are correspondingly inconsequential. There is a reason why most of humankind's spiritual orthodoxies require the commitment of soul before the soul can be redeemed. It is the same reason why our satisfaction with our religions, for worse and for better, depends entirely on our ability to give ourselves over to them. This same maxim explains why authentic adventurers are such single-minded types whose experiences can be emulated but seldom duplicated.

A year ago a musher from Cologne, Germany, named Ingabritt Schloven answered a question of mine: How does night travel engage the spirit?

"If you are ready for it, there is calm," she began. "This is what you want to do. When the sun goes down, you must concentrate. The dark is when the dogs want to hunt and run. The sounds are more intense. It is getting colder. The energy isn't physical as much as in your head. You can see the mountains around you. And then, above, the northern lights. You see the green and then a swirl. And then a hand comes down to touch you. Athabascan natives say the North is where you have room to dream. Here is where the mind can walk. You stop thinking about people and hassles. All that goes away when you are standing on the runners. You are taken with calm. The dogs do the same, I think. It is like when you wake up and a dream stays with you."

Some Eskimos believe the northern lights are alive and if you whistle they will come closer out of curiosity. Scientists believe otherwise. They say the aurora borealis is an electrical light storm. Solar winds shower the thin gas of the ionosphere with electrons, forming a ring of visible energy around the top and bottom of the earth, according to the magnetic field of the two poles. The result is a colossal discharge of electricity, one thousand billion watts, or as much as is consumed by people in all of North America. The energy can be seen as bands of color. To be rather everyday about it, the same thing happens in a television as electrons bombard phosphor in a picture tube.

Because of the symmetry of the polar magnetic fields, auroras in the Northern Hemisphere can be seen in mirror image in the Southern Hemisphere, where they are known as the aurora australis.

Through history, northern peoples and travelers have reported hearing swishes and crackles from the aurora. That's perhaps why some early tribes believed they were seeing torches lighting the way to heaven. Scientists say they are puzzled by these reports and have never been able to record the sound.

From Pelly Crossing, the trail of the Yukon Quest is like nothing so far, like nothing else in competitive long-distance mushing. For the next 203 miles, dog teams will cross no roads and encounter no settlements. And then, right at the end, they will confront the first of three great climbs—this to the top of King Solomon's Dome. From there, they'll go past the headwaters of the Klondike's legendary Bonanza Creek and into Dawson City.

The route follows the Pelly River due west for thirty-five miles to an occupied cabin on a bluff called Stepping Stone. Then the mushers veer right, once again aiming northwest, and travel overland up a canyon, across a hilly pass, and down another canyon, seventy-five miles or so to a sagging, low-lying cabin called Scroggie Creek, where the cold is often extreme. The last part of this leg is the most demanding, sending mushers up another canyon and into the Black Hills. Along the way, some springs have bubbled over and broken through their caps of ice. The water spills out in strange, translucent hues of aqua blue. Mushers call it overflow. When overflow refreezes, it creates impossibly slick and much dreaded patches of ice, which are known colloquially as glaciers. Sometimes a solid crust hides pools of overflow underneath, a trap that can result in a frigid dousing. At the end of these obstacles, the trail begins the winding, seemingly endless climb up King Solomon's Dome, which, at thirty-eight hundred feet, is the high point of the Quest route and notorious for its howling winds. Because of the distance of this leg, mushers begin the trek with massive loads, 350 pounds or more. Deciding how much food to carry is one of the most danger-fraught decisions of the Quest. Too much can exhaust the team; not enough leaves them exposed if pinned down by weather.

Joe May, in particular, worries that mushers are gambling on favorable conditions and not taking enough food. It has been a few years since blizzard engulfed the Quest. But Joe remembers his last race and the great storm of 1986, when he nearly died on the long march to Dawson. That year, the race started in Fairbanks and ran east to Whitehorse. Two days before reaching the halfway mark of Dawson, several teams bunched up in a white-out snowstorm. They traveled by caravan, taking turns breaking trail. Soon the weaker teams could not lead but only follow. That left the work of pushing through a trail to three mushers, Joe, Sonny Lindner, and Jeff King. Eventually, King's dogs balked. All the teams were out of food now and unsure where they were. For the next twenty-four hours, Joe and Sonny Lindner kept the group advancing, sometimes steering by nothing except the bite of the wind in their faces. Temperatures plummeted to 40 below. During a momentary stop, Joe fished in his pocket and found a small piece of frozen pepperoni encrusted with hair, dog shit, and old matches. He gulped it down. Breakfast, lunch, and dinner. There was no chance to dig in and wait for the storm to pass. The teams had used up their dog food already because of the slow pace, and the animals would soon perish in such cold, whether moving or not.

Joe recalls having a "morbid conversation" with Sonny. They were worried for their lives. "We had no idea where we were."

For the final push, the men could not see even the front of their teams, and they trusted themselves entirely to two rotating pairs of lead dogs. At 4:00 A.M. on the second day, the men thought they saw a faint glow in the relentlessly swirling snow. It proved to be Dawson. Five teams scratched on arrival. Joe went on to finish but would never race the Quest again.

Better more food than not enough, Joe tells the rookies.

This year, the weather is holding fair. In fact, temperatures rise above freezing in the hills before plummeting 60 degrees.

Bruce Lee, the forty-four-year-old comeback musher from Denali National Park in Alaska, realizes that this Quest will not follow the pattern of earlier races, or any of the seven other thousand-milers he has run. The old rule about saving one's team for later is not going to be good enough. A disciplined and methodical man, the blond, handsome, mustached Lee now faces two pivotal moments.

His lead dog Miles falters. He has other leaders who can follow a trail and pace the team, but Miles is the alpha dog on whom Lee depends for leadership and emotional strength. Miles, however, is not up for the race now. Lee makes the tough choice to drop him. Good luck in a dog race is the absence of bad luck, and his luck has turned sour. "A trump card was played, and it isn't in our favor," he tells his wife, Jeralyn.

Starting out on the longest leg of the race without his best dog, Lee tries to hold his focus on his computer-like prerace game plan. Rather than contemplating 1,023 miles, he divides the race into individual runs; he travels the optimum distance for his team and then stops, no matter where in the trail that puts him. For this section, it means he must pass by the chance to warm up at cabins. The strategy of former winners like Schandelmeier and Mackey has been to stop after thirty-five miles at Stepping Stone and rest. Lee figures his dogs are good for fifty miles, and travels on. No need to warm up, he tells himself. He learned mushing by traveling and exploring in the utterly remote Brooks Range mountains, where there are no cabins. If he wanted to be warm he could live in Key West and go fishing.

Lee synchronizes his travels by the clock. He rests in the heat of the day. He rests again after midnight, when human biorhythms cry out for sleep. Like an automaton, he travels his fifty miles in the evenings and early mornings. The rule of sixes, he calls it. Leave at 6:00 A.M. and break camp again at 6:00 P.M. Lee is a nighthawk. Almost all his travel occurs in darkness. He makes the first hundred miles in two runs, instead of three shorter ones. He gains on the traditionalists.

At Stewart River, where the thermometer dips to 30 below, Lee is tending to his team when Rick Mackey arrives.

"You just get in, too?" Mackey asks.

"No, I'm leaving," Lee says.

Damn. Things are changing.

Andre Nadeau has an even more radical plan. He is loping along at six miles an hour, instead of the nine miles an hour of faster teams. He stays ahead of them by resting less. Lee is now shadowing the mystery musher from Quebec, almost catching up by virtue of his faster team and then falling behind again to rest. Just before the big climb up King Solomon's is Granville Cabin, another inhabited homestead. It is warm and there is food. Lee is on a schedule to rest his team there. But he stops just short of the cabin. He walks ahead quietly and peeks. Nadeau is there. Lee walks back to his dogs and camps out of sight in the cold.

"I figured if I showed up, he would feel compelled to leave," Lee explains.

Lee hopes Nadeau will feel secure and rest longer at the cabin. One thing about being in front, you have no idea what's happening behind you. Nadeau is blind; the stealthy Lee knows his every move.

Nadeau ultimately will keep the lead by pulling out of Granville in a few hours, but Lee has gained precious rest by not spooking the leader back onto the trail early.

Lee doesn't yet know if this newcomer is for real. He has seen more than one mystery musher bolt into the lead and burn up before the finish line. Then again, he watched helplessly in 1991 as one little-known musher beat him to the finish line by five minutes. Maybe Nadeau really can travel with less rest than anyone and still lead for a thousand miles. Who the hell knows? For the first time in the race, Lee deviates from his game plan. He cuts his rest by an hour to keep from falling too far behind.

The Canadian and the Alaskan lead the pack over the summit toward Dawson. First man in wins a poke with four ounces of placer gold.

Misery and pleasure are brothers who live on the high passes. Venture up, and you never know who will greet you.

For some of the mushers, King Solomon's Dome becomes a spectacular clear-weather climb to a million-dollar vista. Starting at the mouth
of a canyon along a stream called Sulphur Creek, they stare up at the
massive hump of the mountain blotting out the horizon before them.
They ponder its bald and windswept summit. The trail winds upward
gradually through the spruce and then folds into ever steeper switchbacks. As they climb, they look behind them and watch ridgelines
appear, one after another, until all the Black Hills take form. With that
perspective, they can measure their progress over the rough corrugated topography. Then they rise above the tree line, exposed, and the
whole world seems to be spread before them.

I wait atop the dome on a borrowed snowmachine with the wind
rattling in my ears. I can see a hundred miles in all points of the compass. To the south all the wrinkled Black Hills. North, the jagged and
distant peaks of the Ogilvie Mountain Range. To the east, the famed
gulch of Bonanza Creek, and its tributary, Eldorado Creek. I ask myself,
Are there words strong enough to convey the play of sunlight angling
on all this vast, empty snowscape? Or words for the collision of the
sun's marmalade rays against the white reflections of the snow? Or the
empty feel of sunbeams that carry not the slightest touch of warmth? If
there are such words I have not learned them.

So dry and sustained is the wind over the dome that the snow has
taken on the shape and texture of cornflakes. It crackles underfoot. The
Eskimos have a word for this snow, but I do not. I will ask the next
group of native children I see. What kind of snow is it on the top of the
dome?

If I try, I can summon ghosts here. Not so long ago, really, only as far
back as my grandfather's age, men were hunkered down, shivering,
digging holes along these many creeks that drain King Solomon's
Dome. Beneath the permafrost, they peered by lamplight into the slush
at the bottom of the dark, pebbly holes they dug in the ground. They
looked for their dreams. Their campfires sent coils of smoke into the
winds, and the ice-stiff canvas of their coats crackled when they
emerged from the holes.

Did they share my feeling of awe? I wonder.

I have read the histories and the thrilling accounts of the Gold Rush, of the violence, the danger, the rowdy saloons, and colorful characters. Writers have staked claims all over that part of the story. But what about those long hours in dirty miners' tents when a man's body rested and his mind could walk?

George A. Huntzicker headed north for the "Clondyke" on July 29, 1897, leaving Neillsville, Wisconsin, with four other men. His granddaughter, Anne, shared with me his unpublished journal of the expedition, written in pencil in a black, pocket-size notebook. Then, as now, ink pens are useless in the subarctic winter. Even ballpoints freeze in an instant.

I meditated over Huntzicker's journal, as I have over journals of other nineteenth-century North American wanderers. There is a uniform deadpan in their writings. They burden their histories with neither self-pity nor awe. The paper they carry is precious, and their entries understandably concise. They leave us to fill in the blanks.

During one period of eleven days—the amount of time it may take for the fastest mushers to travel the Quest trail—Huntzicker writes this account of winter days in the Yukon a century ago:

11/15   *Chas. and I went back to camp for more grub. 16 degrees below zero.*

11/16   *Got our grub and went back to prospecting camp. 32 below.*

11/17   *Prospected up a gulch but was driven out of the hole on account of water. 25 below.*

11/18   *All went back to camp on the Lewis River and moved into our new log cabin. 45 below zero.*

11/19   *Worked inside cabin. 36 below.*

11/20   *Hauled rock for fireplace. Gates froze his nose very badly. 52 below.*

11/21   *Hauled rock for fireplace and worked on chimney. 30 below.*

11/22   *Worked on fireplace. This is the Canadian Thanksgiving day. 20 below.*

11/23   *Hauled rock for Jerry's fireplace. 16 below.*

11/24   *Hewett and I whipsawed lumber for table. Gates set snares for rabbits. 6 above zero.*

> *11/25   Built chimney on fireplace and for our Thanksgiving dinner*
> *we had bread beans & . . . 40 below.*

The group wintered partway up the trail to Dawson. Huntzicker's black notebook records that his group found a scattering of good colors and in one location "struck coarse gold." There was a team of dogs with the party, although the source or type of dogs is not specified. In the spring, these Argonauts continued north to Dawson City, then known by its nickname "Louse Town" because of the filth. They camped, and on May 23, 1898, the boys "went downtown and took in the sights. Nothing much to see only saloons, guys and pretty girls dressed to kill." The following day, Dawson's miners challenged and easily beat the Northwest mounted police at a game of tug-of-war with a long rope. Then Huntzicker moved up the hillside to have a look.

26 (May) Went up Eldorado and watched them sluicing and pan out lots of gold.

These good creeks had long ago been staked. But there was no hint of melancholy or resentment in Huntzicker's neat longhand. He was an adventurer, not a miner, and like all adventurers he lived entirely in the present.

Me? With Huntzicker's ghost, my own pencil, and notebook, I wait for Andre Nadeau and the others, stomping my feet to stay warm.

"These young dogs, they can break your heart. You want them to make it. Then they break your heart."

Paddy Santucci had lectured himself not to set expectations. Not for his dogs and not for himself. That way he will not have to cope with disappointment too, along with other difficulties of the trail. He will do what has to be done, exactly when it has to be done, the cooking and feeding, the resting and the rising, booties on and booties off, liniment rubs—all of it. He will show his team nothing but determination. He will look his dogs in the eye, trying to reassure them, but probably just reassuring himself. Together, they will do the best they can. That's the way the old-timers did it, and they spared themselves contests against the unbeatable foe of frustration.

But still, Paddy raised these dogs, including the five youngsters he brought to Whitehorse. Yearlings and two-year-olds can be very strong, but you cannot teach them fortitude. You can only hope they have it, or pick it up from the more seasoned dogs in the team. You won't know, though, until they've run out of it.

Now Santucci's yearlings are fading. It's not their bodies but their will. Just as dogs can gain strength from one another in a team, a drop in spirits can be a contagion that brings the whole outfit to a sputtering collapse. Team dog Teacher develops the "thousand-mile stare" during the second day of the run to Dawson and caves in. To keep him in harness risks spreading gloom through the entire team, ruining the young dog's drive permanently. So Paddy loads him into his sled bag and the team hauls him into Stewart River. Teacher is calm as they arrive, perhaps sheepish.

"I suppose he's probably a bit dejected, not that he let everybody down but that he let me down. He knows what his job is, and it's not sitting in the sled," Santucci observes. "Oh, they break your heart."

Teacher is dropped, a financially costly decision because the dog will have to be flown out by bush plane at Paddy's expense.

"You know, I remembered about fifteen miles after I started the run: shit, I was going to drop that dog."

At Stewart River, mushers have a painful duty. The longtime sourdough who lived in the cabin and hosted Quest racers over the years has died. In a city, one might only pause at the loss of a casual acquaintance. But in the bush, this man opened his cabin, gave warmth and shelter, food and companionship. Just knowing he was there made the long passage less fearful. He wasn't really a friend, because they saw him only then. They knew, though, he would always help. His son now occupies the Stewart River cabin, and the mushers string through like a funeral procession.

Up the long climb to King Solomon's Dome, the last three of Paddy's youngest dogs start to break down. Paddy worries about the impact on the team. What impact this may have on Paddy's own "head" he keeps to himself. He works with what he has. He coaxes the dogs on. He balances pairs of dogs by their gait and moods. He runs checklists in his mind. He mentally prepares the next meal. Exactly where has he packed the alcohol for the stove? He'll want to get to it quickly. Which bag of food should he use for the next meal? Be ready. He measures the movements of each dog, looking for that hitch in a step that might signal a bootie rub, or the rolling gait that could be the start of a sore shoulder. He flashes his headlamp up the trail, alert to danger. He kicks, one-footed like a skateboarder, to help push the load up the mountain. His eyes are narrowed, his field of vision as focused as if he's looking through a peashooter. If you stood ten feet off the trail as he passed, Paddy would be aware but unlikely to acknowledge your presence. He fills his mind with the journey so there will be no room for other things.

One of the logistical challenges of the Quest is putting in the trail each year. In the weeks before the race, volunteers at each checkpoint gas up their snowmachines and begin pathfinding through the local ice jams and tree falls. The trail generally follows routes established a century ago. But each winter poses its own obstacles that must be routed around or chopped through with ax and chain saw. Snowmachines pack down a rough trail first. The mail drivers and dogsled freighters of earlier this century relied on similar help from families that ran the roadhouses, although those sourdoughs did the work solely with dogsled and hand tools.

As race time approaches, tens of thousands of wooden stakes, marked with reflective tape, are hammered into the ice and snow for the entire 1,023 miles. A good trail is one where a musher can look ahead with a headlamp and always catch a reflection from one or two of these upcoming stakes. But that would be in fair weather, if the wind does not carry off the stakes and blow away the path of the snowmachines, leaving only a vast glaze of ice. Or if snowdrifts don't bury all signs. Or if the river doesn't open a lead and swallow up part of the trail.

Then, a day in advance of the leaders, less if the weather is stormy, three Canadian Rangers mount their snowmachines and give the trail a final grooming, marking open leads and trailside glaciers with crossed stakes, the warning sign. For mushers at the head of the pack in good weather, the trail and its dangers are apparent, confused only by the crossing trails of local trappers. In one of the cruelties of the race, mushers farther behind, usually those with less experience and unseasoned lead dogs, face higher odds that wind or snow will make havoc of a straightforward passage. Rookies get tough quick or quit. Everyone feels very close to the whims of nature.

Sure enough, conditions atop King Solomon's Dome do not remain auspicious for long. In the twilight of the following afternoon, Aliy Zirkle makes her approach. Clouds sweep in from the west, a haze first and then wind-snorting, gunmetal storm clouds.

"I knew this race would be the hardest thing in my life. And it fucking is," she says.

In the lead, she has plain-brown Kronk and Chip, the powerhouse with the yellow eyebrows, steady dogs but none too smart. As the winds rise and the trail grows steeper, the team is engulfed in blowing snow. Aliy stops and installs Flood and Rubia into lead. Flood is the dog on which she depends in every tight spot. Rubia can match him. Aliy finishes and lumbers back to her sled. She looks ahead and the leaders are invisible in the swirling snow. She whistles and they respond over the shriek of the wind.

The higher the team climbs, the fiercer the winds. Snow blasts her eyes like sand. She tries to squint ahead but can barely discern the shaggy rumps of the wheel dogs just in front of her. Beyond that, all sense of depth fades into the impenetrable white rage of the storm. She cinches down the hood of her parka and heads up the summit as blind as if she'd buried her head in a feather pillow.

She mutters to herself, Flood, old boy, you'd better keep us on the trail or we'll all be fucked but good.

9

*With the aurora borealis flaming coldly overhead, the stars leap-
ing in the frost dance, the land numb and frozen under its pall of
snow, this song of the huskies might have been the defiance of life,
only it was pitched in minor key, with long-drawn wailings and
half-sobs, and was more the pleading of life. . . . It was an old song.*

—Jack London, on pulling into
Dawson City one dreary afternoon

Today: Dawson City, Yukon Territory. Population 1,999. Temperature zero, light snow.

If Jack London walked these old wood-plank sidewalks now he
could measure the progress of a century by the advent of pickup trucks,
snowmachines, and garbage Dumpsters. Otherwise, the capital of the
Klondike, with its Wild West facades and stovepipe chimneys, is recognizable from the black-and-white photographs of the Gold Rush.
Saloon doors still swing until late and hairy men stagger forth bleary-
eyed and broke. Music wafts down the frozen streets. Some old clapboard buildings have been slapped with fresh paint while others, bare
wood, sag into the permafrost. Dog teams still ride into town on dreary winter days and stop on Front Street, and you have to wait until the
hoarfrost melts from the newcomer's face to see if it's someone you
know. Merchants are proud to post signs saying that they accept payment in gold dust.

Indeed, gold still rules in these hills—the tailings of the old claims are being turned over and worked for the third time. Fewer nuggets are found, but there's plenty of powder gold for those with modern technology.

Jack London might wonder, though, what happened to all the people. A century ago this was the largest city north of Seattle and west of Winnipeg; it teemed with thirty thousand Argonauts. And maybe one of them really did earn wages by panning gold from the sawdust under the bar. For a brief time, Dawson City was the wildest, craziest place on the continent.

Back then, saloon keepers shut down a few hours every so often, not because of laws but to make repairs. Gold Rush dog puncher Arthur T. Walden remembers the townsfolk getting drunk one holiday and shooting the stovepipes off each other's tents and buildings for the fun of it. Scared the hell out of dog teams, and some ran off. Arthur lost a couple of dogs himself.

Like other boomtowns, Dawson was an edgy, greedy place. No one could be bothered to pick up garbage or dig deep-pit outhouses, so the miners died of their own filth. Typhoid killed ten a day when the city thawed that first spring. But at the same time, Walden, and no doubt thousands of his fellow adventurers, believed their outpost lacked "the insane feverishness that you meet in a large city."

Why sure, Art. I know what you mean. I'd rather be in Dawson for the Yukon Quest than any town in the world.

Christmas passed six weeks ago but a string of holiday lights still twinkles at the saloon they call The Pit.

There isn't much else for lighting. They keep The Pit dark, for reasons I suspect have less to do with living up to its name than keeping us from looking too closely at the sour old carpet that squishes underfoot, or the plastic paneling that is peeling off the walls. The windows are curtained in threadbare red velvet, and rotting acoustic tiles dangle from the ceiling, along with a Kmart fan that evens out the hanging cloud of cigarette smoke. Formica tables wobble under the weight of elbows and pitchers of beer, some of which is now sloshing over and recharging the carpet. The Pit is not known for its stylish decor. Or for its smell, either, which perpetually recalls mornings after. Better to judge this landmark by its clientele, a babbling throng of people in need of showers, crammed wall to wall, so many that you can feel the whole building shudder with their movements and so loud you can hardly hear yourself think. About one-third are local miner types, one-third Indians, and one-third from the Yukon Quest. Almost all are drunk or on their way. Although, to be truthful, it is hard to judge who has a snootful because the floor sags so horribly that even a prim matron from the Women's Temperance League couldn't walk to the john in ten-pound bunny boots without staggering like a wino. Cardboard six-pack holders have been shimmed under the pool table in a vain effort to level it. But no matter: people who winter in Dawson have known worse.

On a small stage, a band is emitting screeches that I take to be blue-grass. A seventy-five-year-old gold miner in pinstripe bib overalls and a spade beard howls a jaunty "Mind Your Own Business." He is fol-lowed by my Eskimo friend Walter Newman, of Beaver, Alaska, who belts out soulful renditions of "Cold, Cold Heart" and "Have I Told You Lately?" Walter is a dog handler and Quest gadfly, and he receives mountainous applause, never mind that his singing voice has a dis-tinctive mumble on account of a shortage of teeth.

Around the tables, men with beards outnumber those who are clean-shaven eight to one. Men without a Leatherman strung on their belts are rarer than those with shaves. Men whose smiles cannot be distin-guished from their snarls also seem to be a majority. Across the table from me, a husky native woman has unbuttoned her flannel shirt, and her breasts swing ominously as she paws the reluctant stranger next to her and tries to stick her tongue in the man's bristly ear. Behind me, I watch another man approach a blond woman in a biker shirt and moosehide vest. He says something to her by way of introduction. But I think she misunderstands him. Over the roar of the music, her lips spell out "Fuck you."

I worry that my notebook might mistakenly identify me as a health inspector or a parole officer. I put it away, because a woman who drinks her beer with her shirt open, or a bottle-blond who wears a Harley T-shirt and a moose pelt might be the kind who are itching to kick someone's teeth in for almost any excuse at all.

I have watched men stagger outside, strip off their good shirts, and pound each other into raw meat. At 20 below, such fights have the virtue of ending quickly. I know a man who comes here every year with the Quest, and his theory is that you need to keep drinks working simultaneously on both sides of the room to properly socialize and enjoy yourself.

The Pit is the best saloon in my favorite winter town. Jack London might wonder who rolled everyone's cigarettes so neatly for them or what Harley means on the blond's shirt, but otherwise I think he would be comfortable here too. I notice that no one seems to have a cell telephone.

In the ammonia-smelling men's room, I jot my favorite lavatory wisdom on the wall: *I sure feel a lot more like I do now than when I got here.*

The patron behind me, wearing standard Far North Carhartt bib overalls in brown duck canvas, squints and asks to borrow my pencil.

Me to, he writes.

Touché.

As I've said, there are traditions besides hardship to uphold in the Far North.

In frosty darkness, Andre Nadeau's string of dogs climbs up over the riverbank at the far edge of town and glides along a levy before he turns the team down the center of Front Street. He wins the four ounces of gold as the first musher to Dawson. It is 8:10 P.M. on the fifth day of the Yukon Quest. Snug in his forest-green parka, his face icy, the French Canadian is all business on his arrival, walking through his team and mumbling what seems to be encouragement while checkers log him in and inventory his mandatory gear. Nadeau's wife is here. She greets first the dogs, then Andre.

The mystery musher's arrival will be the talk of Dawson: instead of his dogs looking weak or stressed for lack of rest, his Siberians are squirming and howling in their harnesses as if they're ready to start fresh. Their tuglines are tight and Andre's sled must be anchored on the ice of the street to restrain them. When he maneuvers the team out of the checkpoint, I sense their power and eagerness. In mushing, these are said to be "happy dogs." There is no higher compliment to a musher.

Onlookers shake their heads in disbelief. Nobody doubts Andre anymore.

Later, after he tends to his dogs' food and feet, and beds them down on straw sprinkled over the snow, the squat, dark-haired dog driver declares psychological warfare on his opponents. In monosyllabic replies translated into English by his wife, Andre Nadeau seems to be saying, What's the big deal about the Yukon Quest anyway?

Aren't you rushing this early in the race?

"This speed is normal," he replies.

Is it disconcerting to be out front by yourself on a strange trail?

"Doesn't matter."

Are you worried about those behind you?

"No. They are all copying the same strategy. I just go on my own experience."

Can your dogs maintain this pace?

Nadeau answers and his wife explains: "He says the dogs can run a hundred miles a day for a year. Not him, but the dogs."

What is his secret?

"He has done three thousand miles training this year, forty miles a day, with a loaded sled, behind which he drags a truck tire and still another full sled. These are not made to be fast dogs. They are strong, tough dogs."

How hard was the climb up King Solomon's Dome?

"Easy. I didn't do anything but stand on the runners. I'm keeping my energy for the last two hundred miles."

What's your feeling about the Quest so far?

"It's the first time he's done a race so easy."

Uh-huh.

Nadeau unintentionally reveals cracks in his cocksure bearing, however, by allowing himself to get into a sputtering, rage-filled argument with Quest officials.

Dawson City is not only the halfway point but a mandatory thirty-six-hour layover for the Quest mushers. This is both for the benefit of the dogs and to uphold tradition. Whether a century ago or now, no dog driver should be asked to pass through Dawson without a rest and the chance for a little fun, or even a lot of fun. Here, and nowhere else, mushers are allowed assistance from their dog handler. A city campground is opened up across the river as the designated layover dog yard. Handlers and mushers for each team stomp out a depression in the snow and line it with straw for dog beds. Plastic tarps, strung between trees, keep off wind and snowdrifts. Handlers stand watch over the dogs. Mushers venture back into town, where each is hosted by a local family. The lucky ones will get a bath in a steaming tub and a queen-size bed with clean sheets.

Nadeau is incensed because the motorized camper that his wife has driven up from Whitehorse is not allowed inside the dog yard. A loner, Nadeau has not accepted the local offer of hospitality. He wants to sleep here with his dogs in the warmth of his camper. Rules prohibit vehicles in the campground, say the Quest officials. They refuse to yield.

Nadeau storms off, and he is seen later behind the wheel of the camper, glowering and driving through the empty streets of Dawson, looking for a private place to park.

Some regard Nadeau as unpleasantly standoffish and temperamental. If everyone was like this the Quest would be a sullen affair. Plus, he is threatening to disprove the standing theories of driving dogs—which is to say, he is mocking the locals. But Nadeau has a growing fan club too. Joe May, for one, thinks the hardheaded Canadian is just what the Quest needs.

"Somebody to shake things up. Scare the hell out of these guys who have been doing it the same way for years." Joe grins.

Fulda is posting flyers offering a $300 reward for information leading to the arrest and conviction of the "person(s) who slashed a tire on the Fulda truck in front of the Downtown Hotel."

The Fulda legions and their wads of marks may have bought the temporary servility of the people of Whitehorse, but the new sponsor receives little except grief in rough-and-tumble Dawson. I'm thankful my parka is gunmetal gray, not red. Last year, an expensive custom paint job on a Fulda truck was vandalized in Dawson. This year, the first of the company's big four-wheel-drives was parked for only a couple of hours before someone unsheathed a knife.

"Wonder what took them so long?" remarks Mel Basharah, a Dawson fur trapper and all-around character who is assisting the Quest as a volunteer race judge. Mel is just about the nicest, most easygoing man in the whole race organization, which can come as a surprise to strangers because just the sight of his fierce, weather-beaten face would be enough to clear the sidewalk in front of him in a more refined city.

Dawson's grudge is not against Germans but against the big-money arrogance of a corporation. Actually, Germans have deep roots in the Yukon. Colonies of them settled here after the Gold Rush, and many businesses in Dawson cater specifically to Germans. The reason why Fulda provided its sponsorship in the first place and stamped a tire as the "Yukon" is the fascination that the Far North holds for Germans.

It's not the Germans that rub like a sharp pebble in the boot of the Yukoners, it's the presence of an Outside corporation exploiting the hard fun that the people here took to be theirs alone.

Last summer, my California friend Frank Clifford and I floated up the Yukon in a canoe from Dawson 255 miles to Circle, Alaska, one of the later checkpoints on the Quest trail. I wanted to see this country with the snow off.

Only once did we meet any fellow voyagers, a young German couple, Walter and Elizabeth, from Nuremberg. One night torrential rains drove them ashore and they happened to make camp nearby. Long ago, Europeans filled in and tamed all their own wilderness. Now their young people, particularly the Germans, are crazy for the Yukon and the Yukon River. The man who rented us our canoe said that half the paddlers who travel out of Dawson and Whitehorse each summer are Germans. Visions of Jack London inflame their imaginations, just as the cowboy myth excites the Japanese. Who can blame them? They know best what it's like to live where there is no space left for the mind to work up a sweat.

Walter, a car mechanic, and Elizabeth, a waitress, flew to North America to go wild. They brought a tiny butane backpacking stove, but the airline refused their fuel bottles. Replacements to match the fittings on their stove could not be found in the Yukon. They set out anyway, determined to cook with firewood just like old Jack and the sourdoughs did. They'd read the stories, but it soon became apparent they had not built that many of their own fires before. When they pulled in near us, it had been raining for twenty-six hours. They'd failed to gather bark and kindling twigs before everything became soaked. I offered to cook their food on my stove.

From his rucksack, Walter produced a box of cornmeal and a bag of powdered milk, to which he added murky river water. I boiled the mixture for him—cornmeal mush.

Somewhere, I suppose, Jack London wrote about cornmeal mush. So the two young visitors squatted in the mud and, under the hoods of their dripping raincoats, grinned like they were eating caviar.

"Yes, good, good," said Walter.

Walter carried a shotgun at all times. He walked in a perpetual crouch, as if he was on a jungle patrol. The couple pitched a tent, and Walter rigged a cord around it. He connected the cord to some sort of battery box. He demonstrated: if something pushed the cord, a homemade alarm would screech. The two were frightened of bears. But don't make fun of them: that's exactly why they came. To experience nature, to feel what they could only read about back home, to flush the carbon monoxide from their spirits, recalibrate those internal gyroscopes by which we set the course of our lives, to exist, momentarily, in the present, and no doubt to spice their lovemaking with the knowledge that honest predators lurked outside their rope perimeter, ready to challenge them for the top rung of the food chain.

As the proverb says, we must travel in the direction of our fears.

Even, I guess, if it means gagging down cornmeal mush.

During this summer trip, Frank and I encountered black bear on the river and a single gray wolf, as well as foxes, both red and brindle. Moose were common, if not plentiful. One morning I awoke to the clatter of hard feet on river rocks and watched a goofy young bull moose feeding twenty feet in front of my tent. Nature has achieved nothing quite as preposterous as an adolescent moose, his head as big as a beer keg with antlers the size of oven mitts.

We saw fresh grizzly tracks circling an island and, improbably, happened across the trail of an errant bull musk ox who'd wandered down from the Arctic looking for babes. Wild musk oxen are only now filling in the territory from which they were extirpated by hunters a century ago. Bachelor oxen are known to travel great distances in search of females, but no one could recall one coming this far.

A logbook at an unoccupied public-use cabin where we sought shelter during one storm contained a whole spring's worth of entries from visitors who'd felt harassed by a small bear that would claw at the door and peer in the windows. We saw no bear here, although were alarmed to hear strange noises outside. It sounded like someone was bombarding the outhouse roof with pinecones. And someone was. The rain had just ceased and the stand of trees outside was enveloped in a spellbinding orange mist from the setting sun. High above, a squirrel had emerged to harvest pine nuts, dropping the cones *bang-crunch* onto the unfortunately situated commode.

Our one-room cabin was built before World War II by a hermit trapper named Christopher Nelson. Whenever a visitor stopped by, Chris would let fly with all the thoughts pent up in him. He talked without interruption and so fast that everyone called him Phonograph Nelson. A framed picture screwed to the wall showed that Phonograph had also killed every large animal who came within range, and hung the pelts outside to dry.

Winter travelers, of course, will see no bear. But wolves are fairly common, as are coyotes and wolverines. I had never seen a lynx in the wild until I drove the lonely winter highway into Dawson, where I surprised four of them feeding on hare. They exploded in all directions at the sight of my car.

Moose pose the gravest danger to mushers, and almost everyone who has spent a winter driving dogs up here has had an unpleasant encounter. Many mushers carry guns. A bull moose can weigh up to eighteen hundred pounds, a cow twelve hundred, and naturally they prefer the packed snow of a trail to wallowing in soft powder. For them, it can be a matter of survival. Thrashing around in deep snow leaves the moose disadvantaged against wolves, so the moose will fight to hold the trail. The Alaska Railroad kills several hundred a year in these right-of-way disputes.

Confronted with a dog team, which resembles a wolf pack to the atavistic moose brain, the animal sometimes chooses to attack rather than run. Rusty Hagan's lead dog was killed two years ago when a cow moose charged his team on a trail near Fairbanks. In the 1993 Yukon Quest, a pair of mushers warily made their way around an angry cow on the trail. One of them had to stomp out a detour trail. The next musher to pass, Jeff Mann, was horrified to watch the bleating, angry-eyed cow charge directly down the center of his team, hoofs flashing. Amazingly, no dogs were seriously injured, but the cow clambered over the sled and sent Mann leaping. He grabbed his ax and, with two blows to the head, killed the moose on the spot. Quest rules required Mann to gut the animal and report the kill, so the meat could be salvaged for distribution to the needy.

Two hours and eleven minutes behind Andre Nadeau, Bruce Lee pulls into Dawson. Rick Mackey arrives three hours and thirty-two minutes later, followed by Paddy Santucci, John Schandelmeier, Jerry Louden, and Frank Turner.

Dave Dalton is a half day behind; Tim Mowry and Aliy Zirkle are a half day farther still. Aliy has fully recovered from her flu and, despite her hair-raising climb over King Solomon's Dome, she swoops down Front Street grinning and waving to the ten or so spectators as if she'd just scored a gold medal. Her huge ruff of wolf fur frames a face reddened by cold and blushed with achievement. The only indication of her struggle up the mountain is that her eyes seem a little wider than when she started. Her dogs have frosted faces and ice beards and they roll in and nuzzle the snow. They seem to sense they have reached some break in the action.

Rusty Hagan and Brenda Mackey mush into town two days behind the leaders. Their spirits, too, seem higher. They have passed the psychological Wall and climbed the first mountain pass, and they have a day and a half to rest. If they weren't so bone tired, we'd probably see them jump for joy.

With the striking exception of Andre Nadeau, the Yukon Quest is shaping up just as everyone guessed.

Oddsmakers still seem to favor the traditionalists over the newcomer. Nadeau's strategy is now apparent. He is not pacing himself for a one-thousand-mile race but for two back-to-back five-hundred milers. Mid-distance races are his specialty. He's counting on his dogs recovering fully during their thirty-six-hour rest and never having to slow down.

"We just don't know him," says a reflective Bruce Lee. "Nobody knows him. I know Mackey's style, and he knows mine. That's true in most sports. But this guy I don't know at all. He's trying something that's never worked. People have tried this before and have crashed and burned. He may not. But the worst thing any of us could do is abandon our own plans and start trying to run his race."

In his own form of psychological warfare, Lee insists the teams behind him are more worry than Nadeau: "They're like freight trains back there, building up power."

Lee has studied the records of all the past Quests. There is no correlation between winning the race and being first into Dawson. Hear that, Andre? All Lee wanted to do was not fall further than six hours behind Nadeau—just in case the bastard isn't listening and doesn't slow down on the rough trail ahead.

The Quest, as now becomes obvious, is a mix of celebration and ordeal. At the finish line in Fairbanks, dogs from winning teams will get blood tests for drugs; a microchip injected under the skin of their necks is used for identification. There are no drug tests for the mushers, though. Whether one approves or not, marijuana is very much a part of life in the Far North. And, for some, it's an integral part of the Quest. Nothing like a few hours gliding along under the northern lights and having the brain charged with cannabis, they say.

Until this decade, Alaskans could legally grow their own pot and possession was not a crime. State courts held that personal use of marijuana was safeguarded by Alaska's privacy statutes. With the growth of politically active Christian organizations and the national "war on drugs," a signature initiative recriminalized pot in 1990, but most police agencies still consider personal possession a low priority.

At least in their own culture, few of the white outdoorsmen and women of Alaska attach a stigma to pot. And by writing about this ticklish question I do not mean to imply that all the Quest mushers are dopers. I know a half dozen who are and I'd guess there are others. They're not all also-rans either. Getting stoned is part of their lives and, oddly, does not seem to leave them in a stupor, as it does the urban pot smokers I know. The only explanation I can offer for this, purely supposition, is that I understand marijuana to be a mood enhancer. So perhaps these hyperactive mushers only intensify their gusto for living by puffing their pipes. Either that or their drive is so strong it overpowers the tranquilizing effect of the drug.

The question these mushers ask each other is not Do you have any pot? but What kind do you have? And it so happens that along the trail, the question is answered in the form of a side competition.

I had been hearing references to some famous "best butt" contest. Then I was told I had misunderstood; it's the annual "best bud" competition. There is a single judge, and apparently the judge is an individual whose experience and opinion is beyond question. The winner is never disclosed. Or maybe the judge is too stoned to remember who won anyway. But surely the best weed will come from the Matanuska Valley north of Anchorage, one of the few places in all the North where agriculture is viable outside of hothouses. In the summer, farmers grow fifty-pound cabbages and pumpkins the size of easy chairs under the perpetual sun. They also produce a sweet, sticky resinous marijuana that goes by the name Matanuska Thunder Fuck. The bud of champions.

This year's Quest poses a special challenge for potheads. The twenty-fifth starter in the race is Doug Harris, of the Royal Canadian Mounted Police—the officer in charge of undercover operations in the Yukon.

Mounties patrolled the Far North by dog team until the 1960s, and a few traditionalists like Harris honor the memory. With a neatly trimmed black beard and an easy manner, Harris, forty-three, is both tough and popular. No one expects him to have time for plainclothes work this February, but just to be on the safe side several mushers casually inspect Harris and his outfit before the race. They want to remember the color of his parka and his sled bag and be able to recognize his dogs, thus reducing the chances of an awkward encounter on the trail.

On the second night in Dawson, the lights of town reflect, moonlike, off the low clouds and a gentle snow falls. I guess the temperature at 5 below.

On the sand spit on the east side of the river lies Dawson City and the boozy blare of The Pit, the Sluice Box, and Diamond Tooth Gertie's Gambling Hall. Tonight, I dance clumsily with a few strangers. But I'm feeling melancholy. Earlier in this story, I said the people up here would change my life. And they have.

Last month, before leaving Fairbanks, I asked a woman to go out and have a beer. Liisa Penrose is general manager of Apocalypse Design, the tiny specialty company that made and later repaired my cold-weather parka. I had known her for a year—a tall flirt of a woman with a banquet-hall grin. Apocalypse made gear for most of the mushers and officials, and so Liisa was caught up in the pandemonium of race preparations. Her cheerful air lightened and brightened any room.

One afternoon, the words just blurted out of me. You know, I told her, I've had just about enough of dogs and people who smell like dogs. Wanna get a beer later? She smiled. And we did. During the next few weeks, I felt myself falling hopelessly in love. This love, I might add, was not entirely reciprocated in kind. We spent time together, but Liisa maintained enough distance between us to provide her an easy escape route. Spirited and strikingly good-looking, she has her pick of the boys at home. But she promised to meet me in Dawson, where I could have the first dance.

Now bad flying weather has intervened. She is not coming. Downcast, I wander across the ice bridge over the Yukon to the west side of the river. Here, in a thicket of oversize spruce, campfires crackle. Mushers and dog handlers have retreated from the raucous town to the woods, where they feel at home.

The murmur of conversation is inconsequential, and timeless. The weather, the standings, the trail behind, the trail ahead, old stories from other trails, how the dogs are eating, how they are shitting. Men and women laugh, and pause in long silences as people do around campfires, poking sticks into the flames and watching the coals melt into the snow. They brag about their good dogs, and bitch because they don't have enough of them. Hardly anybody, apparently, has leaders worth a damn, though I wonder how any team has made it this far if that's so.

I look at the faces. Tough. Reddened even in firelight. Their hands are scabbed and chapped. Lips are cracked. Their insulated trail overalls are smeared with dog food and dog shit; their white rubber bunny boots have grown gray and scuffed, and the laces dangle loosely. For camp chores, these dog people wear fleece work gloves that are filthy, stiff, and scorched. Even with many hours of Dawson City rest, their eyes are red and puffy. Altogether content, I'd say.

I'm at the campsite of Tim Mowry, the Fairbanks newspaperman who has run two Iditarods and six previous Quests. He has never scratched, but neither has he ever finished in the top five. A particular transformation comes over Mowry during the Quest. Back home, he is a baby-faced, thirty-four-year-old columnist who writes about the outdoors by making fun of his own foibles. He has never seen a live wolf; he is a comic hunter. But Mowry gains stature after five hundred trail miles, when his dogs are bedded down in the woods behind him and firelight shimmers in his eyes. His handlers and friends listen with admiration when he talks. From where they are sitting now, they actually are looking up at him, as he stands there with a fresh dusting of snowflakes on his big shoulders.

Someone opens the ice chest and hands out another round of beers. The cooler is not to chill the beer but to keep it from freezing. The beer bites in the throat, and we all shuffle position when the smoke shifts and blows in our faces with a faint breeze. In this snug embrace of the campfire, I forget I am sitting in winter snow 150 miles from the Arctic Circle.

Because he is so gregarious and because we practice the same craft, I presume to understand a little about Mowry. I know his wife, Kristen Kelly, herself a one-time reporter who now teaches high school. Just days before the race, she learned she is pregnant with their first child. Kristen shares Mowry's love of these dogs, but I know that she has other dreams, too. She wanted to go to Hawaii once before having children. She would like to go out to dinner at a fancy restaurant and order whatever she feels like. The family lives in an old and intimate miner's log cabin in Two Rivers, outside Fairbanks. They use wood for heat and must add a new room for the baby. Wouldn't a new house be lovely? Mowry is sympathetic to these dreams. He has his own: to build a tourist lodge in the remote bush. But as he stands here, I see that mushing makes him tall. The Quest brings him alive. Kristen has seen it too. So everything they earn and all their time has gone to the dogs.

Before the race, Mowry's mother sewed him one thousand fleece dog booties. Each winter, his friends gather at the Big "I" saloon in Fairbanks for a fund-raising auction to benefit Mowry's race effort. This year, Kristen took the microphone and announced that Tim would auction off his scraggly blond ponytail; the high bidder would get to snip it off. Surprised, Tim had no choice but to consent.

There was an opening bid of thirty dollars. Then an old biker in the back of the room with his own ponytail bellowed out an offer of thirty-five to save it. Kristen's face dropped. At the least, she'd figured, Tim would be forced to clean himself up. The bidding carried on until the biker won at sixty-five dollars. The ponytail stayed.

"Jesus Christ," the biker muttered. "Didja see that? They tried to ruin the man."

I bid five dollars for two cans of Trusty Husky paw ointment, which I donated so Tim could slick back his ponytail. Trusty Husky is concocted locally from eucalyptus oil, wax, and who knows what else by Kris Krestensen, a friendly fiftyish man who calls himself a former LSD chemist.

By the dance of the campfire and in the gauzy envelope of softly falling snow, Mowry is talking now about the ups and downs of the trail. Coming into Dawson, he caught up with John Schandelmeier and

Jerry Louden. That was at the bottom of the Black Hills, and Mowry's single lead dog, Alf, was pacing the team.

"My eyes lit up when I saw those guys. I was going to stop. But I said, Shit, I'm not going to now. For at least one night, I'm in the race . . ."

Mike Ott, an Alaskan from Wasilla, had never been part of a big dog race until his neighbor Larry Carroll invited him along as dog handler. Low-key and shy, the black-bearded Ott was thrilled to join a mythical undertaking.

After he accepted the invitation, he began pissing blood. On Wednesday before the race started, Ott underwent a CAT scan and other tests. On Thursday he was diagnosed with kidney cancer. On Friday, he flew from Anchorage to Whitehorse to do his part for Carroll and the Quest. He deferred treatment until after the race.

"After I took that test, my wife asked what was I going to do if it came back bad," he recalls. "I told her I wasn't going to let Larry down. If I only had six months to live, I'd still come. I might as well do what I wanted. And I've always wanted to do this."

As Mike's story makes the rounds, many of us declare a moratorium on our own complaints about lack of sleep, hard floors, sore backs, caustic coffee, and frigid outhouses.

"I love this, I love these people," Mike says, smiling and looking out over the flophouse scene inside the checkpoint headquarters at the Dawson visitors center. Strangers a week ago, this band of mushers and fellow-travelers has been molded by common interest and the harshness of the surroundings into a nomadic family: natives and whites, women and men, parents and children and grandparents—characters all, and many with character.

Reflective moments do not linger long. Before anyone has a chance to fully unwind, anticipation and anxiety return. The last half of the thirty-six-hour layover is devoted entirely to preparations. The trail is about to get ugly, mushers are told.

All along, trailbreakers have been worrying about horrible ice north of Dawson. "The worst in twenty years," says Sergeant Sylvian Gagnon of the Canadian Army Rangers.

Jumble ice begins right outside of town, where the mushers leave the far end of the campground and drop onto the Yukon. The trail is said to be exceedingly rough, with numerous hairpin corners around and through broken slabs of ice. There also are steep, short climbs and drops over ledges. The trek promises to be exhausting. Then, about twenty-one miles down the river, the ice has collected into an even more frightening jam, a jagged labyrinth of interlocking icebergs two stories tall. Again, the only rough trail that could be chopped through this maze leads mushers along a traverse of constant sidehill hairpins, drop-offs, and rises—sometimes all occurring simultaneously within the length of a strung-out dog team, which is about the same as that of an eighteen-wheel trailer-truck. Vast tracts of bank-to-bank jumble ice are then sprinkled at intervals farther down.

Group dynamics in the Dawson campground transform worries into dread. The crisis over booties now seems minor. There will be enough to get the teams to the next couple of checkpoints at least. But will they get that far through the ice? A story passes from team to team about the trapper who took ten days to chop his way a mile and a half past one section ahead. Mushers know they will hit the worst when they and their dogs are already tired. Mushers double-check their departure times, which are adjusted here to account for the two-minute gaps between each team at the relay start. From Dawson on, everyone will be on the same clock. Those who will have to pass through the tangle of ice in darkness feel an extra measure of apprehension.

William Kleedehn is particularly disquieted. The thirty-eight-year-old Yukoner lost a leg in a motorcycle crash when he was a teenager. He's been racing dogs for ten years now and working summers driving construction equipment, but the trail being described to him will require agility beyond the ordinary capabilities of a man with a prosthetic limb.

"You wait a whole year and then this. Shit," he says to race marshal Dave Rich. "I've got a disadvantage—I can't get off the sled and work it like these other guys, shit. Shit."

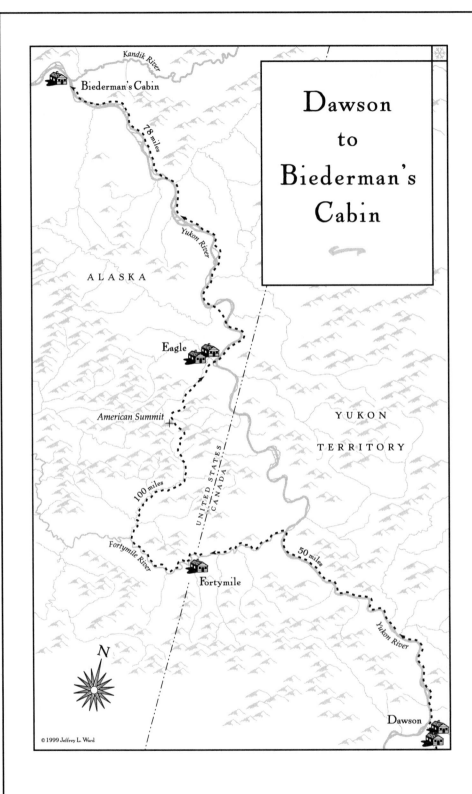

Kandik River

Biederman's Cabin

78 miles

Yukon River

ALASKA

Eagle

American Summit

YUKON

TERRITORY

100 miles

Fortymile River

UNITED STATES
CANADA

50 miles

Fortymile

Yukon River

N

Dawson

© 1999 Jeffrey L. Ward

Dawson
to
Biederman's
Cabin

Dawson to Biederman's Cabin

ARRIVING AT DAWSON CITY

1. Andre Nadeau, *Sainte-Melanie, Quebec**
2. Bruce Lee, *Denali National Park, Alaska*
3. Rick Mackey, *Nenana, Alaska*
4. Paddy Santucci, *Fairbanks, Alaska*
5. John Schandelmeier, *Paxson, Alaska*
6. Jerry Louden, *Two Rivers, Alaska*
7. Frank Turner, *Whitehorse, Yukon*
8. Brian MacDougall, *Whitehorse, Yukon*
9. Dave Olesen, *Hoarfrost River, Northwest Territories**
10. Louis Nelson, *Kotzebue, Alaska**
11. William Kleedehn, *Carcross, Yukon*
12. Doug Harris, *Whitehorse, Yukon*
13. Dave Dalton, *Fairbanks, Alaska*
14. Keizo Funatsu, *Two Rivers, Alaska*
15. Cor Guimond, *Dawson City, Yukon*
16. Tim Mowry, *Two Rivers, Alaska*
17. Aliy Zirkle, *Two Rivers, Alaska**
18. Amy Wright, *Tok, Alaska**
19. Larry Carroll, *Willow, Alaska*
20. Walter Palkovitch, *Two Rivers, Alaska**
21. Rusty Hagan, *North Pole, Alaska**
22. Keith Kirkvold, *Fairbanks, Alaska**
23. Brenda Mackey, *Nenana, Alaska**
24. Thomas Tetz, *Tagish, Yukon**
25. Brian O'Donoghue, *Two Rivers, Alaska**
26. Gwen Holdman, *Fox, Alaska**
27. Bill Steyer, *Fairbanks, Alaska**

Scratched:

Michael Hyslop, *Grizzy Valley, Yukon**

Kurt Smith, *North Pole, Alaska*

Ned Cathers, *Whitehorse, Yukon*

Mike King, *Salcha, Alaska*

Stan Njootli, *Old Crow, Yukon**

Jimmy Hendrick, *Denali National Park, Alaska*

Dan Turner, *Haines, Alaska*

John Nash, *Nenana, Alaska**

Terry McMullin, *Eagle, Alaska**

Tony Blanford, *Two Rivers, Alaska**

Dieter Dolif, *Trebel, Germany*

* rookie

Slump-shouldered, Kleedehn sulks off, vowing to reinforce the sides of his sled with sheets of plywood and disconnect the tuglines of all dogs in the middle of his team, leaving only the leaders and the wheel dogs to pull. This will slow him down and give him extra time to react to problems.

"I don't care if I have to go one mile an hour. Shit."

Other mushers are beefing up their equipment, too. Tim Mowry laces ash hockey sticks to the sides of his sled to absorb blows from the hard ice.

So high is the tension that word filters ahead to Sebastian Jones, the caretaker at the Fortymile mining ghost town, which is located, confusingly, fifty miles up the trail. Sebastian sends back a handwritten, mile-by-mile guide to the worst of the trail. He includes a cheery summary: "Lots of people have heard the river is a bit rough this year. I can tell you that it is, in places. But I don't think Quest teams with 500 miles on them will have any trouble."

While the mushers agitate, bitch, stew, and pack their sleds, the rest of us plan our paths out of Dawson. This is the end of the road in the Yukon. Dog handlers and families traveling by truck must now double back to Whitehorse, then travel west to Alaska and north up to the road-accessible checkpoint at Circle City. They will travel one thousand miles over snow and ice. For the mushers, Circle City is 308 trail miles away—over a meandering route that penetrates some of the most isolated wilderness in the Far North.

I have arranged for a bush pilot to fly me to the intermediate checkpoint at the Yukon River village of Eagle, 150 miles away. From there, I will pack my gear in a sled and take to the trail by dog team. I can attest to the uneasiness that an unknown ice-choked trail ahead adds to one's state of mind.

10

The heavens themselves run continually round, the sun riseth and sets, stars and planets keep their constant motions, the air is still tossed by the winds, the waters ebb and flow . . . to teach us that we should ever be in motion.

—Robert Burton

In the first milky light before dawn on the sixth day of the Yukon Quest, Andre Nadeau drives his string of twelve remaining Siberian huskies through the Dawson City campground. At 8:16 A.M. the team caterpillars over the riverbank and down onto the craggy surface of the Yukon. The dogs look fresh, strong. A moment later Andre's hulking silhouette disappears behind a block of sharp ice as big as a riverboat. Next stop, Alaska. Five hundred and sixty miles to go. Three hours later, Bruce Lee is given the go-ahead and follows with his eleven remaining dogs. His team also looks strong and eager. Neither man smiles. Both are bundled in parkas, their hoods drawn over their heads against the icy breeze.

Everything so far has been prelude. Now the race begins.

That afternoon I join the exodus from rollicking Dawson City, advancing westbound in the blue, orange, and yellow Super Cub, the "circus plane," flown by Gary Nance, a thirty-six-year-old Fairbanks food distributor and longtime pilot for the Quest. Gary is a cold-

weather bush pilot, costumed in regulation Far North pilot's garb: jog-
ging pants and a pilled and dirty fleece jacket, with a ratty knitted bal-
aclava perched back on his head like the floppy hats conceived by Dr.
Seuss.

"Go ahead and smoke," Gary says over the screechy intercom. He
pauses and adds, "But don't drop that cherry. Or you'll blow us up."

I see that Gary has lit a cigarette already. He turns and coughs, then
grins conspiratorially, wiping his runny nose on the sleeve of his
hunter's camouflage fleece. The bush pilot's creed is rigid on matters
of personal presentation. Nonchalance is achieved by appearing as
though you bolted out of deep REM sleep five minutes ago, possibly
with a throbbing hangover, with no time to wash or comb your hair.
This conveys the lack of time or interest for anything except flying. On
matters of dress, bush pilots stick with the cheapest, grimiest, lowest-
tech clothing they can buy from, say, the sale racks at Value Village in
Fairbanks. If necessary, these garments are then rinsed in engine oil
and allowed to ripen in a dog yard for a few days. This suggests that
all the pilot's spare cash has been more usefully spent for something
mechanical. Likewise, the seats of bush planes are torn on arrival in
Alaska, then patched with duct tape; the paint on the instrument panel
is hammered and chipped, and the outside skin of the aircraft profes-
sionally wrinkled and dimpled. Any aircraft not so weather-beaten
might be suspect as having not yet proved itself. Under the engine
cowling, however, everything gleams and is surgically disinfected.

It's freezing cold in the tiny two-seater as we pass over Dawson and
the lumps of mine tailings that make the banks of nearby Eldorado
Creek and the Klondike River look like they are infested with giant
moles. I grab the flexible vacuum-cleaner hose that leads from the
engine and delivers warm air into the cabin. Like a hair dryer, the hose
heats only the small area in its direct aim. I spray the weak flow around
the cabin with little effect. From time to time, Gary calls for the hose,
which he places on top of the instrument panel to defrost the windshield.

We are flying low over the Yukon to see for ourselves the horror of
the ice jams ahead. Down here in the canyon of the Yukon, against the

bluffs and hills through which the river carves its path, headwinds buffet the small plane. When Gary coughs, the plane lurches. With alarm,
I'm watching the glowing cigarettes bounce horribly in our hands. I'm
also quite aware that we are so close to the ground that I can see the
reflective markings on trail stakes outside the window, and can plainly
identify the tracks of a moose in the snow across the Quest trail.

Ahead of us, the ice rises—great broken walls of it, a jumbled
labyrinth continuing for miles. Gary pulls back on the stick to lift us
over the craggy blue-tinged mass. Just as unsettling are the periodic
open leads we see on the Yukon. Some are just cracks; others are geo-
metric rectangles a hundred feet long where the ice has vanished and
the wind froths wavelets on pure blue water. In summer, the Yukon is
loaded with so much soil runoff that it churns like chocolate milk. But
in winter, the sediment drops and the deadly open sections of river run
cerulean.

Our departure from the tiny Dawson airfield was delayed more than
an hour because of an emergency. A longtime Quest volunteer had broken his arm fifty miles down the trail. The man was traveling ahead of
the race on a snowmachine but couldn't make it through the jumble ice.
He flipped and crashed, and had to hike injured to the caretaker's cabin
at the ghost town of Fortymile. A Quest two-way radio had been for-
warded there for just this kind of incident. An SOS call was relayed to
the airport. Gary was asked to medevac the injured man. At the last
moment, another airplane passed over the accident site and the pilot
agreed to make the rescue. This is not the only misfortune to occur at
Fortymile. Cor Guimond, the fierce and crowd-pleasing Yukon trapper,
can no longer nurse along his ailing team, apparently another victim of
the corona virus. He becomes the twelfth musher to scratch.

I've been flying in this dwarf airplane with Gary for a year now. You
get attached to your bush pilots up here, superstitious about your luck.
The cold and remoteness call for pilots with special skills, guile, and
equipment. The aging Super Cub is a workhorse. Gary's was built in
1961 and is considered "new." It has only two liabilities that I can discern. One, I can barely squeeze myself into the miniature passenger
compartment behind the pilot. When I do, my knees splay awkwardly

around Gary's seat and my elbows jam against the frigid aluminum skin of the aircraft. Another inch or two on my waistline and I'd have to walk. Two, the Super Cub carries only minuscule payloads. The manual specifies no more than four hundred pounds with full tanks of fuel. In my arctic garb, I weigh two hundred and so does Gary, plus the tail is loaded with mandatory survival gear and we've shoved my bulging duffel and Gary's pack into the space behind my seat. Also stuffed back there somewhere is a portable engine heater, a tin of white gas, insulated coverings for the wings and cowling, along with a few quarts of high-grade oil. Snowshoes are lashed to the starboard wing strut.

How the hell can we fly loaded down with all this?

"Amazing, isn't it," Gary replies with a wink and a maniacal grin.

On the upside, the Super Cub is so dinky and slow that it can land on a space only slightly bigger than a suburban backyard. Using skis, floats, or wheels, the Super Cub is at home on sandbars, ponds, and mountain glaciers, or between ice jumbles on frozen rivers.

One time Gary and I left an Indian village where there was no liquor allowed. We were en route to visit a friend at a cabin in the bush, and we couldn't very well arrive without an offering of beer. So Gary detoured to a mountaintop roadhouse, where an enterprising bush rat was known to sell a little booze. In a vicious crosswind, Gary buzzed the roadhouse. Protocol demands a greeting when a plane arrives, but no one emerged. If the roadhouse was empty, there was no need to risk landing in the driveway during such a gale. Gary made another pass to double-check. He reduced throttle, dropped to just a few feet off the ground, and flew up next to the front window of the roadhouse. Against the buffeting wind, we virtually hovered. Gary worked to hold the plane steady.

"See anybody?" he yelled over the intercom.

Through frosted windows, I could see the kitchen table with a magazine on it, and dirty dishes in the sink. But no inhabitants. No smoke from the chimney.

"Are you sure?" he asked again, the airplane bucking and lurching.

Jesus, Gary, I'm real sure.

"Okay, but you'll tell them we tried to get beer, okay?" He nudged the rudder left and the wind blew us off the mountain.

Now our destination is Eagle, Alaska, the next checkpoint on the Quest trail. A pint-sized village with a population of 180 on the Yukon River, just downstream from the Canadian border, Eagle can be reached during the brief summers by taking a rough gravel road 160 miles north of Tok. In winter, the road is impassable and Eagle is wholly isolated except by bush plane, snowmachine, or dogsled.

Eagle is the most welcoming village along the Quest trail. There are two inns with a few rooms each, a small café that specializes in doughnuts and burgers, a general store with free hot dogs, and a couple of living-room craft shops—but otherwise, it is an elemental bush community of whites and natives. Much of the village celebrates the Quest as a winter festival, and children gather with their parents around a bonfire that roars all night in front of the one-room schoolhouse that serves as the official checkpoint.

I have a friend in Eagle who has made for himself a quiet, mostly subsistence life as a fisherman and trapper. Wayne Hall also sometimes brings in cash as a wilderness guide for a few intrepid backcountry travelers, and he does occasional taxidermy. He is one of those surprising characters—a man you almost surely would take for one thing but who is really quite something else. Almost frightfully rugged in appearance, Wayne's face and body are a mat of scar tissue from burns. One hand is misshapen like a claw, with only three burned fingers. His beard sprouts in clumps between the scars, and he speaks with a low growl. His movements are sometimes slowed as a result of a youth spent on the Texas rodeo circuit riding bulls. Yet Wayne, at age forty-six, is also one of the gentlest, most deeply centered people I've ever met. His thoughtful curiosity is far ranging. Like some other bush rats scattered around up here, he does not see himself as retreating or running away. He lives on the far edge of civilization with his wife, Scarlet, less an escape from contemporary society than a determined pursuit of a more harmonious way of life.

Wayne has assembled two teams of shaggy, oversize trapline dogs, and together he and I will mush down the Yukon River over the next leg of the Quest trail. At least that's our plan. Finally free from roads, from the German press, from edgy race officials, I am overcome with happy fatalism.

I've lost track of the day of the week, but I am acutely aware that it is growing dark as Gary circles Eagle and buzzes an open field in between houses to make sure there are no children or moose in the path. Then he drops over a stand of spruce, cuts the throttle, and glides to a stop in a rooster tail of spindrift, the landing skis on the Super Cub punching deep into the soft snow. Now it is quiet. The temperature is 15 below and the breeze is dying. On the horizon, the sky glows in bands of yellow and orange. But above, the gemstone colors of huge night stars already flicker in the descending indigo. On the far horizon, the inky black shadows of stratus clouds advance toward us. Wayne Hall steps up with a handshake and a shy cowboy grin.

We are now many hours ahead of the lead mushers in the Yukon Quest. Wayne's dog teams are harnessed and burrowed in the snow, just a quarter mile away at the Eagle schoolhouse. The nightly bonfire crackles nearby; the townsfolk of this outpost are beginning to gather. I smell hot coffee. Behind us on the trail, however, the unfolding journey is not so serene.

The snowstorm clouds we see in the distance now engulf Aliy Zirkle. Fresh powder accumulating on the trail slows her to a crawl. No longer running, her team now wades. The sled does not glide but plows. Her mandatory thirty-six-hour wait in Dawson ended just a half hour before noon, and she now heads into the scary ice jumbles under these awful conditions. Aliy's mood is gray, like the inside of the descending storm. Before long, fierce winds swirl up the exposed river, driving the snow sideways: a ground blizzard. She cinches down the cuffs and ruff of her parka to block the biting drafts.

As day drifts into night, she is blinded by the fury of the weather. With her headlamp off, she can sense the world around her only by the noise of the wind, muffled through the fur flaps of her trapper hat and the two-inch-thick insulation of her parka's hood. There is no light whatsoever on the scene, and she feels attacks of vertigo as the sled rises, drops, and skids over the irregular ice underfoot. Turning on her headlamp, however, is just as bad. The hot, white beam of halogen light bounces off the blowing snow like a million car lights aimed right at her. She blinks and tries to focus her vision down the trail. Impossible. The reflected light is claustrophobic, making her feel as if her head is trapped inside a cardboard box full of dancing strobe lights.

Aliy finally stops. I cannot go on alone like this, she says to herself. She turns her back to the wind; the dogs burrow in. Another Alaskan rookie, Amy Wright, catches up later. How much later? Sometime later. Together they resume the march, taking turns breaking trail, a few hours at a time. In the inky gloom, a fog descends on Aliy's thinking. There are long blank spots in the experience, the drudgery of movement, the sweat that builds up from exertion and then freezes around her like cold candle wax. Hot one moment and bone-chilled the next. Mentally, the hours pass like sleepwalking. She talks to herself. These are the hardest miles of the race, she says.

When time comes to feed the dogs, she climbs up the bank of the Yukon River looking for a sheltered spot. Finding none, she remembers that behind her just a mile she'd seen the shadows of a plywood shed on the bank. She turns around and gives back a hard-fought mile, breaking a fresh trail over the distance she just traveled. Here she rests the dogs. At least they are eating. They haven't lost heart. But Prince worries her. The tough, fast veteran, a blond dog with a liver-pink nose, seems lethargic. Not at all normal.

After the feeding, she puts fresh boots on the eleven dogs remaining in her team and clips them back to the gangline. Before resuming the trek, she walks ahead to check conditions on the river. Even worse now. I can't see shit, she says. Then her headlamp starts shorting. She mutters more profanities. That old demon frustration begins to poison her disposition. She decides to await sunrise. But when she turns around, she cannot find the short trail back to the shed and her team. For a panicky instant, she is lost and alone. She wonders to herself whether she should turn back for Dawson.

Amy Wright decides to move on.

When night yields to a brooding, zinc-gray dawn, Aliy follows ahead. She doesn't really decide to so much as yield to habit. She lets the woozy Prince ride in the sled bag for the next leg of the journey— to Sebastian Jones's cozy caretaker cabin at old mining ruins of Fortymile. She is three and a half hours behind Amy. She snacks the team. Prince eats along with the others.

Now the Quest trail departs the Yukon River. Mushers veer ninety degrees left and travel up Fortymile River. They turn right after about thirty miles and follow another drainage along the route of an old gravel road, which is not plowed in winter. For twenty miles, the trail winds steadily uphill to a windswept dome, barren and exposed. The forbidding top of American Summit rises 3,420 feet into the jet stream, where the trail crosses a ridge of local mountains.

I'm leaving Fortymile between a rock and a hard place, Aliy says grimly to herself. Ahead is a long pull to the top. Behind, the hardest fucking part of the trail. And this worrisome dog. Yes, I knew it would be awful, this Quest. But does it have to be so many awfuls all at the same time? Shitty ahead, shitty behind. Shitty weather. And poor Prince, looking forlorn. Shit, shit.

No matter the turmoil in her mind, Aliy's body moves forward automatically. Booties for the dogs. Tuglines clipped to the gangline. Pack the sled bag. Step on the runners. Kick the sled loose. Okay, guys. Now moving, Aliy turns from the Yukon River without a glance back and begins the winding climb up Fortymile Creek, past hulking lumps in the snow that once were the mining shovels and detritus of the gold seekers. Somewhere back there in the spruce are the rotting timbers of the famous Fortymile Opera House. A century ago, a crowd would have gathered in amazement to watch such a handsome, formidable woman disappear into the bush with her dog team.

In summer, Fortymile Creek runs with an oily metallic sheen, residual evidence of mining. In winter, it's just more lumpy ice and drifting snow with spruce thickets on both sides. Aliy advances on autopilot, ten dogs pulling and one riding. Four hours up the trail, she passes by a heated cabin without stopping in order to complete a full fifty-mile leg before camping. She reaches the unplowed summer road, called the

Taylor Highway, and stops where a bridge crosses Fortymile Creek. All the dogs eat, a good sign. The team rests.

Ahead, the trail climbs more steeply. When Aliy rouses her dogs, she decides to give Prince a try in harness again. She hooks the big yellow dog into the wheel position, right in front of the sled, so she can watch him closely. He seems willing.

Okay, guys, let's go.

With the steady cadence that has now become their existence, the dogs shoulder forward. Up front, Flood's ears bounce like metronomes. The dogs behind him bob in a rhythmic string. Storm winds still swirl around her.

"In your heart, you never think anything bad is going to happen to your dogs," Aliy recalls later. "Half the time, you think to yourself that the dogs get as much out of it as you do. . . . I didn't cry until Eagle."

Less than an hour up the trail, Prince stumbles and collapses. The team, unaware, continues as the big blond dog drags limply, plowing up soft snow. Horrified, Aliy jumps on the brake with all her weight and rushes forward to the downed dog's side. Prince finished the Quest last year, a smart but never very demonstrative dog. He is five years old. But he is not breathing now. Aliy squeezes his muzzle in her hand and puts her lips over his snow-covered nostrils. Her cheeks swell out as she puffs: mouth-to-nose resuscitation. The voice in her ear screams, No, No! The other dogs in the team, their fur rippling in the wind, turn and watch. Their eyes meet hers. A charge of emotion passes between species—but exactly what dogs feel in their hearts at such a moment is a question for which humans have no answer.

Further back, Rusty Hagan has joined with three other rookies in a traveling caravan. Four teams arrived together in Dawson, and they band together again after their departure. Hagan and young Brenda Mackey are teamed up with Thomas Tetz, a thirty-three-year-old native of Germany who now lives in the Yukon and works as a butcher, sausage maker, and tour guide; and Keith Kirkvold, a forty-five-year-old Alaskan carpenter from Fairbanks. Someone has begun calling them the "party pack," not owing to any high-spirited antics but because of their close-knit trailside fellowship. They have gained perseverance from each other, and after those rough first days they seem to be having a grand adventure. Just like Joe May said, they found the light at the end of the tunnel.

With so many casualties in the Quest already, the sight of this lively foursome becomes an inspiration for others.

Patricia Jones, the business editor of the *Fairbanks Daily News–Miner*, feels a swell of emotion as she watches the grizzled Hagan, the baby-faced Brenda Mackey, and the two other men. Jones, herself a musher, is covering the race this year for the Fairbanks daily, which considers the Quest a page 1 story each day. Late at night she hammers out a personal column: "My eyes moistened. . . . Watching the four rookies pull into Dawson with their dog teams Saturday afternoon turned on the waterworks for many bystanders, myself included. I felt such a tremendous surge of pride for these four. . . . No longer will they wear the rank of rookie."

They leave Dawson in the fading light of afternoon, feeling ever stronger. At first, Hagan recalls, it was not important to him to be part of any traveling group. Then, approaching Dawson, they realized that it was easier to break trail if a couple of teams took turns. They found security in numbers and pleasure in camaraderie. If something awful did happen, at least they would not be alone. None of them was really racing. Their goal as individuals, and now as a collective, was simply to make it 1,023 miles to Fairbanks with their dog teams intact. Soon, they found themselves adjusting their plans to account for one another. Rusty waited two extra hours at one spot so that Brenda would not fall behind.

One night out of Dawson, they arrive together in a string at Fortymile. They leave together before dawn and begin the steep climb up American Summit the following evening. It is snowing, with the temperature about 5 below. They have been fighting wind most of the way, and it seems not especially worse now. A couple of other rookie teams have bunched up with them, including Amy Wright. It is a regular freight train heading up the hill.

The winds grow more authoritative the higher they climb. Like Aliy, they begin to experience the dizzying sensation of sightlessness in the dark, with the swirling snow. They no longer have the perception of going up. They cannot actually see themselves moving at all, only feel it. Once in a while, someone illuminates a headlamp, the others catch its faint flicker and the world is, momentarily, a three-dimensional place again. Otherwise, they exist in the flat space inside their own heads.

One by one, the members of the convoy begin to awaken from autopilot with feelings of foreboding. The extremes of cold, wind, and perpetual travel have become ordinary and familiar, but this, kicking them in the teeth now, is something different. The wind shrieks at thirty miles an hour, then forty. The brittle nylon of their parkas rattles with the fury of gunshots. But pulled by the momentum of their own cortege, they continue. This is where the training comes in. Will your dogs go on, even if they want to quit? This is where a lead dog leads. Don't worry about the others—just get one of those crazy sons of bitches who can't bear not knowing what's on the other side of the hill. Keep him in lead. Just as long as he doesn't quit. Sometimes he quits. The trail sometimes drifts over so deeply the whole team founders. Then you're finished.

Keith Kirkvold is in the lead when his team stalls. He pulls himself up the gangline to the front. Then he breaks trail himself, swimming into chest-high drifts to pound out a path so the dogs, with their shorter legs, can gain footing. When Keith is exhausted, his breath coming in short pants, his throat burning in the dry cold, Thomas Tetz, a square-jawed Ironman athlete with a crew cut, takes a turn.

Surely they must be nearing the top of the summit now. The wind increases to maybe fifty miles an hour. The dogs plod on, their heads cocked to meet the force of the gale and the sideways blasting of snow. There is no longer any need for a human trailbreaker. The mountaintop is wind-scoured and crusty hard. A person couldn't find or follow a trail, anyway. There is no choice but to hang on to the sled and give yourself over to your dogs. No one is driving them now. They drive themselves by instincts that are impossible for humans to decipher. Their trail sense and determination is all a person has. Without them, these mushers would be as helpless as babies out of the crib. A false step by a single leader will pull the whole outfit off the edge of a cliff. Nobody would even know for days. If measured by a windchill chart, the temperature is 75 below, perhaps 80 below. Tired, sore, cold, and scared, a musher feels sobbing spasms of gratitude and admiration for these small, hard-muscled animals. You have led them here, and now they must lead you out. You hope to God they don't hear the same voices you do, screaming inside to quit.

Against a particularly fierce gust, Brenda Mackey has the sickening sensation of being lifted off the ground and blown away. Her sled is thrown sideways. She ducks and aims her shoulder into the blast, and the dogs pull her straight again. The rookie caravan now worries less about progress and more about survival.

The rounded top of American Summit is wholly exposed for five miles. Brenda and Amy decide to turn back and seek shelter in a faint hollow just down from the crest. Keith and Thomas say their dogs won't go back. They argue to stay put. Rusty turns back with the women. He looks at his watch. It is 10:00 P.M. As his dogs burrow and make themselves sheltered nests, Rusty empties his sled bag into the snow. He turns the sled on its side to block the wind and crawls into the nylon sled bag, shivering. Brenda is in worse shape. She is approaching hypothermia. Her movements are slow and clumsy, her thinking fogged. Keith attempts to proceed against the wind, but is blown backward. He lies down in place, exhausted. Thomas Tetz, a man who was barely known among other Quest mushers at the start of the race, recognizes the peril. The dogs will instinctively find shelter in the snow, but the mushers are in jeopardy of freezing to death. One by one, he rouses them. Get up and walk and keep the blood pumping, he orders. Brenda rises groggily and moves, her shoulders slumped and her back hunched against the screeching wind. Then Rusty. They stumble like ghosts in the fury of the storm.

At 2:00 A.M., the wind steadies to about forty miles an hour. The group decides to push on. Keith leads. But his dogs quit after only minutes. They just stop, and nothing he says will budge them. Thomas takes the lead and barely gets any farther. They have gone only a quarter mile and are stalled. Rusty thinks that maybe his dogs can lead. He moves up past the other teams, with Kid and a dog named Gator in front. Let's try, guys, he says. The two shoulder into the wind and blowing snow. Then the trail imperceptibly begins to angle down. They have crossed the summit. With gathering speed, the dogs lope ahead. They are moving. And safer ground lies ahead. They gain speed, and Rusty finds himself having to stop his high-spirited team from time to time so the others can catch up. Now, in the wind shadow of the dome, the blizzard slackens. The mushers take a quick count of themselves to make sure someone hasn't been left up there.

It is barely fifteen miles to Eagle. Rusty feels his hands shaking, and not from the cold.

11

In the worship of security we fling ourselves beneath the
wheels of routine—and before we know it our lives are gone.

—Sterling Hayden, wanderer

In an unheated outhouse behind Eagle's one-room school, I unpack
my duffel and dress for the trail.

My outfit is this: two pairs of Capilene long underwear, over which
I wear a pair of two-ply nylon wind pants, a lightweight fleece shirt,
and a puffy synthetic-insulated vest. On top of that, I pull on a heavy
fleece T-top. On the waistband of my pants, I clip a battery pack con-
taining four fresh alkaline D-cells. I thread the power cord under my T-
top so the loose end dangles around my neck. Then I climb into Arctic-
insulated bib overalls, the kind that Prudhoe Bay oilfield workers wear.
I wear two pairs of Capilene mountaineering socks under white bunny
boots, originally designed by the military for Arctic combat. They
encase the foot in inch-thick felt, with twice that much under the sole;
the outside is rubber, with an air bladder for added insulation. My
extralong parka goes on next, along with two neck gaiters, one of them
fitting tightly around my Adam's apple and the other a looser version
that I can pull over my mouth and nose. I have a beaver-fur hat, also

called a trapper hat or a bomber cap, with furry earmuffs that hug my
cheeks and a thick patch of fur to insulate my forehead. The guard hairs
dangle down to shield my eyes. Over the hat, I strap a halogen headlamp and connect it to the power cord. If I slap my right side hard, I can
trigger the plunger switch to the headlamp. I have extra batteries and
halogen bulbs in the pockets of my bibs. I carry an extra set of neck
gaiters to swap with those I'm wearing when they become heavy with
ice from my breath. My parka has an insulated hood and a ruff of
Finnish raccoon that I can snug down in the wind, pulling even more
guard hairs around my face. I wear thin fleece wrist warmers, which
are like fingerless gloves, and over that a midweight pair of fleece work
gloves, with a spare pair in my parka. Heavy musher's overmitts with
eighteen-inch gauntlets are tied to a harness that hangs over my shoulders. I twist their leashes behind me to keep the mitts handy and out of
the way. In another pocket, I carry a Ziploc bag with matches and birch
bark shavings for emergencies, plus a Leatherman and a half dozen tea
bag–sized packets of iron oxide crystals, which heat to 107 degrees
when exposed to air. Those can be placed in the toes of my boots or the
palms of my mitts. I arrange my duffel so that, in the event it gets really cold, I can quickly get to another layer of fleece pants and jacket. In
case I get wet, I carry a spare set of underwear, fleece, socks, gloves,
and a backup pair of felt-insulated mukluks, all double-wrapped in
garbage bags. I also carry a 20-below synthetic sleeping bag and a full-
length Therm-A-Rest pad, along with a quart of dark rum, a thermos
for coffee, painkillers of assorted strengths, a large Ace bandage, and a
shaker of powdered toothpaste. One must be careful with the rum,
however. Chilled to 30 below, it pours like syrup and will freeze your
mouth and esophagus badly enough to cause you harm. In other
words, I'm pretty much outfitted in the getup of a dog musher.

Ready at last.

Wayne Hall's massive, heavy-coated dogs growl ominously as I
approach, wary of strangers. We'll try to make friends later. For now,
I'm anxious to get down the trail.

Race marshal Dave Rich is now fretting about my trip down the
Quest trail. If I screw up and lose control of a dog team at the wrong

moment, I may cause grief for Quest mushers. Wayne is confident we can stay far out of the way. But the least I can do for Rich is hurry myself along and try to keep ahead of the race. So I tell Wayne we should hit the trail immediately and travel through the night. He rolls his eyes in doubt, but we strap the sled bags closed and I load my thermos with thin schoolhouse coffee into the quick-access pocket below the handlebar.

No less than race dogs, a trapline team rises and shakes off the snow with pent-up energy, howling to go. Wayne catapults out of the school yard with seven dogs in harness. I yank the snow hook, and my team of six leaps to follow, staying only inches from his heels. Across a playground, we race into a stand of spruce, the dogs at a full run and the trunks of trees blurring past on each side. My sled skids around a corner and I'm holding on with both hands. Then we are climbing up a steep berm and turning ninety degrees onto one of Eagle's back roads. The dogs claw for traction. My sled jolts over the berm and then spins sideways when the gangline pulls taut. With my knees bent to keep my weight low, I struggle to stay upright as the whip-sawing sled tips onto the outboard runner. I heave back with all my weight. Too much weight. The sled rocks back and over onto its side with a bang and I'm dragging behind, holding on, worrying, again, about that double-sharp snowhook bouncing along somewhere with me. Wayne sees the beam of my headlamp sweeping crazily through the treetops and stops his team. We come skidding to a halt behind him, me facedown.

Wayne spares me unnecessary reminders about the dangerous jumble ice downriver and kindly forgoes comparisons between the ease of travel on city streets and the difficulties that await us on the chaotic Yukon River trail. But he does vaguely suggest the wisdom of postponing our departure until first light. So we mush eight miles back up the road and along a bush trail, the night air biting our faces, to Wayne's log house, where the rum at least has a chance to warm up. The distant clouds have moved in and cover the sky, and the first fine crystals of snow begin to fall gently.

Biederman's cabin awaits us eighty-six miles down the Yukon.

Dawson may be my favorite winter town, but Biederman's sagging old wilderness cabin is the place I really want to be in these dark winter days of February. It is hard to imagine a more remote or storied habitation. The nearest roads are back at Eagle and, in the opposite direction the same distance, at the small settlement of Circle. In anticipation of the Quest, a dozen trappers, homesteaders, and regular Alaska visitors bundle up and make their way overland by dogsled and snowmachine to Biederman's, joining a veterinary crew shuttled in by Super Cub. The ninety-year-old, two-room log cottage is abandoned in winter except for these few days when the woodstove is brought to a cherry glow and the cabin fills with the smell of bubbling game meat and boiling coffee, and the laughter of lonely friends gathered together. The lopsided plank table in the kitchen fills up with elbows, coffee cups, cans of beer, children's toys. Amiable smiles emerge on the hard, weathered faces of those whose lives define the frontier. It's winter rendezvous on the Yukon, better then Christmas, time to catch up with your extended family of fellow bush rats. How was the fishing? Trap many marten? Might get cold, eh? That a new lynx hat? Swap some books? How about we fry a beaver for supper?

I meet Tim McLaughlin, a small man with a huge spade beard, who introduces himself as a musher, trapper, and roustabout. For some reason, I ask if he has a telephone.

"Hell, I don't even have a floor," he laughs. He lives year-round in a tepee heated by a woodstove.

As usual, the history in these parts is so fresh, its fingerprints are still damp. Ed Biederman and his wife, Bella, built this rectangular log house in the summer of 1916. It is now sinking into the permafrost like a boat with a slow leak. Ed was an immigrant from Bohemia; his original name was Adolph Biederman. A veteran of the Spanish-American War in Cuba, he came north and carried the mail between Eagle and Circle City. He put his house at the exact midpoint. The story is told of the summer of 1925, when Ed lost his dog team in a barge accident on the river. That winter, he had to rely on a new team of inexperienced dogs. Lacking trail experience, they pulled him onto thin ice and he broke through to a warm spring below—mushy overflow. It was 42 below and Ed's feet froze before he could pry off his boots and build a fire.

"He knew he was in for it. He had frozen his feet before, but this time he knew it was for good. . . . A doctor amputated the fore parts of his feet, a little at a time. He was running the mail again next winter." So wrote popular newsman Ernie Pyle after meeting Ed in Eagle in 1937.

Pyle continued: "Beiderman wears regular shoes in summer, and has phonograph springs in them to keep the toes from flying up. In winter, he wears three pairs of socks and stuffs the toes full of rabbit fur. And over these he wears moccasins."

Biederman brought his son into the business and they mushed the mail until April 1938, when an upstart bush pilot underbid them for the government contract. That was the beginning of Alaska Airlines. Ed died in 1945. His son Charlie took the old man's hickory sled to Washington, D.C., in 1995 for display in the National Postal Museum. Charlie died later that year, the last man to mush the U.S. mail.

Ernie Pyle, the most popular newspaper reporter of his time and the man who humanized the ordinary-Joe side of soldiering in World War II, said that the strangest stories in all his life, the finest "examples of great strength of character," he found along this stretch of the Yukon River.

During my first trip to Biederman's during last year's Quest, Joe May and I took a stroll outside. It was 30 below under an indigo sky.

"On a night like tonight," he said, "with a three-quarters moon shining off the hills and the wolves out prowling in the trees, you can slide back a hundred years. Can you hear it? Your mind talking to you. This is the Old Dawson Trail. And out there, under a spruce tree, you can hear anything you want—music written on the wind. . . . There are people I know who want out of their lives. But for me, the passing of time is the only sadness."

Joe already knows his dying wish. He'd like to be out here in a cabin in the bush, with a fire and a bottle of Jack Daniel's and B. B. King on the stereo and two old girlfriends to see him off. Then he'll be buried under a small black obelisk, carved with these words: "He cared not for money or indoor plumbing."

"John?"

Yes, I reply.

"You know—the days are different here. They don't run together. Each day is like a page. At the end, you say, that's a good one. Or that wasn't so good."

Later, Joe retired to his sleeping bag. Some of us stayed up and watched the night sky. Then my eye caught sight of a weathered four-by-eight plywood box, half-buried in the snow: a bush sauna.

Mark Richards agreed to build a fire. Richards has since become one of the people in Alaska who most fascinates my imagination. A former Californian, he is an avaricious reader and deeply, meditatively intelligent. From childhood, he never thought of a life for himself except in the woods. Sixteen years ago he and his wife, Lori, homesteaded in a tributary drainage a couple of days' drive by dogsled from here. They now have three children, Amber, Megan, and Keene. Mark supervises Biederman's for the Quest.

Mark brought the small cast-iron stove in the sauna box to a translucent red. We peeled off our itchy trail clothes and climbed in, followed by Quest veterinarian Darren "Woody" Woodson of Farmington, New Mexico. The heat was stunning. We quenched the stove with melted snow from a bucket, and closed our eyes against the resulting blasts of steam. I could feel the grime and smell ooze from my pores. We laughed and told stories, and Mark quizzed us about the latest books, about classical books, about any kind of books until he'd exhausted our knowledge. Against all sauna rules, we drank whiskey and chased it with icy beer. My head was so light, I felt it drifting off my shoulders.

There was a knock. A little boy's voice came from the other side of the flimsy plywood. "You want some more beer?" Richards's seven-year-old son, Keene, had been dispatched by his mother to keep us big boys happy. And also, presumably, to keep us from dehydrating in the melting heat.

Why, sure, let's have more beer.

Woody cracked the wooden door just wide enough for Keene to insert a six-pack. With it came a blast of polar wind and sandpapery spindrift, by way of reminder that we were just seventy-five miles or so below the Arctic Circle.

"Jesus, I'm burning up. Oh, Christ, here, change places with me. I gotta get back from this stove."

Three naked men, all careful not to touch, shuffled places in the lightless box.

"We need more water. Oh, God. And hand me another beer."

Giggles. We rotated position again to rescue one another from the direct heat of the corner stove.

Then we heard another noise. Dogs whining outside. Then barking. "Okay, boys, let's go," a voice said. Then the clatter of a sled breaking out of the frozen ground.

We winced. While we sat there like drunken frat boys at a beer bust, yelping about burning the hair off our legs in the unbearable, luxuriant heat of the sauna, musher Larry Carroll was on the other side of the quarter-inch plywood, quietly putting booties on his dogs. Later, Larry confessed that nothing in his life was so unpleasant as heading out on the trail in the 30-below darkness of that night while every nerve ending in his body screamed for him to stop, rip off his snowsuit, and leap into the fiery sauna with us, a beer in each hand. Graciously, he bore no grudge afterward. He said he would have done the same thing had he not been racing. Besides, the plywood radiated enough heat to keep his hands warm while he hooked up his team.

So that night we cranked up the stove and splashed it with water to bring on more explosions of steam. And we drank more beer and whiskey and laughed and told more stories. What stories? Our best stories. And when we could no longer endure the heat and the sweat and the dizziness, I unlatched the door and we jumped, steaming and half-drunk, maybe wholly drunk, into the northern night, where the other voices speak. They complimented us on our good fortune.

I can hardly wait to get back to Biederman's this year.

Long before dawn, I hear Wayne's heavy boots clomp down the stairs from his loft. I'm out of my sleeping bag in a heartbeat, and repacked before the coffee is done. I've dashed out to pee in the snow and check the temperature: 15 below. But rushing is futile. I have come to the conclusion that dog mushing is the perfect endeavor for putterers.

First the whole yard of twenty-three dogs must be fed, a pan of fish and kibble mixed and delivered to each caterwauling animal. Then the pans are retrieved and each dog given a good morning rubdown and hello. Some of them insist on a longer conversation. Wayne and I finish the tedious business of dressing ourselves for the trail. With so many layers, I'm puffing from just lacing my boots. Our two sleds are broken out of the fresh snow that fell while we slept and the ganglines unrolled. Harnesses are brought from inside, and each of thirteen dogs rodeoed into position. Naturally, one clip or another breaks and a replacement has to be spliced into the rig. We rest with another cup of coffee. Then we load our gear and food into the sled bags and tie them closed. By now, the coffee has worked through my system and I must get half undressed to relieve myself. Then a final check of the lines, clips, and knots. All the time, of course, the dogs shriek and lunge and sometimes snarl at one another and make everything difficult and nerve-racking. During the process, however, I seem to be making myself accepted among the six dogs who will be pulling me. They are not growling anymore as I approach, but my face and hands are starting to smell of fish, kibble, and sticky dog drool. I pay particular attention to Paleface, an eighty-pound brute with the heavy dark coat of a black bear. He will be my leader. Wayne trusts him to keep me from screwing up. Squatting down and looking into Paleface's big, wet brown eyes, set narrowly in a white mask that covers his muzzle and forehead, I speak in the reassuring tones that I've heard from other mushers. I cannot tell if the dog is just being polite and tolerating me or laughing inside. But he damn sure wants to get going, and I have to stop and catch my breath after wrestling him into a harness.

It is still pitch-dark when Scarlet bids us off, along with the couple's six-year-old son, Matthew, who answers to the name Garf. Then we're slip-sliding back down the narrow Eagle road that leads to the river. Paleface positions my team exactly one inch behind Wayne. With every shift of position, Wayne manages to kick the veteran dog in the chin. Which seems to suit Paleface just fine.

"Paleface!" I bark as commandingly as I can.

In the beam of my headlamp, I see the big dog's pointy ears rotate in my direction, like radar dishes. He's listening.

"Ease up, buddy. Okay?"

His pace changes not a iota. He's not listening. But he's traveled thousands of miles in this country. Who am I to argue?

"Good boy, Paleface."

The dog's ears rotate forward.

We pass back through the village of Eagle, where not a single light yet glows. Then we leave the road and skid down a quarter-mile-long gulch and onto the ghostly Yukon. To my left, I can feel the presence of a massive bluff, an Eagle landmark where the Yukon is forced into a sharp bend by three hundred feet of towering bedrock. The ice underfoot is uneven; riding over it is like traveling over a parking lot after a magnitude-8 earthquake.

Paleface throttles back. From his vantage point, only two feet off the surface, the up-and-down, zigzag trail requires more concentration than he can give it while sniffing the soles of Wayne's boots. We drop back fifty yards and all that remains of my trail partner are reflections from his headlamp.

Now the dogs have burned through the adrenaline of our departure, and they settle into a rhythmic lope. Although obviously moving at the same steady speed, each dog has its own cadence. The gangline bobs and quivers. With my headlamp, I study each dog, one by one.

Paired with Paleface is a smaller blond female named Foxy. The two are particular friends, and Foxy intermittently brushes close to the larger leader and nuzzles him. Without breaking stride, he responds by rubbing his head against hers. I can only guess, but they seem animated, like kids after hearing the last school bell of the year—trail friends on the go again, the dog yard behind them and nothing but open space and possibility ahead. Never mind the strange lout back there and his mumbling reassurances.

"Good girl, Foxy. Attaboy, Paleface."

Behind the leaders are my two team dogs, Hawk, a bruiser as big as Paleface, and Sox, with naturally light-colored feet below a dark rust-colored coat. The wheel dogs are Brown Nose, a black dog with, of course, a brown muzzle and mask. Next to him is Sable, another light-colored dog. Brown Nose is a mellow fellow, his partner more nervous. Sable frequently looks back, as if wondering what strange planet I came from. Or perhaps she is hoping to find that I have fallen off, never to intrude on her life again.

"Good girl, Sable." Smother a dog with kindness, I say.

Almost imperceptibly, the sky begins to lighten. The snow has stopped, at least for the moment. There is an inch of fresh powder on the trail—not enough to slow these dogs down. Trapline dogs like these normally do not wear booties. Their feet are scabby hard. Even so, I watch carefully for limps or even the slightest hitch in stride that may indicate the formation of ice balls between the pads of toes. From time to time, I stop the team to let someone chew the lumps of ice out of a foot. We also stop anytime a dog has to shit. Race dogs learn to crap on the run, hop-skidding along with their hind legs splayed and tails lifted, their little butts heaving left and right.

"But these trapline dogs," Wayne explains, "they share a team etiquette. It's a social event for them."

I smack the plunger switch with the heel of my hand and turn off my headlamp. The day has broken oyster gray and overcast. There is no discernible difference in shade or hue no matter where I look: above, underfoot, across the river and beyond. I resist the temptation to call it a gloomy morning. But it does have the somber feel of a workday.

Here, the Yukon is a half mile wide. Its banks are high and steep, and topped by shadowy stands of spruce. Our route wanders from bank to bank as the miles pass, following the lay of favorable ice. Hills rise back from the banks, sometimes miles back, often barren and snow blown. Beyond, on both sides, six-thousand-foot mountains loom, the Ogilvies on the right and the Mertie Range on the left—places unknown outside the Far North, immense landscapes, roadless and uninhabited, big enough to swallow up any of the national parks in the Lower 48. In this slowly passing panorama, I am struck by how amazingly small the musher's world becomes.

Sometimes in the outdoors, like at the bottom of the Grand Canyon or hiking in the high mountains of the Brooks Range, I've found myself dizzy from the enormousness of space. Against the majesty of the surroundings, I've felt shockingly reduced. In other circumstances, however, something quite different happens to one's sense of self and space. Once I sailed across the Pacific in a sloop. In this largest of wildernesses, I was surprised to see that I didn't shrink. Instead, the world around me did. Everything came down to the compact sixty-five-foot deck of the sailboat and the narrow path it cut through the sea. Now, as I travel the Yukon River in winter, the sensation is something of the same. The buckled ice crust, the trees, hills, mountains, and sky stretch before me—but in abstract, distant monochrome. My worldly reality lies inside all the puffy layers now encasing me, cocoonlike. Sounds are muffled. I am shielded from the cold and the harsh touch of the wind, even as ice slowly builds around my face and neck. I am acutely aware of my body working as its own efficient furnace. I can hear my heartbeat. Mine is the tiniest of worlds, the self alone.

I'm even vaguely removed from my dog team. Yes, we are joined by this springy gangline, and I watch their movements intently. I try to remember to give them encouragement from time to time. They obey when I command "Whoa," because stopping is part of the training of a trapline dog. Likewise, they resume their canter when I tell them "Okay, guys, let's go." But their reality is apart from mine. Their feet prance in high-speed rhythm. Their tongues dangle and sway to the beat of fast puffing. Mile after graceful mile they move in an unbroken, purposeful tempo. By contrast, my movements as part of the "team" are cumbersome and irregular: pedaling to push the sled, shifting weight to offset the pull of sidehills, grunting and wheezing, dismounting and pushing whenever we reach a steep climb, trying to balance and ride the brake on the careening downhills. The dogs and I seldom have eye contact; we touch only when stopped. Mostly, my view is limited to the steady dance of paws and the swaying of six hairy rumps, each with a wrinkled bull's-eye staring at me from dead center. Yes, I've heard that old wheeze about how only lead dogs get a change of scenery. Well, ditto for the musher.

Along a more or less flat stretch of river ice I pull my hands from my mitts, break the crust of frozen breath that has formed on the neck gaiter over my face, and I expose my mouth. I unzip my parka and fish into an inside pocket for a pouch of tobacco. Hooking an elbow under the handlebar, I peel a paper from the sheaf, add a pinch of tobacco, and roll a cigarette. The most difficult part of the procedure is licking the paper and getting it to stick in the subzero temperature. It is no good to touch the corner of the paper to the tip of my tongue and draw the gummed edge of the cigarette across, as I would do elsewhere. By the time my tongue reaches the far end of the paper, the moisture already has frozen at the other end, and the whole creation unwraps. By trial and error, I've learned to stick my tongue out as far as I can and immediately bring it into touch with the gummed edge of the entire paper, all at once. Then instantaneously I spin my fingers. Usually this works, as long as the wind is moderate. I have to remember to zip my parka and don my glove liners or I quickly feel an achy cold. Sometimes I have to wait for the circulation of blood to carry away the stiffness in my fingers before trying to light up. After a few drags my exposed face begins to sting, and I find it takes longer to recover than it does to pull down a few drags of nicotine.

I look in the distance and see that Wayne, with his team's one-dog advantage, has moved ahead a half mile. He is little more than a drab dot in the chunky ice ahead, preceeded by a string of smaller brownish dots. They barely seem to move. I summon Paleface to stop, and I unzip and remove my parka, which requires undoing and detaching the rope harness for my mitts. I unzip and shoulder out of the suspenders holding up my bibs, then loosen the belt on my wind pants and fish through in the layers of Capilene for the appropriate and, might I say in this cold, diminished apparatus by which I can relieve myself. Quest mushers, at least the men, accomplish this while under way, standing on the runners. But they have years of practice, of trial and error. By the time I've threaded myself back together, I see that my stall has worked. There are no moving dots visible ahead. I now enjoy the remarkable sensation of being alone on the ice. Just to make sure, I reach into the ready pouch on my sled bag and pour a cup of coffee. Already, ice is forming in the liquid. I gulp it down before it's too late.

"Okay, guys."

I first met Wayne Hall last year at Biederman's cabin. I was assigned a metal-spring bunk in a small log cabin adjacent to the main homestead.

I had just built a fire in the barrel stove and unrolled my sleeping bag when I felt the thumps of a stranger kicking the doorjamb to dislodge the snow from his heavy boots. Then he was standing there, this man with the scarred face and three-fingered hand, his eyes red and wet from the trail, his nondescript trail clothes old and greasy, the random clumps of his beard encrusted with ice.

"Howdy, I'll be bunking here," he said, closing the door behind him.

Everything about my first impression was entirely wrong. I was sure I detected menace behind the soft growl of his voice. The sight of him raised the question of whether I had found myself in some subarctic sequel to *Deliverance.* Wayne introduced himself as a trapper but otherwise said little. We both walked back to the main cabin and sat at the edge of the growing crowd inside. Wayne mostly listened. Then he motioned me aside.

"I've got a favor to ask," he began.

My response, I think, was tentative.

It was about the sleeping arrangements, he began.

Hmmm?

Wayne explained that his lead dog was in a pinch of trouble, off her feed, not doing well. Just something wrong.

Gee, that's awful. What can I do?

"Well, would you mind if she, sort of, came inside and, ah, bunked with me? In the warm and all, it might help."

Sure, Wayne. I recall feeling both mystified and relieved. Whatever his troubles, this did not sound alarming.

That night, drunk and exhausted, I stumbled into the cabin, fed the fire, and looked over to see that I'd been wrong about the fierce facade of this man. There he was, curled up in his old sleeping bag with his main dog at his feet. This is how they lived out on the trapline trail, and he couldn't bear to leave her out in the lonesome cold this night. Just another Alaska softy.

As a thirteen-year-old New Jersey boy, Wayne Hall went flying in a small airplane with his grandparents. Grandpa lost control and they crashed, and the plane exploded in a ball of fire. Everyone died except the young teenager. He would live with the scars forever. Three years later, he drifted from home. At twenty-seven, he traveled the professional rodeo circuit as a bull rider. He took up flying himself.

"People ask why would I fly after that crash. Well, my grandfather made a mistake. It wasn't the plane's fault. I became a pilot to further my rodeo career. I could get more places and get more sleep if I flew myself."

At one point, Wayne rose to fourth place in the professional bull-riding standings. But he couldn't hold it. In his best year, he finished twenty-fourth in the nation. When his rodeo career was over, he flew crop dusters in Texas and South Dakota. Then his wife left him.

"That put me on my own," he recalled. "So I said I'd go see Alaska. From the moment I touched the ground, I knew I'd never leave."

That was 1987. For six years he flew as bush pilot on the Bering Sea coast, living in Eskimo villages, carrying freight and passengers. Then he struck out for independence, for "a higher quality of life." He came to Eagle and built his log home on a bluff eight miles from town, overlooking the Yukon River. Here, at last, he could live according to the immutable rhythms of nature. Wayne Hall had returned to his ancestral home: the wild. His new wife, Scarlet, shared his dreams.

"There are only two considerations up here: winter and preparing for winter," Hall explained. "But every month has a season to itself. In June, the garden goes in. In July, you fish for kings [salmon] on the Yukon. In August, it's chums [another salmon] by fishnet or fish wheel. September is moose season and it's real important to be successful. In October, you prepare for the trapping season. From November to February, you trap. In March, you get next winter's four cords of wood. In April and May you do everything else to fix up your cabin and equipment."

I ask, and Wayne has no idea in the world what day of the week it is.

12

The Indian name, Yukon-duye, means "the river of you never know what next." . . . Its men are, as a rule, cast in large mold, and no man can mix or come in contact with them without being advantaged.

—Joaquin Miller, July 20, 1898

B ring your cup," says Wayne Hall. On foot, he leads up the river-bank.There are signs of human habitation, the first we've seen.

It's now midday and we've pulled over to the eastern edge of the river for a break. Wayne has snacked the dogs with chunks of frozen fish, which they gnaw momentarily and then gulp. Then they resume singing to strange, unseen dogs that answer from up there behind the trees. This is Dick Cook's camp. Back in 1972, there were thirteen year-round homesteads along the Yukon and its main tributaries below Eagle. Now there are three. Dick has been here the longest, thirty-three years in the bush. As in other places in the North American West, it is of no consequence where one came from or who one's parents hap-pened to be. But it does weigh heavy how long you've been here. Dick's been rooted long enough to be described, both respectfully and euphemistically, as "authentic."

I unscrew the cup from my now-frozen thermos and follow Wayne up the bank.

As I understand it, Dick was educated as a scientist and worked as a real-estate appraiser in Ohio before coming north. I relate that as if it mattered for anything except curiosity, which it doesn't. A quarter century ago, the writer John McPhee passed by and Dick explained that his purpose in homesteading was to transform himself "from a professional into a bum."

I can now report: Mission accomplished.

Dick lives as rough a life as anyone I've ever met in North America. Wayne and I bring our own cups when we call, because Dick has only one in his dark, dugout log shack with its dirt floor, sooty walls, and three decades of accumulated debris. Dick pours us coffee from a tin pot that once was enameled but is now only crusty black from the woodstove. I sit on a log. Dick has a folding chair. Wayne takes the edge of the cluttered bunk. We've come at the saddest of times. The deeply lined, bony, and grimy face of this old sourdough—Dick must be seventy now—is the picture of grief. Last summer, he'd made a new friend out here in his lonely landscape. A young raven began to hang around the cabin. Dick began to talk to it. The bird talked back. You cannot imagine how joyous it was to have conversation again after so many years of isolation. The raven greeted him at sunrise. They talked over the weather. Ravens and homesteaders, it turns out, have plenty in common. Everyone else puts up a defense against the long winters. Foxes and ptarmigan change colors to blend in with the snow, geese fly south, bears and squirrels hibernate. But the raven and the sourdough, they just tough it out. It never gets too cold for them.

Dick pours us more gritty coffee.

During the days, after their talks, the raven did its work and Dick his. One of the things the bird did was scavenge through Dick's small dog yard, grubbing for bits of food. Just yesterday, the bird grew too daring and wandered near one of the new pups. The dog feigned indifference, luring the bird closer. Then with a flash of teeth, the pup pounced and snapped the raven's neck. Dick is heartsick.

"That bird, he meant a lot. You know what I mean?" he says, his voice forlorn.

On his porch, Dick lifts the edge of a dirty tarp. The frozen carcass of the raven lies in its folds. The old man looked as if he might weep, but I think there are no more tears in him.

Dick wonders if any of the Quest mushers will stop by this year and say hello. Sometimes they do and sometimes not. He asks if any women are running the race. I tell him about the four rookies. He mentions that a lot of the women mushers are big girls, kind of fat really, not his type at all. His watery eyes seem to drift into thought.

Oh, yes, he says to Wayne, his sled is broken and he could use a couple of bolts so he can get back out and check his trapline. Wayne says he'll help. When we get to Biederman's there will be a ham radio, and Wayne will call back to Eagle and fetch the proper bolts. A pilot will be flying down in a couple of days to shuttle in one of Wayne's friends, a man who will mush my dog team home while I continue ahead with the Quest. Maybe that pilot can fly over and drop the bolts for Dick. Wayne goes over the plan a couple of times to make sure the old man understands that a plane might be buzzing him. Otherwise, Dick has been known to grab his rifle and step outside to enforce his claim of vertical property rights on airborne intruders who fly too close.

Suddenly, Dick remembers that he is a host and offers to fix lunch. Popcorn. Cooked in a hand-scoop of rendered animal fat. As I look around, I see nothing by way of food in the cabin except the tin of popcorn and a single blackened pot. Wayne declines. We've got many miles to go, he explains.

Dick sees us to the top of the riverbank, nods good-bye, then turns and walks back to his solitude. He may see no one else for three months.

"I thought you ought to have a chance to meet someone who's authentic," says Wayne. "He's authentic. But you understand why we didn't want to stay for lunch?"

As a matter of fact, there will be no lunch at all. We travel, as the cowboys say, on hard stomachs. The ice becomes rougher now and the gunmetal clouds descend low around us. It is lightly snowing again. At one particularly awful section of jumble ice, the trail detours up the riverbank and through several miles of foothills. I jump off the runners and help push on the toughest climbs. The path is so steep in places that I find myself standing on slippery vertical slopes, shoving on the handlebar like it was a barbell above my head. Each time, there is an awful moment of truth where, exhausted and panting, I must leap forward and catch up so the sled doesn't plummet downhill with me dragging dangerously behind. The twisting curves of the descents reawaken my lingering fear of crashing into a tree. Wayne, who otherwise is a patient teacher, has only one instruction in this regard: "Don't hit a tree square-on."

This kind of mushing is a bit like having the flu. Your body heats up from effort, then breaks into sweat, followed by the shivering chills. Muscles throb and ache, and time passes in strange, hallucinatory intervals where minutes cannot be distinguished from hours. Only with the abrupt and seemingly random returns to consciousness do you realize that your mind has been drifting and your sled is about to plunge down another ravine. I suspect that long-distance dog drivers spend many of their hours in the accordion rhythms of this kind of trance. One minute you are acutely aware that you are passing through a silent and mysterious grove of trees where other people almost never venture, lightly falling snow softening all the edges of the scene. Then alarm bells. You're flying downhill and torquing the sled to miss the trees at the bottom turn. Then . . . then, well, long empty spaces in the mind. A message from your stomach brings you back. You haven't eaten for hours. Where the hell is Wayne? Don't trappers eat? What is he carrying in that damn sled bag, if not food? That thought passes, but another takes shape in the fog-spell of your thinking. You are having trouble breathing through all the ice that has built up on the gaiter covering your nose and mouth. You carefully calculate when, in between the millrace of hills, to remove a glove and scrounge around in your pockets for a fresh gaiter. When you expose your face you are reminded of how stinging cold it is.

Finally, the trail emerges from the woods and back onto the Yukon, sort of. The jumble ice is still horrible, and rather than tackle the big obstacles head-on, the trail breakers have chosen to chop a torturous path along the edge of the river—a slanting, lumpy sidehill course that requires a musher to kick and scramble to keep the sled from sliding down into the crevasses or smashing into the glass-sharp edges of the ice blocks. The jarring, heaving, crashing traverse seems to go on forever.

"Good boy, Paleface. . . . Quit loafing, Sox."

I am falling way behind now. Wayne decides to give me more horse-power, replacing the smaller Sox with a huge, friendly brute from his team. The new dog, Dozer, with a long butterscotch coat and an endlessly happy countenance, pulls just like his name, and we're not lagging anymore. As Wayne kicks and skids along the trail, his boot again clips the chin of tailgating Paleface.

At 5:30 P.M., eleven hours after we started down the trail, Wayne barks, "Haw! Haw!" His team turns sharply and plunges into the deep snow on the left-hand side of the river. We clamber up the bank and drive a quarter mile, to a clearing. It's now dark again but in the beam of my headlamp I can see the welcome shadow of an empty cabin. This is the way stop called Trout Creek, forty-eight miles downriver from Eagle. In the days that follow, many Quest mushers will stop and rest here. The cabin is privately owned and used as a summer retreat. In winter, it is left unlocked for the occasional traveler. As the first to arrive, Wayne starts the fire.

Into the lining of his parka, Wayne has sewn half of a fly-fishing vest. In its many pockets, he stores matches and fire-starter, all carefully wrapped and sealed to stay dry. He carries three types of tinder, his favorite being small shavings of dried birch bark. Wayne carries a back-up fire kit in his pants pocket, just in case. Some years back, he explains, he was cold on the trapline trail. It was 40 below and he stopped and bent down to build a fire. His tinder was damp and the fire fizzled. When he tried again, he was horrified to realize that his hands would not function. They were like two frozen clubs dangling from the sleeves of his parka. He could no more strike a match with them than he could pick a seed from his teeth with a boulder. Only because a companion happened along to rescue him did Wayne survive. His frostbitten fingers later blistered and turned black. He is now fanatical about being ready to build a fire under any conditions.

My job is to load pans with snow, which we slowly melt over the barrel stove. A full kettle of dry Alaskan snow yields only a tiny inch of water each time, so it is a tedious process. My gloves become soaked and my hands grow numb and throb. Eventually, after we have accumulated three gallons or so of steaming water, Wayne adds a bag of dried kibble mixed with chopped, frozen meat. Under the soft yellow light of an oil lamp, the stew steeps for twenty minutes and we ladle out thirteen helpings, which we deliver one by one to the grateful beasts waiting patiently outside.

At 7:30 P.M. I locate my thermometer and see that we've warmed the cabin to a cozy 22 degrees. I peel off most of my trail clothes and relax on a squeaky folding chair. At this temperature, I find the rum to be wonderfully drinkable. Wayne digs into a cooler pack to see what Scarlet has sent along for our dinner. He offers me a snack first, the trapper favorite: flattened and hard-frozen peanut-butter-and-jelly sandwiches on white bread, crunchy and delicious. Wayne lights a small white-gas stove and produces a freeze-dried packet of chicken and rice. Forget being authentic: I gulp down my half. I only regret that I left my bottle of Tabasco in my shoulder bag, where it froze and shattered the glass and made a mess of everything. Rookie mistake.

We scrub our plates and take one more inspection of the dog yard. The snow is falling heavier, and the animals are curled up and disappearing under blankets of white. We retreat to the cabin, roll our bags onto the plank floor, and blow out the oil lamp. I put on a pair of fresh and wonderfully dry socks. I have no memory of my head hitting the fleece jacket that I use as a pillow.

The dogs' caterwauling yanks me out of a dreamless coma. The glowing hands of my watch say 4:10 A.M. Otherwise the cabin is as dark as a mine shaft. I hear Wayne tromping to the window as the alarm cries grow more urgent.

"Musher coming," he says, after a second.

My right arm and shoulder are immobilized from the unyielding floor, and I squirm out of my bag as if I were a combat casualty or a character from a Monty Python skit. Through the window I see the approaching beam of a headlamp cutting through the black night like a comet. Wayne quickly feeds fresh wood into the jaws of the stove and strikes a match to the wick of the oil lamp.

The oil lamp is one of those dying cultural remnants that remains superior to all inventions superseding it. Compared to the unnatural hot white of incandescence or the unbearable glare of the Coleman lantern, the moody light of oil adds texture to whatever you're reading, and throws a halo of softness around your surroundings. Of course, it was a dropped oil lamp that started the fire that burned down half of Dawson City one night ninety-nine years ago when the temperature was 45 below. So you have to be careful.

The strange dog team follows our trail into the clearing in front of the cabin and stops. Our teams and the new dogs eye each other across the snow, and their barking dies down. Then something in the shape of a mighty bright red parka lumbers forth—but not without stopping to scratch, rub, pet, and approvingly jostle with his eleven dogs, one by one. They are small, nervous animals with what seems, compared to Wayne's bushy string, mere peach fuzz for coats: a race team.

Boots clatter and stomp on the wood porch and the door squeaks open. A broad-shouldered being that appears to be made of ice presents itself, and begins to melt. Bruce Lee eventually materializes from the dripping glaze, his nose snuffling but his eyes bright and dancing in the buttery warm glow of the cabin. He removes only his gloves, offers a friendly but brief hello, and quickly gets down to business. He slides a chair close to the stove, unzips a pocket, and produces a notebook. Intently, he reads over his game plan. He holds the notebook to one side so as not to smear the pages with snot draining from his thawing nose and mustache.

This far down the trail, a musher cannot rely solely on his frazzled brain to tell him what to do. So he must triangulate—compare what he thinks is happening out on the trail with what he thinks he should do and what the notebook tells him he planned to do. Lee mulls over his next play.

What is happening outside Trout Creek Cabin is this: two miles ago, Lee passed a resting Andre Nadeau and took over the lead.

For one wonderful and entirely futile moment there are only four people in the world who know what is happening at the front end of the Yukon Quest: the two dueling mushers, Wayne, and me.

"He may be letting me pass so I'll have to break trail awhile," Lee says pensively.

The handsome blond musher says he found the trail from Eagle rough, "poorly marked," and slow. Three inches of snow have accumulated since nightfall, and Lee struggled most of the way to see because of the blinding reflections of his headlamp against the falling snowflakes. On the upside, Lee left Eagle before any of the other powerhouse mushers, like Rick Mackey or John Schandelmeier, even arrived.

Lee made the trip here from Eagle in six hours. It took us eleven. But he is uncomfortable being in the lead. He'd rather hang behind for a while longer if possible. Let Andre wear himself out pushing through the fresh snow. Besides, Lee likes being able to chart his rival's every move—noting, from studying the trail, how often Andre is stopping to rest or snack his dogs, calculating the relative speed of the two teams. Looking closely, Lee can even tell what Andre is feeding his team for snacks. But now the French-Canadian voyageur seems to want a turn playing the cat to Lee's mouse.

Well, at least the race has started.

Lee calculates the miles to Biederman's cabin, thirty-eight, and to the next cabin after that, another thirty-some. What is the smart move now?

I am making coffee from the water we melted last night and kept hot on the stove. If Wayne and I decided to stay at Trout Creek for the duration of the Quest and were willing to help every musher, Lee would be free to share in the precious water. But since we are moving on, it would be an unfair advantage under the race rules. He avails himself only of the warmth of the fire and must trudge outside again, unpack his sled, assemble his alcohol cooker, and begin the tedious gathering and melting of snow for his dog food. Later, while his five-gallon pot of food steeps, he trudges through the fresh snow a quarter mile back to the river to see if Andre has moved ahead again. He has.

"He has the strangest schedule," Lee remarks as he returns to the cabin and drops a puny tinfoil packet on the stove. When it sizzles, he peels open his dinner—a single small slice of pizza.

"I think this will be my last Quest," Lee says, out of nowhere. "Not that I'm not having fun. But there are other things in life."

I look at my notebook and calculate that Lee has raced some nine thousand cumulative miles in his long-distance mushing career. He says good night and reflexively folds himself into a ball, falling immediately into a heavy-breathing sleep. In one hour exactly, Lee jumps to life again. I have spent most of my adult life in motion, traveling, and I've never seen anything like a dog musher when it comes to making a departure. I have shared roadhouse rooms with mushers who could rise, dress, brush their teeth, pack, and have the pickup truck warming before I could put in a single contact lens. They weren't even in a hurry. Lee blinks his eyes once or twice, automatically inventories his things—his notebook, his hat and headlamp, the little ball of tinfoil garbage left from his pizza—zips up his parka, says good-bye, closes the door, hurries down the gangline of his stirring team whispering encouragement, and pulls the snowhook. I see a brief flicker of his headlamp on falling snow; then he disappears.

I notice that Wayne has also packed himself as well as our traveling kitchen, swept the cabin floor, and is now putting on his parka. I'm still staggering around in my socks and long johns, stupidly wondering where I last put my coffee cup, and contemplating the chore of breaking a trail through snowdrifts to the outhouse, which ominously overhangs an eroding gulch and has to be entered by slithering through a cut-out window in the back. My thermometer says 20 below.

Forty minutes behind Lee, in the first emerging hint of a blue-gray morning, a freshly fed and watered Paleface leans into the harness and we follow Wayne, back down the trail to the Yukon. We will use headlamps to supplement the dawn light for a couple of hours still. I aim the beam of mine and watch a tiny rooster tail churned up by Wayne's sled in the newly fallen snow.

Naturally we have skipped breakfast. We are dog mushers. I now gather that authentic mushers are supposed to regard eating as an activity associated primarily with dogs. So acid coffee sloshes freely in my stomach and I find myself daydreaming about little slices of pizza, about Steve Watson's Braeburn Roadhouse and those hot, dinner plate–sized cinnamon buns that drip with frosting, and, finally, I fixate on those squashed and frozen peanut-butter-and-jelly sandwiches that Wayne is hoarding up there in his sled bag. These distractions are soon overcome by the difficulties of the trail, which once again follows a slanting, twisting, undulating sidehill route along the riverbank and through the insistent jumble of snow-capped translucent cakes of ice. I slip, fall, bang my leg, slip again, carom one way and then fishtail the other, huff and puff, run and push, jump aboard and brake, sweat and shiver—a thoroughly absorbing and satisfying endeavor. I can understand why people get hooked and end up with fifty dogs in their front yard, never to step on a jet airplane again.

Under these circumstances, time and distance release their grip on me. So I can only say that it is a while later when we turned off the trail, after the steely morning light fills in behind the overcast and I can scan the bends and bluffs of the Yukon for landmarks I might recognize from last summer. Wayne barks, "Haw! Haw!" and the teams, in tandem, bound again into the glades of spruce. With the physics of the dog sled now more familiar to me, the winding trail past blurry tree trunks becomes exhilarating. Too soon we arrive at another clearing, where the baying of strange dogs welcomes us to stop.

The cabin here is six-sided, built in traditional log fashion. That is, logs rise as high as a man can lift them, then the inside floor is dug away to provide headroom and space for a loft. This is the property of Tim and Tova Henry, a Mormon couple and the second of three homesteaders in the many hundred square miles of this region. In contrast to Dick Cook's dark and squalid habitat, the Henrys maintain a cheery, bright, and spotless home with rugs on the floor, bookshelves on one wall, and a battery-powered CD player for special occasions. Four new puppies squirm and play inside.

And what's that I smell?

Tova offers a square of her fresh-baked berry-and-nut breakfast cake, which is as sweet and warm and wonderful as anything I can remember. I notice that Wayne accepts seconds, no doubt just being courteous.

With his long blond hair and goatee, Tim looks like a time traveler from the 1960s Merry Pranksters, dressed in a pajama-print shirt, with red-and-white-striped socks. He built a raft in 1980, floated down the Yukon, and has lived at one bush cabin or another in the region ever since. Four years ago, tired of living alone, he drove his dogs to Eagle, then took a bush plane to Fairbanks and a commercial flight to Salt Lake City; there he announced he was looking for a bride. A reception was held in his favor. Tova happened by, curious to see what a wilderness bush man looked like. Three days later, Tim proposed marriage and Tova gave up her seventeen-year career as a schoolteacher. A pretty woman but less flamboyant than her husband, she is now pregnant with their first child, and the couple's friends in Eagle are trying in vain to get her to come into town to have the baby.

As sometimes happens when cultures collide, I find myself on a different wavelength from my hosts, as charming as they are. Tim is a news addict. He follows NPR faithfully on the battery radio and is excited at the opportunity to kick around the state of America's political affairs with a writer from Outside. I'm a fresh ear for his rants and opinions, and he can hardly contain his enthusiasm. Meanwhile, I'm enjoying the illusion of having escaped this very thing and full of wonder about wilderness life, a shopworn topic of conversation for Tim. We talk, but less from the heart than from politeness. I'm afraid I'm a dud as a visitor here; with profuse thanks for the cake and a stove to warm ourselves, we leave.

Downriver, the Yukon gives us a break. The jumble ice yields and our trail becomes flat and marble-smooth under the fresh snow. My dog Hawk is picking up ice balls in his splayed feet, so we stop and Wayne puts bright orange booties on the dog's hind feet. He seems to run more comfortably now, and he looks rather dashing too. We wind around islands and undertake long, mesmerizing straightaways.

Now all the work is shouldered by the dogs. I ride along in a magic spell, my world becoming this world. Sometimes we see trampled spots in the snow where Bruce Lee or Andre Nadeau stopped for a quick snack. But we sight neither. With a loose, one-handed grip on the handlebar, I relax and lift my eyes to the generous scene, now more familiar but hardly less breathtaking. Around me I see crystal snow, windblown naked rock, and thousands of square miles of spindly, cake-frosted spruce forest; a single tree may require fifty years to reach three inches in diameter and still have, thankfully, virtually no timber value. This is a place in the middle of no place, and I feel both disconcerted and comforted by knowing that no roads or cities or power lines intrude on the raw country—not here, not over the next ridge or the next. Much of this country is now park land, Yukon-Charley Rivers National Preserve, one of America's least-visited holdings in the national park system. According to a government study, some of the river bluffs here expose shales, cherts, and limestones that chart an unbroken 760-million-year geologic chronicle of the earth. This rock history is "incredible and perhaps unparalleled" anywhere on the planet, scientists report.

Our privacy is disrupted by a noise. At first it is a buzz that could be just a ringing in the ears. No, this is a real buzz. I look back and a low-flying airplane is headed up the river. A blue, orange, and yellow Super Cub. Gary Nance. He passes so low that his draft sandpapers us with blowing snow, and I can see his maniacal leer in the window. He circles tight and throttles to a landing fifty feet away. I stop the dogs and walk over, and we smoke a cigarette: a perfectly ordinary convergence of travelers from different centuries. He is bound for Biederman's too. He warns Wayne and me to hurry and not be late for dinner, because it's going to be a doozy. He winks and points a thumb to a big cardboard box stuffed in the back of the little plane.

"You'll see," he says.

Well, don't let them eat it all if we're late.

Then Gary roars away, and I'm reminded how wonderfully quiet it is to travel by dogs in the subarctic winter, where the wind and the sled make the only sounds, and these are muffled by powder snow.

Even with Dozer in my team, I'm beginning to fall way behind again, a half mile, then a full mile. At every bend of the river, I lose sight of Wayne for a half hour. Paleface has gone from a trot to an amble. It's apparent that the whole team is beat. I'm trying to help by skateboard kicking. I offer coaxing words of encouragement but fail to lift anyone's spirits. So I try singing. I give them a couple of verses of "Oh My Darlin' " and some old Marine Corps endurance chants.

I don't know but I've been told/Eskimo pussy is mighty cold.

Six pairs of ears rotate in my direction. Their pace increases. I'm thinking they like it. So I sing even louder. And Paleface lopes a little faster still. Well, maybe they don't like it. Maybe they're just trying to hurry away from me. I laugh and stop the team, and walk down the line, giving each dog a half nelson hug and a scratch by way of thanks. I now think I understand the profoundly deep feelings mushers develop for these animals that work so hard for them.

You want me to sing? I ask.

Paleface cocks his head, now frosted white with dangling icicles on his chin.

One reason mushers advance for their absorption is that every time you stand on the runners and go catapulting down the trail, you know for certain the experience will be different than all other times you have done it, no matter how many times that may be. But there is another reason: the indescribable, primordial kinship between humans and dogs. Dogs joined with us first. They nosed around our ancestral camp-fires and finally, one day, came to lie at our sides and gnaw the bones left from our dinners. They followed our wanderings and began to join in those long-ago hunts. They accepted the harness. In all the animal kingdom, they were our original friends.

Okay, Paleface. We resume our march. It seems I've waited too long to finish my coffee. From the pouch in the sled bag, I retrieve my steel thermos, but the contents are frozen solid. So I roll a cigarette. And I make a mistake.

When I last checked, it had warmed to 15 below. Perhaps I hadn't registered that the wind was picking up briskly. Now I see it blows the tobacco right out of the paper. So I twist my back into the bluster and try again. I continue to be amazed at how critically important one's gear becomes in these conditions: when you break the seal of your own micro-environment by taking off a glove to pull down a neck gaiter, you are always a little startled by the hostile world around you. This time, I fumble and cannot get the gummed edge of the paper to stick. I try a third time and finally get a wrinkled little cigarette that looks more like a teenager's first joint. I'm not paying attention to the chill I feel in my hands or face. But after just a puff, the cigarette falls out of my fingers and I realize I can no longer move them.

I fumble as fast as I can to get these clubs of hands inside my over-mitts. I think to myself that I wish I could unzip my pocket and get a couple of those packets of iron oxide, but I know I can't. I cannot even pull the neck gaiter over my exposed face. I wrinkle my face, and I real-ize that it, too, is entirely numb. I turn away from the wind and wind-mill one hand while hooking the other forearm over the handlebar to hold on. It seems like an uncommonly long interval until I can summon the *thump-thump* throb of feeling in my fingers. As soon as I can, I can tug my neck gaiter over my mouth and cinch down the ruff of my parka. Soon my fingers and cheeks sting and then burn furiously.

Even after as many stories as I've heard, I'm shocked at how fast you can go from euphoria to serious trouble in this country without even asking for it. A single lapse can bring you down. Had it been 40 below or had I found myself wet from overflow, the cigarette might have cost me much more than a week's worth of blisters on my fingertips and cheeks.

I recognize this landscape. After a sweeping bend to the right, the Yukon straightens out. That's the Kandik River coming from the north. Across is a bluff, and in the trees just before the bluff is Biederman's cabin. The wind is too stiff or I could have also seen a curl of wood smoke through the trees.

My friends are waiting outside and I push the sled up the steep fifty-foot grade of the bank, and their waves and smiles fill me with happi-ness.

Andre Nadeau is here too, and he watches our arrival with surprise. In broken English, he asks how far behind are Rick Mackey and John Schandelmeier. I'm busy trying to unharness and stake out my dogs with my burning fingers, so I miss the point of his question. I tell him I have no idea where anyone is. He frowns. Only later will I realize the source of his worry. He has mistaken us for competitors. He knows hardly anyone in the race, but he's seen my face along the way. Surely I'm a racer, and now I'm breathing down his neck, only a few hours behind. He has surprised everyone by the performance of his large Siberians, so he has to be prepared to be shocked by these strange, hairy, oversize trapline dogs who run barefooted except for those silly orange things on Hawk's two hind paws. Jesus, he must have said to himself, that one guy with the pot belly has only six dogs and, look, he's catching me. If I'd paid attention, I might have heard a squeak as Andre's sphincter tightened.

13

*A lady wot leaves a fine home an' fine friends and luxuries
to take up with hardships what's hard enough for strong
men to bear [ought] to be locked up in an insane asylum.*

—A Colorado miner to Mary Hitchcock, Klondike, 1899

I have a problem. A problem . . . problem." The words ping through
Aliy Zirkle's mind. It is midafternoon as she drops down the long,
barren flank of American Summit and slogs into Eagle. A checkpoint
volunteer walks over with a clipboard. Teenagers mill around the
schoolhouse. The smell of coffee and chili beans wafts from inside. Aliy
is crusted with snow and ice, her face red and miserable. For the twenty-five other mushers who made it this far, the arrival in Eagle is a
moment of relief. For Aliy alone it is agony.

She speaks the words softly. "I have a problem."

The checker quickly motions her ahead, to a far-off corner of the
snow-covered play yard, where she parks her team. A race judge is
summoned, as are the veterinarians. Everyone is trying to appear casual and draw no attention to the scene, although if you look closely you
can see a hitch in their strides.

Aliy has spoken dreaded code words. "I have a problem" means
only one thing: inside her sled bag is the body of a dead dog.

She could not revive Prince. Back on the trail, as she puffed desperately into the dog's nostrils, she thought for a few moments that she had brought him back.

"Then he gave a death shake. But I still didn't think he was dead," she says, her eyes seemingly focused somewhere far away as she talks. "But he was. And all the other dogs were looking back at me. . . ."

The term is denial. We deploy the word mockingly—until it happens to us; until our lives are shaken by events. What we cannot accept we reject, and it keeps us, momentarily, from falling apart.

"I really wasn't convinced he was dead. But I loaded him into the sled bag. In the next two miles, I must have stopped ten times. I'd take him out. I'd shake him. I couldn't believe this." She pauses and sighs. "But then I could feel he was starting to stiffen up. In your heart, I dunno, you don't think this is ever going to happen."

With the body of the dog in her sled, she faced the stormy summit, a six-hour trek under the best of conditions.

"I put him in the bottom of the sled bag. I was already low on dog food 'cause I'd fucked around on the trail. I had to go on. These other dogs depended on me. I ran into Amy, who had turned around and was retreating off the summit. But I was obsessed. I had to get to Eagle. It was nightmarishly windy. But I had no choice. I drove on. You could sulk and feel sorry for yourself and get overcome with emotion. But then you look and you've got ten dogs down the line, and they're half-frostbitten and they have to eat and get some sleep."

Denial helps because it shuts down the reflective recesses of the brain. One can proceed automatically, shielded, as it were, from the overload of despondency that breaks not just the heart but the spirit too. Aliy climbed American Summit like a robot. She put fleece belly warmers on all her dogs because it was so goddamn cold. On three of the males, she also sheathed their penises in fleece jocks as a guard against frostbite. She hardly felt the cold herself. Only when she began to see the outlying cabins of Eagle did she begin to prepare her mind.

"At the meetings before a race, they tell you how you're supposed to behave, what you're supposed to say. You listen, but you never think you'll have to say those words."

Some years, the Quest concludes without the loss of a dog. In other years, two or even three have died. Aliy relinquishes Prince's body to the veterinarians, who will package it in a cardboard box and fly it out on the next bush plane to the University of Fairbanks for necropsy. Scientists at the university and a team of blood researchers working for the Quest are attempting to find the cause of these sudden deaths that continue to beset mushing.

Sled dog myopathy is one syndrome that has been identified by veterinarian John Blake of the Institute of Arctic Biology at the University of Fairbanks. He has been studying sudden dog deaths for eight years. Myopathy is a breakdown of muscles. It has been recorded in horses for a century and is also known to afflict human athletes. Sometimes dogs show warning signs, like passing extra-dark urine or collapsing suddenly on the trail and then appearing to recover, only to die soon thereafter. Sometimes there is no warning at all—and the phenomenon is even more mysterious because it can strike dogs who are in prime condition.

Aliy wonders if she should blame herself. She tangles with her own emotions. For three hours, she sits outside in the snow with her remaining dogs, who are curled up asleep. No one approaches her, although from a distance some people do stand and look, until it is too painful and they turn away. Tall, strong, hard-bitten, tough-as-nails Aliy Zirkle cries. Big chest-heaving, shoulder-rolling, sobbing cries that drain her. She is left empty. Nothing to feel except rising exhaustion. She stands and clomps heavy-footed into the schoolhouse and walks silently past the table where high school students sell candy and potato chips for a class fund-raiser, past the chili buffet, past a dozen pairs of eyes that follow her in the sudden quiet of the school. At the very end of the room is a door into a windowless storage area, set aside for mushers. She collapses on the floor.

She is awakened by Dave Rich, the race marshal. He has moved ahead in the race, and calls her by satellite telephone.

She recalls the conversation. "He told me, Look Aliy, this is really fucking serious. I said, What? You don't think I give a shit? This is my own dog! And you don't think I give a shit?"

She pauses, then adds, "I guess he rubbed me the wrong way."

Rich realizes the conversation will go nowhere now. He tells her to sleep, but to contact him if she decides to continue.

Race officials, like mushers, grieve the death of a trail dog. They are mushers themselves, after all, and understand the bonds that grow over thousands of miles and months of travel. They also know that some racers push too hard and give critics ammunition to use against the sport. Dave Rich in particular feels entrusted with the reputation of the Quest and long-distance mushing. Those competitors who know him are aware that if the worst happens, he is not inclined to adhere strictly to the legalism that one is innocent until proven otherwise. As mushers see it, Rich, a former college football player with a decidedly cold "game face," is the inquisitor who represents the dog.

Mushing has, in various degrees, become a controversy.

As it rose in public awareness in the 1980s, it became a target for some in the animal-rights movement. They called it cruel to run dogs this hard and long for sport. They pressured national sponsors to withdraw support and peppered their newsletters with vitriol. More important, they defined a vast divide between people who love dogs one way and those who love them another.

To their credit, animal-rights advocates succeeded in raising the standards of mushing. There is more attention than ever to the care of dogs. There is less tolerance for those people in the sport who still have medieval attitudes about animals. And in public, such as during a race like the Quest with the press around, there is no tolerance whatsoever anymore. Last year, a member of the Quest board of directors was accused of cruelty to dogs—and the angriest outcry of all came from mushers themselves and other race supporters. Dog mushers and, even more so, their dogs owe a debt to mushing's critics.

But the argument over sled dogs, like many glib debates in today's society, asks people to take sides, make their choices, and hold on to them—and that's that. And since most of us are plenty busy, we choose sides by the word of those we trust—say, the Humane Society of the United States. We're comfortable with our friends, period. Which leads to the fact that animal-rights supporters draw little satisfaction from having made things better. Mushing must still be bad, they think, because someone told them it was. Therefore, they say, competitive dog mushing should be abolished entirely. And a good many would go further and say that dogs should never be put in harness at all, even for recreational trips. Mushers are the enemies of dogs.

On the other side, mushers do not gratefully acknowledge that their critics have made dog sledding a more humane endeavor. They call them the enemy. They cast the issue as another unbridgeable gulf between their "authentic" way of living and that of modern urban dwellers, who have lost connection to the natural world—the kind of people, they say, who gratefully roast a chicken, never allowing a thought to how this chicken was hatched in a tiny wire cage and not once walked free or even saw the sun until the hatchet fell, yet all the while are ready to condemn mushers as "cruel" for running sled dogs.

In sum, neither side has taken the smallest step toward understanding.

I find the circumstance maddening and inexcusable. And, if I may say so, I can speak with some authority. In the past decade, I've traveled from Florida to Alaska, from New York to California and written stories that give voice to some of the more sensible crusades of the animal-rights movement. I have been a guest at the dinner table with leaders of this cause. I have been invited to their celebration banquets. Some of them I regard as friends, and I don't say that lightly. Theirs is a big task, and I share the view that the cruelty humans inflict on one another is inseparable from the cruelty they impose on animals. I say proudly that I too am an advocate for animals.

When it comes to mushing, however, I fault the animal-rights crusaders. An incredible amount of their emotional conviction is based on dubious or secondhand reports. That, in turn, becomes doctrine, and the public must choose sides accordingly.

The fact is, dogs sometimes die while running races like the Iditarod and the Quest. Many more die, I'll bet, from being inadvertently launched out of the beds of pickup trucks over any equivalent period of time. Pet owners with pickups are just a more diffuse target. How can you tackle them in a neat sound bite for the Associated Press? And if you're not out making news, then how can you convince contributors that you're standing up for the rights of dogs?

As is often the case in these emotion-laden debates, both sides are right, so far as they go. But they don't go far enough to bring any progress, not by a long way.

I have an acquaintance Outside who owns a big dog and keeps it fenced, alone, in a small yard all during the workday. Her love for this animal is unbounded. But, one might ask, is that enough? Dogs are social animals, creatures of the pack. This dog has never known and will never experience the joy of the companionship of its own species. How cruel is that? Moreover, dogs are born to run. You cannot deny that. So is it enough to let this one scramble up the stairs each night, and take a turn around the block on a leash? I hesitate to pass judgment on a friend. But when I invited her to Alaska to take a mushing trip into the wild, I was surprised to hear that she wouldn't even consider it. Mushing dogs just isn't right, she said. Her mind was made up, and closed. As best I could tell, she wasn't even curious about handling a string of dogs all at once. How odd, I thought.

In Los Angeles, taxpayers finance the killing of 54,000 unwanted and stray dogs a year. That's almost 150 a day. In just one city. More lonely, abandoned, and mistreated dogs will be put down in Alaskan death chambers—generically called "humane" shelters—in an average week than will ever perish on the trail. And these dogs will never know the devotion of a musher, the camaraderie of a pack, or the joy of purpose. If they ever had a chance to run, it was only for their lives.

It's not just the killing of strays that should concern us. What about the untold thousands of dogs in every city that come home as Christmas or birthday presents and then are sentenced to lives on the end of chains in crummy backyards, fed once a day and loved never; dogs who howl, not for the joy of the impending run but from the despair of loneliness? What about the street hooligans who raise pit bulls to fight with the pit bulls of rival hooligans on the boardwalk in Venice Beach, California?

Or, more sharply to the point, what about the very doyens of pure-breed dogdom, the members of the American Kennel Club—the people who encourage and participate in the breeding of dogs almost solely to conform to appearance standards? The working characteristics of these animals become concerns of no consequence, their temperament only a matter of casual consideration. No points are given for soundness. As a result, the genetic health of some breeds has declined scandalously. Yes, true enough, many of the fine ladies and gentlemen of the kennel club are generous donors to the humane movement and might object to criticism about their entrenched traditions. But if you cannot call bullshit on your own kind, who are you to call it on someone else?

I find all of these challenges to dogs' well-being noble; each one deserves more than the animal-rights movement can currently give. I understand, or at least I appreciate, how difficult and intractable these problems are in a society beset with so many other problems. But if the animal-welfare movement was mine to lead, I would not turn my back on mushers—I'd enlist them as allies in these crusades. As a group, they live closer to dogs and depend more profoundly on dogs than any pet owners I know. I would continue to keep a wary eye on competitive mushing to guard against backsliding, and I'd denounce those who would train dogs by fear, or those who would cull puppies looking for only the strongest. And, again, I'd enlist mushers as allies.

Although it would separate me from many inside the sport, I would continue to object to big-money sponsors and television coverage of dog racing. Money leads to ever more determined professionalism, to larger and more impersonal kennels. Invariably, it provides the incentive for some mushers to take too many risks. Just look at what TV and millions of dollars have done to other "sports." Lastly, as a show of goodwill and for the sake of dogs, my animal-rights movement would offer financial support for the medical studies of canine myopathy.

As for mushing on the scale it's reached today? Yes, the Quest is dangerous and demanding. Yet what do the dogs say?

Listen to them howl and watch them run.

Aliy Zirkle never really considers quitting. Sometimes mushers succumb to despair at the loss of a dog. Or they suspect other weaknesses in their team and decide to quit. Or they lose confidence in themselves or their dogs or both. But Aliy feels strong, at least physically, and her remaining dogs are unfaltering. It is anthropomorphic, but she tells herself that all of them have worked so damn hard to get this far, they've invested so much of themselves. They haven't lost their head or their drive. Why should they be loaded into a bush plane and flown home just because their musher is brokenhearted? Look at them, they're barking and agitating to go again.

Melanie Donofro, a volunteer veterinarian from Tallahassee, Florida, encourages Aliy. There is no indication the musher was at fault in Prince's death. Melanie tells her so. And the judgment proves correct down the line, as the postrace necropsy and analysis determine.

Still fuming a little about Dave Rich's accusatory approach, Aliy disregards his order to call him first before continuing. She feeds her team, loads the sled, and signs out with the checker.

Rested and newly resolved, her mind is no longer a blank. As she lurches down the rough ice of the Yukon, she can reflect on some of the high points already—like that long, wonderful ride one night before Dawson. Gee, how many nights ago was that now? She broke out of a grove of trees and the northern lights flamed green and purple across the whole sky.

It was quiet. That's when it comes to you, she remembers. The dogs looked so good that she couldn't find a reason to worry, even though she watched them closely. God, was that ever smooth sailing. Kicking up the small hills and gliding down. She was high and the dogs were high. She passed Tim Mowry, camped and asleep near the trail. It was so fucking beautiful, she simply had to stop and wake Tim. You gotta take this in! Mowry could barely open his eyes. Huh? Well, hell, go back to sleep, she thought. Your loss.

Aliy now lets her mind drift to another subject. She was supposed to accomplish something out here in addition to finishing the Quest. This was going to be her chance, alone and without interruption, to ponder her future and settle some things in her life. Should she keep her kennel and race again? The question implies so much more. A kennel is a way of life, not a pastime. Is that what she wants for herself: Aliy

Zirkle, dog musher? What about her career as a biologist? So many of the people at Fish and Wildlife throw themselves at their work. She has felt this pull of ambition, if only faintly. Is now the time for her to buckle down as a scientist? Get the fever? But, man, wouldn't it be nice to have some money first. She could hustle up some construction work come summer and stash away a good chunk of cash. That is, if she worked her ass off and didn't spend it all partying. And then her personal life. So complicated . . .

She had intended to resolve all these questions. So why can't she bear down on them now? All she has to do is weigh the options and devise a plan, she tells herself. Why can't she just do it?

Back home, the imposition of telephones, the proximity of friends and family, the schedule of responsibilities, the old nagging doubts that keep you looking over your shoulder, those handy pints of ale—all of these things distract you. Weeks, months, and, finally, years spin by. You move by inertia and seem to have lost the ability, or the resolve, to choose your own direction. Sometimes with aching clarity you flash on the thought that you need some time alone, quality time. Then you can sort things out. Just what is important? And how do you go after it? How do you fill those empty spaces in your life?

She tells herself that she'll go out on the Quest trail, where there are no distractions and life is elemental. She'll settle things out there.

But the Quest trail has a different lesson to teach. Try as she may, she cannot cling to the what-ifs of the future. They come and go, as wispy as tendrils of ground fog, and they slip right through the fingers. Each time you bring out the mental checklist of pending questions, your mind loses the train of thought and doubles back to the immediate present—the ice and the dogs, the quiet and beguiling beauty of a landscape so sharp that it seems to have come right out of the mold. Yes, there is space out here for the mind to walk. But it doesn't want to walk far. Liberated from the static interference of modern life, where does one seek repose? In the wonder of the here and now.

Aliy feels the balance return to her life. Not by settling matters of tomorrow but by escaping the incessant demands to settle anything. Like her ancestors long ago, she builds a campfire and stares into the embers, not because she's searching for something but because it wraps her comfortably in the moment and fills her with contentment.

To all those looming decisions she was going to make, Aliy says, "Well, ha."

Farther back along the trail, the bedraggled rookie caravan of the "party pack" limps down from the top of American Summit at six o'clock the following morning, with Rusty Hagan leading most of the way. Later, they will learn that the winds that pinned them high on the mountain were the worst that veterans had ever encountered. Some estimated the velocity at sixty miles an hour, with the temperature at 10 below, making for a windchill of something like minus 80.

Looking back into the gray swirl above him, Rusty realizes he has never had such a harrowing experience—not even the time when the moose charged into his team and killed his lead dog. He could have perished up there. They all could have. All it would have taken was a mistake, or a turn of bad luck.

"It just felt very dangerous. You could have definitely died up there. I was spooked. I think everyone was. It could have turned into a real tragedy, real easy."

Rusty's grateful ruminations are soon interrupted, however. A couple of interlopers on the trail are pissing him off. Fairbanks area mushers Bill Steyer and Walter Palkovitch, also rookies, had joined the cortege of the party pack in the storm on American Summit. But they did not share in the group's collegiality. Now the two men, safely below the fury of the summit winds, decide to make a race of it. For a man like Rusty, whose attachment to and concern for his friends is now his primary concern, the idea of competition this far back in the Quest pack is absurd, and downright irritating. Steyer passes when Rusty stops to make sure those behind him are keeping up. Imagine that, jumping into the lead and racing this last little stretch after all we went through. Passing me after I got us moving! While I'm holding back to make sure the others are okay! The more Rusty thinks about it, the madder he gets.

We'll see you down the trail, he fumes to himself. "The one thing I didn't want was to get to Eagle and find that we'd left somebody behind."

A man who is both exhausted and dyspeptic is easily distracted. Somewhere just before Eagle, his dogs miss a turn and Rusty goes loping off in the wrong direction. By the time he gets himself turned around, the musher who led the rookies out of harm's way is the third of the group to reach the checkpoint.

Rusty is no longer just glad to be alive. He's fit to be tied.

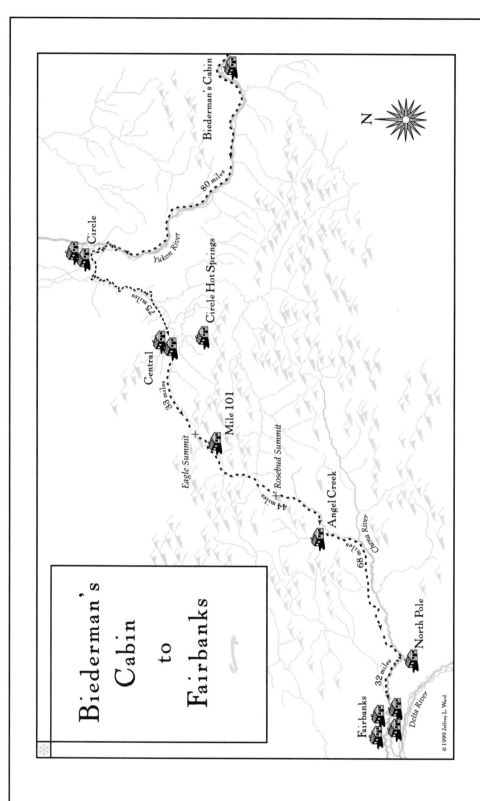

Biederman's Cabin to Fairbanks

N

Biederman's Cabin

80 miles

Circle

Yukon River

75 miles

Circle Hot Springs

Central

33 miles

Eagle Summit

Mile 101

Rosebud Summit

44 miles

Angel Creek

Chena River

68 miles

North Pole

32 miles

Fairbanks

Delta River

© 1999 Jeffrey L. Ward

Biederman's Cabin to Fairbanks

ARRIVING AT BIEDERMAN'S CABIN

1. Bruce Lee,
   Denali National Park, Alaska
2. Andre Nadeau,
   Sainte-Melanie, Quebec*
3. Rick Mackey, *Nenana, Alaska*
4. Paddy Santucci, *Fairbanks, Alaska*
5. Brian MacDougall, *Whitehorse, Yukon*
6. Frank Turner, *Whitehorse, Yukon*
7. John Schandelmeier, *Paxson, Alaska*
8. Jerry Louden, *Two Rivers, Alaska*
9. Keizo Funatsu, *Two Rivers, Alaska*
10. Doug Harris, *Whitehorse, Yukon*
11. William Kleedehn, *Carcross, Yukon*
12. Dave Olesen, *Hoarfrost River,
    Northwest Territories**
13. Dave Dalton, *Fairbanks, Alaska*
14. Louis Nelson, *Kotzebue, Alaska**

15. Tim Mowry, *Two Rivers, Alaska*
16. Larry Carroll, *Willow, Alaska*
17. Aliy Zirkle, *Two Rivers, Alaska**
18. Thomas Tetz, *Tagish, Yukon**
19. Rusty Hagan, *North Pole, Alaska**
20. Bill Steyer, *Fairbanks, Alaska**
21. Amy Wright, *Tok, Alaska**
22. Brenda Mackey, *Nenana, Alaska**
23. Keith Kirkvold, *Fairbanks, Alaska**
24. Walter Palkovitch,
    Two Rivers, Alaska*
25. Gwen Holdman, *Fox, Alaska**
26. Brian O'Donoghue,
    Two Rivers, Alaska*

Scratched:

Michael Hyslop, *Grizzy Valley, Yukon**
Kurt Smith, *North Pole, Alaska*
Ned Cathers, *Whitehorse, Yukon*
Mike King, *Salcha, Alaska*
Stan Njootli, *Old Crow, Yukon**
Jimmy Hendrick,
Denali National Park, Alaska
Dan Turner, *Haines, Alaska*
John Nash, *Nenana, Alaska**
Terry McMullin, *Eagle, Alaska**
Tony Blanford, *Two Rivers, Alaska**
Dieter Dolif, *Trebel, Germany*
Cor Guimond, *Dawson City, Yukon*

* rookie

14

Our camp was so far out in the tall and unserved that there wasn't even an echo. An echo would die of lonesomeness out there.

—Ernest Hemingway

How does one end up in a place like this?

Never by a straight path.

Twice in my life, the Far North has provided me sanctuary when I needed it. The first time, I was on the run. After years as a political writer, too many years, I'm afraid, on the greasy slope of journalistic ambition, I'd had my fill of gasbags, of fellow reporters reduced to shouting inane questions at would-be presidents across a velvet rope. This was not work to raise gooseflesh. Instead, I checked into hotels most nights feeling I couldn't get clean no matter how much I scrubbed myself in the shower. I diagnosed myself as suffering cirrhosis of the spirit. I was becoming a cynic. Then one day, and yes it happened just like that, one day I quit.

Colleagues said I was a fool to give up one of the most cherished titles in American newspapering, *political writer.* Some, I think, secretly envied me, however. Anyway, what next? The *Los Angeles Times* had decided to post a correspondent in Seattle, and national editor Mike

Miller, one of the last of the great, gruff newsmen, who never doubted the nobility of his calling, took a chance with me. I would "cover" the Northwest. Which meant I would have to dig up my own feature stories after a lifetime of being spoon-fed the pap of politics. I remember with acute clarity the joy of landing in Anchorage that first trip north. There was snow on the ground and a bite to the breeze. I glanced around and there wasn't anyone else who looked remotely like a reporter. I was loose from the pack, on my own. Before I got to the bar at the Captain Cook hotel, I started stumbling over stories—good, old-fashioned stories that had not been laundered by press secretaries or already told a hundred times by others. Within a year or so, my closet was choked with boots and parkas, mosquito nets, Capilene, and fleece.

For reasons I still cannot explain very well—although discontent was not a conscious factor—I veered off on another sharp hairpin a few years later. I came home one day with an unquenchable yearning to be a foreign correspondent. Soon I was on my way to Africa. For two years I roamed the continent, that land of beauty and the beast. I soaked in its magnificent vistas and marveled at its wonderful peoples, who for a thousand years have had the worst luck in all the world. I watched skip-loaders scoop up human bodies each morning from the smoky, teeming Rwandan refugee camps. I lay flat-faced in the sand in Somalia while tracer bullets lit the sky overhead. I pinched myself when I interviewed fourteen-year-old soldiers in Liberia's civil war, vicious boys in shower caps with names like "General Buck Naked," who waved RPG launchers menacingly in my face. A stern policewoman wrote me a citation for smoking inside the airport at Freetown, Sierra Leone, while mortar shells fell alongside the runway as revolutionaries attacked the city. I wrote stories about the deaths of thousands of children for lack of clean water; about fourteen-year-olds in Uganda who presided over their village and raised younger siblings because all the adults had died of AIDS. In Timbuktu, I looked for a way to understand why villagers and nomads were still killing each other—but all I found was that I'd arrived in the dry season, when the riverboats could not bring supplies, and there wasn't a beer to be had for five hundred miles.

Then I came home. And for the first time in a long time, I was adrift. I'd had my fill of people bullshitting and killing each other for power. Africa had been life and death; America seemed to be largely a numbers game—the tally on the stock market for the well-off, the daily lottery picks for the poor.

Well, go find a story you think is worthwhile, said Mike Miller.

Any kind of story?

Make it something meaningful, he replied.

How about a sled dog race from the Yukon to Alaska?

Huh?

It's the second most famous sled dog race in the world, I said hopefully. I told him how the Yukon Quest had become a mythical touchstone during my previous travels to the Far North. I bluffed him on the meaningful part. They're authentic people up there, I told him.

Perhaps just to get me off his back, Miller waived me out of his office, muttering, "Okay, fine." I suspect he really meant something more in the vein of, "Poor man, perhaps jungle parasites have eaten away his judgment. Maybe a few weeks in the cold will do him some good."

All of which explains, in a roundabout way, why I happen to be here now, in this empty quarter of North America, with the frail winter sun barely backlighting the overcast and the wind lancing through trees, grinning and hugging fur trappers and homesteaders, and thinking to myself, There really is meaning to life, and sometimes it can be found in the basics.

Mark Richards looks me over as I mush up the riverbank. He smiles and seems ready to say, Well look at the city boy. Instead, he announces: "I got a beer for you."

Mark and Lori Richards came from Los Angeles, too, but they followed a different route to reach Ed Biederman's slumping old wreck of a cabin on this February afternoon.

Some little boys dream of being race-car drivers, cowboys, or fighter pilots. Growing up in the suburban sprawl of the San Fernando

Valley, Mark never dreamed of anything except living in the woods. He never had a sweetheart except his schoolmate Lori. "Since I was five, I've been aware I was born in the wrong century," he says.

In the summer of 1981, the two bid good-bye to the megalopolis and followed the needle-pull of the compass. They had a couple of rucksacks, a few bucks between them, and the dream of being home-steaders. In Dawson City, they bought a hand-me-down canoe, a small cast-iron stove, an ax, a whipsaw, sacks of flour and sugar, and other provisions. The canoe came with only one paddle and they had no money remaining. Mark whittled a second paddle from a scrap board. They launched into the muddy, eight-knot current of the Yukon River so hopelessly overloaded that bystanders on the bank figured they wouldn't make it past the first bend in the river.

Thank God for the doubters.

"People kept telling us we'd never make it. From the very start, they'd say something like, Good luck but no way," Mark recalls. "I think if it hadn't been for all those people telling us we couldn't make it—we might not have."

Today, Mark is stringy-hard with a short brown beard and a vast ponytail. His smile is wry, and private, and his mind challenging—like a graduate student who's fed up with the cautious equivocations of academia and wants to get to the bone. Lori is a robust woman with sparkling eyes and the reassuring, motherly allure that you detect in those old sepia photographs of pioneer women on the Kansas frontier. From time to time you hear that bush life is hard on women—an opin-ion usually voiced by beat-to-hell bush men. The truth is, the bush is hard on everyone. The nearest dentist might be three hundred miles away and require payment in cash, not in moose meat or willow bas-kets. Mark's back has gone bad on him, and he worries that if it gets worse he won't be able to hunt moose or chop firewood. And then how the hell is the family going to survive?

But back in 1981, they were just a couple of young lovers trying to keep their canoe straight in the whirlpools and eddies of the Yukon. When they arrived in Eagle, more doubters were on hand to greet them. It was too late in the year to strike out for a homestead, they were told. This time, they listened. They went to Fairbanks and worked to save up cash for a grubstake, and were back in Eagle in the spring.

They floated to a tributary and then began the miserable process of lining their laden canoe fifty miles upstream, getting out and pulling it with ropes as they waded or scrambled along the banks. The journey took weeks; they banged their shins in the ice-cold runoff and tore the skin off their hands as they heaved on the ropes. The two balanced each other in moments of doubt. Mark broke down crying at one stop. They had lit their little stove and were brewing a pot of tea in a cloud of happy mosquitoes. He stood up and, in frustration, kicked the son-of-a-bitching teapot into the miserable, stinking goddamn willows. In an instant, Lori pounced on him, knocked him to the ground, and shook him by the neck.

"Listen, you gotta get yourself together," she said, her cheeks puffed out and her eyes steady.

He did.

"We finished our tea," Mark recalls. "Been here ever since."

At a clearing 125 miles from the nearest road or settlement, they decided to build. They felled a grove of spruce to make a clearing, and peeled the bark off the logs for their cabin. It snowed on the day they finished.

Amber was born two years later, then Megan, and finally Keene. Amber now has her own dog team and traps with her dad in winter. Last Christmas, she had a choice of presents: her dad would make her a new fur hat or a sled. She picked the sled. She could make do another winter with her old hat, although it was worn and didn't fit well anymore.

The family eats moose from the hills nearby and fish from the river in front of the cabin. They'll take a bear when they can. They grow and can vegetables, and earn cash by weaving baskets and making fur hats. Mark imposes on bush pilots to bring and return library books. He's a ham radio operator and chats nightly with the twenty-five or so regulars of the Alaska radio network—people who sign in from Chickaloon and Trapper Creek, Galena and Chignik, many of them places not even registered on the map. The Richards children, of course, are homeschooled. A teacher flies in a couple of times each year to administer progress tests. Amber is studying Japanese, and for a few weeks in the fall, the family hosted a teenage exchange student from Japan, a shy girl who no doubt had trouble reconciling the America she visited with the one she saw on the TV shows.

This past summer, the Richards returned to Los Angeles to see Mark's and Lori's parents. It was their first trip Outside in four years, and we crowded into my car for a trip to Universal Studios. The kids raced from ride to ride with huge smiles, and Mark and Lori squealed along with everyone else when they got doused in Jurassic Park. These youngsters made their way through the crowds and embraced the urban amusements with more confident aplomb, I suspect, than your average Pasadena schoolkids would show if suddenly plopped down in the middle of Yukon River wilderness and told to enjoy themselves at 20 below. In fact, I could distinguish the Richards offspring from the sea of other boys and girls only by one thing. The rides at Universal Studios are configured so that departing passengers must thread through the aisles of gift shops. Virtually all kids shuffle along, craning their necks to survey the displayed T-shirts, hats, toys, banners, plastic dinosaurs, and souvenirs. The Richards children hurried past, giving none of it so much as a glance. Whatever aspirations these bush children held in their hearts, the accumulation of goodies did not seem to be among them.

By the time Wayne and I arrive at Biederman's, Bruce Lee has driven by without stopping. Nobody mentions any incident involving Bruce's passing, but I will hear of one later—and, strangely enough, it will end up costing me some dear friends and forever color my view of rural life.

Andre Nadeau rests for a couple of hours and then joins us around the big kitchen table.

"By the way, Andre," I tell him finally, "I'm not racing in the Quest. I'm just a journalist. I brought those dogs from Eagle. Trapline dogs." He brightens noticeably to learn that Wayne and I are not threats after all, and I wonder for an instant whether he might actually smile with relief. I resist adding, But we scared the hell out of you, eh?

We have not missed dinner. Gary Nance is boiling a five-gallon kettle of water. And then he reaches into his cardboard box and begins ladling great handfuls of king crab legs. The water splashes with pounds of them, fresh frozen, with gleaming white meat and lipstick-colored shells. In a pan big enough to roast a turkey, he melts a quart of butter. And like famished cavemen around the fresh carcass of a mastodon, we tear in, bare-handed. There is no conversation, just the cracking noise of Leatherman pliers on hard crab shells and the sucking sounds as firm meat is drawn out by mouth. Occasionally, someone offers a satisfied grunt aimed Gary's way. The best kind of bush pilot, I decide, is one who owns a wholesale food distributorship, too. Soon our hands and faces are smeared in butter, and butter runs down our forearms and drools off our chins.

Others who collect around the dinner table include volunteer veterinarian Steve Swank of Oak Hill, West Virginia, and Don Woodruff, a summer seasonal worker with Alaska Fish and Game who winters on the nearby Kandik River and runs a trapline. Two snowmachiners from the Alaska coast come up every February, and one of them has just finished a new cabin nearby. A mechanic has been flown in to try to repair one of their fancy long-distance machines.

Andre departs with a brisk nod at 7:40 P.M. The next musher behind him is still four hours away. At the tail end of the pack, the tennis player Gwen Holdman and another musher are nearly four days behind already.

I check and, sure enough, my rum has warmed up enough to drink. Under the light of a gas lantern, other bottles materialize and are assembled on the table.

Biederman's is a wonderful cozy clutter, full of the rich smells of Ben-Gay, trail dog, wood smoke, B.O., drying socks, cracked crab, and discount whiskey with the brand name R & R that is decanted from plastic bottles and releases vapors suggesting sour-mash Froot Loops. Along the log walls of the kitchen, open shelves are heaped with bush provisions—tins of coffee, boxes of crackers, flour, Cheez Whiz, and

150 other things, some mushed or flown in for this gathering and others left behind who knows when by earlier travelers. Windows at both ends of the kitchen look out onto snowdrifts that reach the bottom sill. Ten feet outside the door, a section of snow has been designated as the proper place to pee, and dozens of yellow caverns have already melted through the crust. Around back, the outhouse features a seat of blue Styrofoam insulation with a hole in its center. This remarkable invention is standard throughout the Far North and, if everyone is careful with their aim, can keep your exposed fanny comfortable and dry even at 40 below. The only reading material is a wrinkled copy of *U.S. News & World Report* from eight months ago. But most people prefer not to shine a headlamp in the outhouse for fear of what else they might see.

Tonight at Biederman's the only one of us not having a splendid time is Brown Nose, my wheel dog. Staked up on a slope above the cabin, he received his steaming bowl of dinner along with the others. But, unseen, he nosed the pan, probably in his rush toward it. His dinner went sliding down the bank, just out of reach. It's there freezing solid right now, with Brown Nose watching sadly. An unjust reward for a long day and thirty-eight miles of trail. Stupidly, I don't notice it, and Wayne will not discover anything until tomorrow's breakfast.

Brown Nose gets a double helping next time around. He displays no grudge. Heaven goes by favor. If it went by merit, you would stay out and your dog would go in. Mark Twain said that.

Question: Dog mushing may not be cruel, but how about trapping animals for fur?

Answer: It's cruel.

But so is industrial livestock production.

Trappers like Wayne and Mark and Don Woodruff are inclined to judge me by how I judge them. And this being Alaska, we do not politely skip over the subject of trapping and seek harmless common ground tonight. Even as we smile, sip our rum and whiskey, and slouch easily on the plastic buckets and tree stumps we use for chairs—brothers in the bush—I can tell this is serious business for these men. And they're going to have their say.

As usually happens when I venture into another culture, I find myself surprised.

Life in the bush may be more elemental and, as I see it, closer to the "natural" way in which humans evolved. But, as in city living, contradictions are inescapable. For one thing, I come to learn—not just tonight, but over the course of my months in the company of such men and women—that trappers (or at least some trappers) kill with a degree of remorse that is difficult to comprehend, and maybe impossible to appreciate, for those who don't kill. They trap to survive. They trap because there is no other way to make honest money in the long winters in the wilderness. They gather fur because it makes possible their lives in the bush. They subsist off the bounty of nature by getting their hands bloody—not by paying the slaughterhouse workers and leather tanners to do the work for them. The trappers I know best feel pangs of guilt as well as gratitude when the steel jaws serve up the frozen body of a marten—worth perhaps $45 at auction. They believe they live closer to and feel greater esteem for animals because of their dependence on nature for survival. They are, by necessity, stewards of the habitat necessary to sustain animals, and they object to the righteousness of those who, for instance, invest in mutual fund portfolios that drive the indiscriminate "progress" that displaces wildlife.

That's what these men suggest tonight, and I'm in no mood to doubt them.

Like all of the rest of us, trappers draw their own ethical lines. Wayne, for instance, will trap for nothing but marten, a nocturnal, weasel-like animal the size of a large house cat. When made into coats, the fur becomes known as sable. He will not set traps for foxes or wolves or other larger, more stately creatures. He cannot bear the idea. He can barely stand trapping at all. If he could gather and sell mushrooms from under the snowpack, I believe he would gladly trade his traps for a shovel.

"I do it because I have to," he says simply.

I have drawn my own lines. I eat meat, although less than I used to.

Sometimes I try to remind myself that I'm party to an assembly-line enterprise of killing. If you think that meatpacking plants are "humane," you might want to avoid visiting one—where fear and panic along the slaughter line is palpable. But usually, I confess, I just pour cumin over the ground beef and my tacos come out entirely bloodless, like everyone else's. I wear the hides of these animals as belts and shoes without sharing the trapper's remorse at the sight of a dead creature with its skin on.

I would never wear fur for decoration. But I have a ruff of raccoon fur on my parka because, as I tell myself, I've learned a little about frostbite, and a ruff becomes a matter of good-sense survival. I wear a hat of beaver fur because . . . well, because it's warm and the woman who sold it to me feeds her family off the trapline.

My own moral position is entirely indefensible, of course. Like millions of others, I hire my killers and don't watch. That puts me on a lower plane, I'm afraid, than the three men I'm with tonight. And many rungs down from my friends at the Humane Society, with their vegan diets and canvas shoes. Odd, isn't it: these two kinds of people have more in common, and are less willing to recognize it, than they do with the remainder of us in the squishy middle. The trapper and the vegan both live in constant awareness of animals and their suffering. The rest of us worry about getting rain spots on our suede jackets and complain because the people who package hamburger these days are always trying to make you buy a little more than you need.

Just past midnight, too late for buttered crab, Rick Mackey leads the next group of mushers into Biederman's. Paddy Santucci is next. They are now eleven hours behind Bruce Lee. Whitehorse veteran Frank Turner is a couple of places farther back, followed by John Schandelmeier and Jerry Louden. The whole bunch of them will feed their dogs, eat from Lori's pot of bubbling game stew, rest, grab a plate of Lori's breakfast, and depart en masse shortly after 9:00 A.M.

The easygoing air of the first half of the Quest has evaporated. Every musher's game plan must now account for the hopscotch pace of

Bruce, the rabbit, and Andre Nadeau, the turtle. More important, these men chasing the leaders are cuing off one another's movements, sizing up one another's dogs. The difference between third place and eighth is the difference between $18,000 in prize money and $4,200. So, along with the cold and bone-weary exhaustion, the creases in the faces of these dog drivers now show the strain of rising competition. They all sleep in a small, detached cabin—trying to discipline themselves not to be disrupted by the noise of someone arriving, while not missing the tiptoe sound of one of them trying to slip out early.

In between their arrivals, I reacquaint myself with my sleeping bag. But it's only for an hour. When someone wakens, most of us rise and stumble around stupidly. Then there is another lull, when heads collectively droop, and no one seems to notice the roar of openmouthed snores. Next comes the rattle of a sled, and someone announces, Musher!—and we're all up again, yawning and blowing our noses and trying to remember where we dropped our coffee cups. For a moment, I am beset with the idea that this is how the North Vietnamese tortured their prisoners, denying them sleep, rousting them at random hours. Then the thought slips away, lost in the fog of a slow-motion brain.

Sometimes the energy rises. We are sitting around the table and Frank Turner, the black-bearded old-timer, makes a confession. He's remembering a seven-hour run where he broke trail while Jerry Louden followed him. Louden declined to take a turn leading through the soft snow. Nobody says that a musher must break trail. But just the same, if you don't share in the work, don't expect to win the sportsman's trophy. Frank and Jerry then hit a long easy downhill, and damned if Jerry, who'd been conserving the strength of his dogs, didn't start demanding to pass. Normal etiquette requires a musher to pull over and let a faster team pass. Fuck him, Frank thought to himself. But Jerry was insistent, riding Frank's heels impatiently, hollering, "Trail! Trail! Frank, I'm tearing off my brake."

"Use your goddamn snowhook," Frank spat back. The two jockeyed, mile after mile, tempers rising. This is the kind of situation that creates lasting grudges if not serious fistfights. And Frank knows that his rival is just about twice his size.

"We came to a flat stretch, and Louden veered out and came around," Frank recalls. "Only it wasn't Louden. It was Rick Mackey."

The look in Mackey's eyes was pure fury.

"By the way," Frank says, interrupting his story with a random thought, "what day is it?"

There is silence in the room. Then someone suggests it could be Tuesday. Yes, it's probably Tuesday, someone else agrees.

"I wouldn't guarantee it, though," says Lori. And she's the most likely to know because, by counting the days, she can tell when Friday comes. On Fridays all through winter, the Richards light their sauna and sweat out the grime and wash their hair.

John Schandelmeier has no opinion on what day of the week it is. He strolls into the cabin and loads a plate with bacon, sausage, hot dogs, pancakes, and scrambled eggs warming on the stove. It must be breakfast time. I'd guess Schandelmeier's waist size at twenty-eight inches, thirty at the most. An office worker in the city who ate this much would be pulling open the pleats on his forty-inch slacks. John is a happy eater, talking as he chews, his Groucho Marx mustache quivering as he amuses himself with accounts of his dogs. By now, he's pretty much worn out the tall tale of that coyote he had to pull out of a trap to fill up his team: "Named that one Lester." Now Schandelmeier has discovered that one of the females in his team is pregnant.

"Wait until you see them pups," he says. "They're going to have a thousand miles on 'em before they're even born."

He keeps shaking his head at the very thought of it. Imagine, that much trail and not even born. Why, give them two years and Rick Mackey and all the rest might as well spend the winter in Hawaii, because there'll be no keeping up with dogs like that. No use trying. Ha, it will be the first time one guy gets all the prize money because everyone else is afraid to enter.

For the rest of us, a day at Biederman's passes in the blissful, sleepy rhythms of a wilderness camp. Outside there is the heavy *thunk-crack* of a maul splitting frozen wood. Mark Richards and his daughter Amber harness up their dogs and mush a half mile across the river to the mouth of the Kandik. They skim fresh ice from a hole they chopped earlier, down to the clean water of the stream. Using a dip bucket, they collect fifteen gallons and mush it back. Don Woodruff arrives with tonight's dinner—a frozen and skinned whole beaver. He hangs it inside near the woodstove to thaw, and then butchers it into kebab-size chunks with his old thin-bladed sheath knife. The cabin fills with a rich, greasy smell of beaver fat. Of all the wild game in the Far North, beaver is regarded as the least appetizing. Lori, however, simmers the red-black flesh in water for three hours with garlic, soy sauce, and pepper and then browns the meat in an iron skillet. The result: delicious. From the sudden wealth of fresh food brought in by air and snowmachine, Lori follows dinner with fresh-baked apple pie and vanilla ice cream.

So what if it might not be Friday? Mark shovels away the snow in front of the tiny sauna and lights the iron stove. In the early blackness of the night, I walk out onto the Yukon, away from the trees, and a meteor streaks across one of those epic skies that demonstrates how our galaxy happened to be named the Milky Way. I'd say life was approaching perfect, except that my frostbitten fingers are throbbing, and someone soon mentions that the rum is finished and the grain whiskey in shockingly low supply.

The sociability of the cabin is both heartwarming and ever so slightly melancholy tonight.

Mark Richards wonders aloud if the time has come to think about leaving the bush, moving his family somewhere closer to civilization, maybe Fairbanks. Amber is growing up. A teenager deserves the chance to have friends and socialize, doesn't she?

"I thought this was right, being here—the right thing to do. I thought she'd look back on it as a good thing," he says, reflectively. Then he weighs the yearnings of his daughter with his own dreads: "A shit job that you hate, with money problems."

Back in Eagle, I have listened to locals cluck and fuss about the Richards family. Imagine, it's said, they live off the land, don't pay much tax, and accept educational help from the state. Who will pay their medical bills in an emergency, except the public? Plus, like all

Alaskans, each member of the Richards family is entitled to a $1,500 annual kickback as a share of the state's Prudhoe Bay oil windfall—a $7,500 payment from the government in a state without income or sales tax. So I suppose it's true that the Richards family receives more than it contributes, if measured by money alone. But the small-town gossip chills me, and I tolerate very little of it. All Alaskans are freeloaders, when it comes to taxes. They singularly benefit from oil development of resources to which all Americans hold the deed. Prudhoe Bay was approved, you might recall, because of domestic oil shortages. Today, this oil is sold to Japan. But to keep their gold-plated state government afloat and the no-tax, oil-fund refunds flowing, Alaskans clamor and win the right to drill in more and more of the federal wilderness, onshore and off. Most recently, the government granted rights for drilling in a national petroleum reserve that was set aside seventy years ago for safekeeping in the event of a crisis. Now the compelling crisis is that Alaskans don't want to pay taxes for services and insist on getting that fat rebate each winter.

If anyone deserves a break in the scheme, the Richards get my vote. They are among the last of their kind. There is no more land for homesteading, even in Alaska. When parcels come up for sale, they are now priced beyond the means of subsistence people. Well-heeled urbanites snap them up for summer cabins or hunting camps. The wilderness homesteader is one of the most powerful symbols of freedom in North America. Apart from the loner bachelors, the Richards and the Henrys are the only nonnative families in this whole expanse of the Yukon River wild who aren't just playing out here. What a puny price society pays to keep that myth from fading into history. Personally, I'll never have the chance to try their kind of life. But it inspires and comforts my soul that they are out here tonight. There are fewer of them every year, and I suspect there will never be more.

My quiet meditation is interrupted by the sound of an engine. A snowmachine belonging to a Canadian camera crew screams up the bank and stops in front of Biederman's. The two filmmakers brush away a crust of snow and step into the cabin. I notice that their clothes carry so much cold that they chill the whole room by several degrees.

They report that the wind has drifted six feet of snow over the trail in some places behind us. They passed Aliy Zirkle as she wallowed in front of her team, trying to stomp out a path.

They pump us for information about what is happening in front of them. By now the Quest is so spread out that no one, even with a fast machine, can keep track of anything except what they can see, or pick up by way of gossip every fifty or a hundred miles or so.

15

The test of an adventure is that when you're in the middle of it, you say to yourself, "Oh now I've got myself into an awful mess. I wish I were sitting quietly at home." And the sign that something's wrong with you is when you sit quietly at home wishing you were out having lots of adventure.

—Thornton Wilder, 1954

A nervous knot has tied itself in my stomach. I went to bed three hours ago but spent most of the time thrashing in my clammy sleeping bag, as if it had shrunk and was too tight. The hands on my wristwatch say 6:00 A.M. and I can bear to lie here on the floor no longer, even though I know it's lousy bushcraft to lie awake when you have a rare chance to sleep. There is no reason to rise in the darkness. But I do anyway. I've got to leave today. I absolutely must get out of Biederman's and catch up with the front end of the Quest.

Of course, I'm helpless to do this. And that is the source of my anxiety. I have never learned to be fatalistic about logistics.

Using my headlamp, I retrieve my familiar layered ensemble from the nails of the log wall. I treat myself to a pair of fresh socks, my last. In the circled beam of the headlamp, my feet look shockingly white and wrinkled from being damp too long. From an assortment of dirty socks, I try to select the driest pair for a second layer over my feet. I pull on the left sock. Then I reach for the right. It's gone. I sweep the space around me with the headlamp. Where is the son of a bitch? I just had it in my hand. Frustration rises. I'm stomping around, making too much noise in the crowded cabin. The fucking sock has completely vanished. Frustration rises and I feel the yearn to kick something—to kick everything, all this absurd, filthy crap that defines my existence. I hate it all. Then I look at my right foot. The sock is on it. I must have dozed off, a microsleep, while dressing. Oh. Now trying to move quietly again, I wriggle my feet into my moist bunny boots. Immediately, I feel the heat of my feet leach into the frigid insulation. I should not have left my boots on the cold floor. I hate bunny boots. In any civilized place, they would be implements of torture.

No sooner am I dressed than I feel an overpowering wave of exhaustion, as if I'm going to pass out standing up. Someone rolls over in the cabin and I hear a contented fart. But none of the other five men rise. I'm jealous, but I cannot begrudge the wisdom that allows them to sleep. I feel the chill of the cabin. As we're all supposed to do anytime we rise, I open the squeaky door of the stove and insert a couple of sticks of kindling on top of the dying coals and add some torn strips of cardboard. Then I turn off my headlamp and step outside.

The mucus inside my nose freezes immediately. I hardly notice anymore except to register that the temperature has dropped. I try to keep my mouth closed so my teeth won't start aching in the cold. I look hopefully for stars, which would signal fair weather for flying. I am supposed to fly out with Gary Nance. Wayne and his trapper friend Tim McLaughlin have already pulled out, driving home to Eagle with his team and the dogs who brought me here. Gary has agreed to advance me to Circle City, the next checkpoint. If the weather allows it. If the Quest can spare him from other chores for a couple of hours. If something doesn't get screwed up. But I see no stars. The air is absolutely still, and I can see nothing. I blink and wait for my eyes to adjust to the darkness. I sense the hulking shadows of spruce trees, but nothing materializes from the blackness. Finally I slap the plunger switch and sweep the scene with a halogen beam. I have the sensation of being in an oyster, closed in by a vague gray all around me. I cannot discern whether this is fog or an impending storm.

Ahead, the relentless advance of the Quest pulls on me. But I am motionless and trapped. For some reason, I feel desperate to move on. No, that's not true. I know the reason that I'm anxious to get to Circle City.

Across a gully, a faint light glows in the main cabin and I clomp through the snow, circling wide so as not to disturb resting dog teams. Bless Lori Richards: the coffee pot is full and scalding. Alone in the lantern light, I sip coffee and wait. My head droops.

Bruce Lee went past Biederman's without pulling off the trail. But he was forced to stop for a minute. A loose dog belonging to trapper Don Woodruff sighted the strange team and gave chase. Lee stopped his team, set his snowhook, and muscled the brawny dog back up the riverbank. It was such a minor occurrence, he did not bother mentioning it later.

With growing confidence, Lee pushes ahead another twenty miles through Yukon-Charley Rivers National Preserve to a park service cabin, where he rests. Lee is now blind to events behind him and must decide for himself what pace to set. For the first time, he allows himself to think that he just might win this thing.

"Nadeau is really easy to put in check. All I have to do is stop resting."

Andre arrives at the park service cabin six and a half hours later. Lee is still resting. Andre pushes on. By sticking with his game plan, Lee has divided the run from Eagle to Circle City into three segments of roughly fifty miles each. To try to keep apace, Andre now forces himself into a tiring eighty-mile final leg. Once again, he has taken the lead. But Bruce is faster and better rested.

When the two last spoke, Andre told him, "You and me, we have the same race."

"Something must have been lost in translation," Lee remarked later.

The trail between Biederman's cabin and Circle City, just as from Eagle, follows the meandering Yukon River. Circle City, a tiny outpost village, is close to the northernmost point on the trail. From there, mushers will veer off the Yukon for the final time, and soon head southwest on a zigzag march to Fairbanks.

Fourteen hours behind the two leaders are Rick Mackey, Paddy Santucci, John Schandelmeier, and a handful of others. With only eight remaining dogs, Santucci's team is the smallest among the front-runners—a subject that gives doubters something to talk about. So what, Santucci tells himself. They're a helluva strong eight. They're pulling their hearts out.

"There's a lot of people out here running egos, not dogs," Santucci says. "You just can't get wrapped up in the idea that you're running with the high-powered teams. You just go."

He goes. Then a little warning light comes on to disrupt his trance. His dogs have tensed, and they break into a fast trot. The trail is hugging the river's edge, and Paddy looks up to see a large black wolf watching him. The dogs have seen the wolf, too.

For fifteen minutes, the wolf trots along with Paddy and his team, sometimes loping ahead, then stopping to watch them pass. It is a majestic sight, rare but not threatening. There has never been a recorded instance of a wolf attacking an adult human in North America.

"The dogs? Well, I would guess that they think to themselves, yes they could be preyed upon. But whenever they are confronted with an adverse situation, they look to the person who feeds them. So in this case, I don't think they feel threatened. Does the poodle in the lap feel threatened? They look back and expect to be taken care of."

The wolf stops on the bank of a small island. Paddy passes, but this time the stately predator stays put, its big head swiveling to follow the sight of the strangers. The trail turns and Paddy sees it no more.

Everyone notices that the weather is getting colder.

The back half of the Quest field is now trickling into Biederman's. Tim Mowry arrived last night and overslept by an hour and a half. His hopes of finishing in the big money have faded, but not his good nature. He just laughs at himself and dallies even more before leaving. Larry Carroll pushes his team up the riverbank in front of the cabin this morning. The memory of last year is sharp in his mind and he wishes he could have gotten here last night, when the sauna was heated.

Hours pass and my anxiety rises; the coffee bubbles sourly in my stomach. $E + C = I$. Exhaustion plus caffeine equals irritability. The first glow of dawn reveals a shroud of clouds draped low over the trees and bluffs. Gary Nance shakes his head. Won't be flying in this. We'll wait. He seems wholly unconcerned, which only heightens my frustration. Why isn't he chewing the enamel off his teeth like I am?

My mind has raced ahead. For the last few days, I have been living entirely in the moment, without thought of past or future. It was a wonderful respite, a return to the ancestral past—a complete escape from the way I usually exist, in the shadows of yesterdays and tomorrows. Whether it was exhilaration or exhaustion, it was always today. I think to myself how seldom I live like this, fully in the present. But now the Quest is heading toward its climax, and it's out of my reach and I'm worrying ahead. More to the point, I'm thinking about Liisa Penrose. I'm only eighty miles from Circle, and then it's just 162 road miles to Fairbanks—that is, if the tiny, dead-end road is even open over the high passes of the White Mountains. Of course, I do not have a car in Circle. But, hell, I cannot get there anyway because of this lousy cloud cover. And who knows if she is interested anymore? What a prize I would be presenting myself: without a bath and in trail clothes I've been wearing for more than a week.

I have been pushing the thought of her out of my mind. But I cannot anymore. I remember her smile, and how she wrinkles her eyes when she's happy, and all the other things that make me feel young and stupid—and anxious to get going. I have no business with these emotions. My life at home has been fixed and carefully charted for a long time. If it had gone dry, I blamed only the erosion of time. I used to say to myself that my only regret was that I would never fall in love again. Then I stopped saying it because it seemed silly. Now, out of the blue, I'm in love in the middle of the Alaskan wild and that's the silliest thing of all.

At 11:30 A.M., Gary takes another look at the sky. The trees around the cabin block the view, so he walks down and onto the river. The overcast seems to have lifted by only inches. He scratches and chews his lip in the standard bush-pilot pantomime.

"I'll give it a try," he says at last.

Gary's plan is to evacuate the snowmachine mechanic and two dogs that mushers have dropped here. Then he will shuttle back from Circle

City and retrieve me. In what seems like slow motion, Gary prepares. Actually, it doesn't just seem like slow motion, it is. He gets dressed, eats another handful of breakfast sausages. The snowmachines are now working again, breaking the tranquillity with their oily screeching, and they transport Gary, the mechanic, and the two dogs across the river to his airplane and the little clearing he uses as a strip. He peels the covers off his wings and cowling. The covers prevent moisture from melting on the warmed surfaces when the plane lands, and then freezing and adding weight for takeoff. He lights a spindly white-gas camp stove and, through a four-inch duct pipe, directs the heat from the flame into the engine compartment to warm the oil and metal. He must take off his gloves to operate the little stove and I watch as his hands grow red and numb. The dogs are inserted into burlap potato sacks, which are snugged around their necks so only their heads are exposed. This is to keep them under control while in flight, and they accept the bag without objection.

At 1:00 P.M., with the sky still gray and low, the mechanic climbs in and the dogs are loaded onto his lap. Gary hoists himself into his seat and brings the motor to life. After a few minutes the oil reaches operating temperature. He guns the engine, the little prop bites into the frigid air, and the Super Cub skids down the short runway, floats upward, and turns west to Circle.

Gary is a third-generation Alaskan, and his love of the Alaska myth is as great as anyone's I know. This is the fifth year that he has left behind his business and family to fly in the extreme conditions of winter in behalf of the Quest.

"I ain't no damned dog musher, but these people who are, are closer to real Alaskans than anybody left. Not all of them, but you've got a better chance of finding a real Alaskan on the Quest than anywhere else. And I'm out here because it's a chance to help them," he once told me.

I watch the colorful little airplane disappear over a hill and feel a swell of relief. I'm next. Back at the cabin, I borrow the satellite telephone that the veterinarian carries and stumble down to the river, where I can achieve unobstructed aim on the horizon. From this latitude, communications satellites do not fly above us but hang way out horizontally, where the earth meets the sky. I walk a couple of hundred yards out on the river to make sure I'm far enough, climbing over ice blocks the size of washing machines. I dial.

Hello, Liisa?

She answers. The sound is distant and crackles.

Liisa, I'd like to see you.

"Where are you?"

I'm calling from Biederman's. Gary Nance will be flying me out in a while to Circle City. Listen, Liisa, I don't know how long the battery will last on this phone. What I'm wondering is, do you want to rent us a car and drive up to Circle and meet me? I don't know if the road is open, but if you can get over the pass, we could follow the Quest back. To myself, I add, Please.

Pause.

Liisa?

"Okay, I guess I could do that," she says finally. "What kind of car should I get?"

Any car, get us a big damn car. Bring music. Bring beer.

Truly giddy like a teenager, I bound back across the ice blocks and up the bank to the cabin. I figure it will take Gary at least two hours to make the trip. I contemplate heating some water and trying to wash, but I have no clean clothes, so why bother? People in the cabin remark about my new mood as if, perhaps, I've just completed a successful mission in the outhouse.

At 2:30 P.M., I hear the sound of Gary's engine. That was fast. I'm not through packing. As he passes overhead to circle his little clearing, I jam everything remaining into my duffel, make one quick survey in hopes that I'm not leaving behind anything essential, and race outside to find the snowmachiner. I don't want to hold Gary up. There is only an hour and a half of daylight remaining.

The wind burns my face as we screech to the other side of the Yukon. When I climb off the back of the machine, Gary is putting the covers on his wings. Something is wrong. Then I see that the mechanic is back, standing to the side. And the two undelivered dogs are loose from their bags.

"Couldn't make it," Gary says, matter-of-factly. "Ran into ice fog out there. Circle is socked in. Fucking impossible. We'll try again tomorrow."

I feel dizzy. Sure, I'm acting like a hysteric. But that's the definition of being hysterical—you've lost control of your senses. I approach him and put a hand on his shoulder. Listen, Gary, I gotta get out of here today. Can I ask you a favor? My voice sounds pleading. Would you try once more? Maybe Circle has cleared a little. *Please.*

In the bush, asking a favor is not a casual matter. Not like borrowing a lawn mower. When you ask a favor here, it's serious business. Gary is a little startled. This puts him in a lousy position. The judgment of a bush pilot is rarely questioned aloud. But, just the same, bush pilots cannot bear the thought of letting people down. He stands contemplatively for a moment. I cannot read his thoughts. Then we hear the sound of another engine. A plane is coming upriver. Gary leaps into the cockpit, switches on his radio, and calls. The other pilot says conditions around Circle are miserable but flyable. That decides it. He yanks off the wing covers as if he's stripping sheets from a bed. In ten minutes we're airborne, leaving the bewildered mechanic standing on the ground. Already I can sense the afternoon light beginning to fade.

The heavy gunmetal sky presses down, and we seem almost to scrape against it as Gary gains altitude. Instead of following the winding course of the river, he charts a straight-line vector to Circle, taking us over river bluffs and foothills. As far ahead as I can see, there seems to be a narrow band of sky between cloud and earth. But of course I cannot see all the way to Circle.

Gary is uncommonly quiet. He smokes and coughs and frequently deices the carburetor, which causes the engine to momentarily lose power. I've never seen him silent like this, and I've never flown when carburetor ice accumulated so fast. He begins to rock the Cub, aiming one wing skyward and then the other. He does it again and looks up. At first, I don't understand. Then I realize he is checking the fuel gauges—little glass tubes, like the ones on a carpenter's level, that are located above his head where the wings attach to the fuselage. When he rocks the plane, he is trying to see how much gas sloshes into the tubes. Not much, I'm afraid. One wing appears to be completely empty. The other glass tube shows liquid only if he stands the plane hard on its side. We bounce along for another minute and then Gary banks hard and pushes the nose down. We are following a side canyon and I can see the ice of the Yukon just ahead.

"Outta gas," he says.

I say nothing, but if I did it would be a sputter.

We are almost at the river. Gary banks again and then doubles back, rapidly bleeding off altitude. He intends to land. I see some branches sticking out of the ice in a line ahead. Apparently they mark some sort of a strip. All I can see is flat, one-dimensional white—no shadows in the diffused, gloomy light of the overcast. Then, in a single instant, there is the shudder of skis touching ground and silence from the engine. We glide to a halt. My heart is, I confess, ker-thumping more excitedly than such a smooth landing would otherwise warrant.

It appears to me that we are in the middle of the Yukon River, smack in the heart of nowhere. And there is absolutely nothing at all in those little glass tubes up by the wings. Oh, great. Then I begin to recognize the landscape from my summer trip down the river. This is park service property and up on the bank, barely visible, is Slavin's cabin—a two-story clapboard monstrosity that the government maintains here. I remember once reading about how the park service was dedicated to maintaining the wonderful heritage of Yukon-Charley Rivers National Preserve and then thinking, as I stopped here on my canoe trip, that I had never seen such an ugly, out-of-place building. At the time, my heart sided with those critics who believed the federal government couldn't pour piss out of a boot even if the instructions were printed on the sole. But now, by damn, a more welcome sight has never filled my eyes. Look at that lovely curl of smoke coming out of the chimney.

"We'll get some gas here," says Gary. His grin is back. He looks like a boy who knew all along where the girls had their private swimming hole.

A ponderous humanlike figure lumbers down the long boat ramp that leads out of the cabin. It is heading our way. And when we meet, a voice speaks from a small opening deep in the hood of a parka. Dave Mills, superintendent of Yukon-Charley, introduces himself. Normally, he lives in Fairbanks. But he's been up here for the Quest, and his airplane is away, shuttling other park service workers somewhere, and he is alone. And he's happy as hell to have company. "Come on up and have some coffee," the voice inside the parka says cheerfully.

Gary is all business. He learns that we can borrow a little gas. There's some up at the park service runway, about three miles up the canyon. But first, the superintendent says, let's have a mug of coffee. Gary can feel the daylight slipping away and just nods. I follow the superintendent into the cabin, where he lights the propane stove. But before I can even unzip my parka, Gary taps on the window from outside and signals me. I spin around and step out to where he is unstrapping a five-gallon jerry can from the back of a snowmachine. He removes the lid, sniffs the contents, nods approvingly, and then grabs the can. He is headed back down the ramp with me right behind him. Realizing that his houseguests are not at this moment waiting anxiously for the coffee to boil and sharing their trail stories, Superintendent Mills comes loping after us. I hear the cabin door bang and see him long-striding, trying to get his arm in his parka and not be left behind.

"This will be fine," Gary tells him. "I'll make sure to pay you back. This will really help."

The superintendent and I watch as Gary climbs up on the wings, unscrews the cap to his fuel tank, and drains about half the jerry can. He moves to the other wing. Gasoline dribbles over the fabric and drips into the snow. Gary is in a hurry.

"Don't you guys want a little coffee?" the superintendent asks hopefully.

"We better go," says Gary, nodding at the darkening sky. "And thanks again."

Yes, thanks, I say.

The superintendent now has his parka on properly and his hood is snugged over his face. I cannot see his expression and no sound comes from the small opening.

With me pushing on the wing and Gary on the tail, we spin the little Cub around so it is aimed back down the smoothed-over strip. I crawl, huffing, into my undersize seat. Gary, smelling of raw gasoline, jumps into his. He fires the engine and we're off in forty-five seconds, leaving a rooster tail of snow. The superintendent turns his back to the prop wash. Then he picks up the jerry can and plods back toward his lonely coffee. I feel a mix of regret at our rudeness and elation at seeing just a little fingernail of liquid in the two glass tubes. Elation, I confess, wins out.

Again our course is a straight line to Circle. We pass over the first bluff, and Gary discovers the carburetor-heating cable has frozen. He works it loose with a vigorous tug, and we alternately climb and deice the carburetor. Approaching a ridge known as Snowy Peak, we scrape the bottom of the clouds and I stare intently at what seems an awfully tiny slit of open sky ahead. Gary glances at the wings. Immediately, he throws the plane into a banked dive. Once again, we descend pell-mell down a side canyon toward the Yukon. And once again I feel the brisk throb of my own agitated heart.

"Icing up," explains Gary.

Even a small coating of ice would add enough weight to bring down the Cub, so Gary tells me that we'll try going lower, where it is colder and may not be moist enough to ice the wings. I dwell on those words "may not." Down here, we'll have to follow the course of the Yukon rather than aim directly toward our destination. Gary is again quiet as he winds down the empty river.

Just before Circle, the terrain changes dramatically. The river bluffs fall away. The hills recede. Ahead of us should be the vast panorama of the Yukon Flats, except it appears that the clouds drop right down to the ground. I feel vertigo as we fly into the grayness.

"Not good," says Gary. He is leaning forward, trying to see.

Stupidly, helplessly, I speak into the intercom: Listen, Gary, I got us into this fix. But I don't want you to take any more risks. You do what you think is right, and I'll be grateful that you tried this hard.

This is my belated offer for him to turn back, even though I doubt if he will. And he doesn't. In fact, I realize, he cannot. Daylight is slipping away. Within a half hour, the people of Circle will be turning on their house lights. My little speech is the quivering of a man who, at the moment, wishes very much that he was in Los Angeles, calmly spading fertilizer into his vegetable garden.

Just then, the engine sputters, coughs, and sounds like it's about to die. I can feel the airplane sag. Gary looks up over his right shoulder at the gas gauge and simultaneously switches to the left-wing tank.

The glass tube on the right is empty. The engine hesitates a fraction of a second and springs back to its workmanlike buzzing. There's still a bubble of liquid in the left gauge. I feel the welcome press of acceleration and the prop digs back into the air. Elapsed time: four seconds.

Outside, we travel through an eerie sky. It's not that I cannot see in the gauzy fog. But I cannot see much. There is a vague sense of motion. The spruce forests move below us, shadowy, like the surface of the moon. Our progress is as much felt as seen. For all I can tell, our direction is purely random.

The law, Gary says, requires one mile visibility to land under VFR, visual flight rules. If asked to testify, I will swear that we had exactly that as Gary throttles back and we clear the trees leading into the large landing strip. I will add, however, that I'm damn glad Gary knows this country blindfolded, as they say. He taxis to the gas pump. My grip is weak as I climb out of the airplane, but I grab Gary in as manly a bear hug as I can and stammer my gratitude along with my apologies. He grins back, starting to unfold the wing covers and put the Super Cub to bed. But I cannot quite tell about his expression. He's either damn proud of himself or he's trying to think of some reason not to strangle me.

My old friend Joe May materializes with a pickup. He is expecting to retrieve the two dropped dogs. He does not seem entirely pleased to find me instead. No, he says, he has not seen Liisa. This is the tenth day of the Yukon Quest. Someone tells me it is 25 below, but I have stopped checking. Too much bother to sort through my backpack for the thermometer. I have been feeling cold most of the day, ever since I put on those damn bunny boots that I should not have left on the frozen floor of the cabin.

Circle happens to be a city in the same way that Gary Nance is an international airline. Since the Gold Rush boom days, Circle is down by twenty-seven saloons—from twenty-eight to one. A roadhouse with four rooms to let, a gas station, schoolhouse, and tiny general store round out the city center. A few dozen log cabins make up the suburbs. This dinky outpost hugs a braided side channel of the Yukon, 252 trail miles from the finish line in Fairbanks. From here, Quest teams wind up the torturous switchbacks of Birch Creek, feared for its glaciers and overflow, and then climb a pair of windblown summits. One of them is the most spectacular and difficult mountain pass of the race, Eagle Summit. The trail then undulates through hills, canyons, and forests before reaching the meandering Chena River for the final dash under the banner that marks the finish line.

For many of the Alaskan competitors, these are home trails, which is both good and bad. Familiar turf can be risky because the dogs begin to think they are heading home. And when the Quest trail crosses a turnoff to their kennels, they have been known to stop dead and refuse to proceed. There have been many frustrating, tearful, yelling-and-screaming, begging hours spent in such standoffs between dog and musher. However, on the upside, a familiar trail takes the pressure off the mushers to concentrate on finding their way—and at this point, fatigue makes rational thought painful. For out-of-town mushers unfamiliar with the local topography, the opposite is the case: their dogs are not going to be distracted by the memory of their home yards, but the interlaced pattern of local trails magnifies the chances of making a wrong turn and getting lost.

Almost everyone connected with the race is bone weary—exhausted more completely than many people will ever know. Gary and Joe May and I adjourn to Circle's one functioning café and order burgers and beer. The cook asks three times if we want cheese, but the question is not registering. We're like three men bobbing in the water. Sometimes our heads are above the surface and we talk like normal people. Then we sink down below, where the sounds are muffled glurbs and everything moves with strange slowness. In my lucid moments, I can see the eyes of my companions drifting in and out of focus. I'm surprised to find food in my mouth. Then I remember I'm supposed to be eating. I've burned through all my reserves of adrenaline. I feel terribly empty and used up.

Right now, Circle is quiet. The mushers leading the Yukon Quest raced by long ago. Andre Nadeau passed Bruce Lee at the park service cabin where Gary and I refueled. Andre took a two-hour lead as Bruce rested his dogs. The trail was rough and tiring, zigzagging across the

Yukon thirteen times to skirt ice jams. Andre was the first to arrive in
Circle, but Lee had made up all but fifteen minutes of the head start.
Andre rested nearly seven hours here before departing. Bruce stayed
for almost a hour more.

Race observers express surprise that the French Canadian has managed to regain the lead. To some, this confirms the staying power of his
Siberian huskies. Andre speaks of his rival, saying only, "His dogs are
faster, but they have to stop longer." Some put the odds at even for an
upset.

Bruce knows better. Ever since Dawson, he has been able to catch,
and pass, Andre almost at will. He prefers to leave the Canadian out
front, where he can watch him and where Andre must break trail. Bruce
is hanging back comfortably, clinging to his rest-and-run schedule. He
feels he has the timing down pat and can calculate just how much lead
to give Andre and how long it will take to reel him back in. Bruce
decides to drop his weakest dog here in Circle. He is now down to a
team of ten.

Ahead, Eagle Summit gives him pause. The mountain is scarily
steep. His young lead dogs have brought him this far without a problem, but they are wholly untested against the kind of storm fury that
can swirl up on the high ground. Again he regrets having to leave
behind rock-solid old Miles. Nothing to do but try. He reassures himself that only a mishap on the trail, a stall on the mountain, or a sudden
surge by Rick Mackey or John Schandelmeier will spoil his plans for
victory.

Mackey, however, is not gaining. He comes into Circle next, arriving
this morning just after midnight, followed by Schandelmeier two minutes later. They are more than fifteen hours behind the leaders. Paddy
Santucci makes his way to the Circle City checkpoint forty-five minutes
later. The temperature was recorded at 32 below, the coldest of the race
so far. All five left here before sunup. Dave Dalton says the early-
morning cold farther back on the trail dropped to 45 below with ice fog
hugging the ground.

Now, at dusk, the first thirteen mushers have all passed through
Circle en route to the hard-bitten mining town of Central, the next

checkpoint. Meanwhile, Aliy Zirkle is just now arriving at Biederman's cabin, eighty miles back. And Rusty Hagan and his party pack are a full day behind her.

Hours pass for me in Circle, and Liisa doesn't arrive. The waitress at the café and the Quest's local ham radio operator both think the road up from Fairbanks might be passable. Probably, but no one has actually driven up since midday. Surely it's storming up on the pass. And down here an ice fog is beginning to form again, a sign of the coldest weather. I ask the ham operator to call his colleague located a hundred miles down the road to see if they know about a woman in a rental car. In reply, the man says he'll keep watch for her. I'm back to drinking coffee with a sour stomach, my head adrift like a half-inflated balloon.

16

Adventure most unto itself
The Soul condemned to be—
Attended by a single Hound
Its own identity.

—Emily Dickinson

In many places, the rifle shots of late autumn sound the opening of hunting season. In the Far North, the same *crack! bang!* heralds the onslaught of cold: birch trees begin to freeze and explode. At about 20 below, moisture in the thin sheath of tissue beneath the insulating tree bark freezes and swells. Sometimes, when a birch has held on to too much autumn moisture or the tree has been damaged, the swelling cannot be contained and the brittle bark bursts with a sudden report of a gunshot ringing through the forest. At 30 below, other trees, here and there, swell and explode. Sometimes another fusillade occurs at about 40 below. After that, everything that can freeze already has and the only sounds of winter are the baying of the wolves and the whirls of the wind.

Cold is both absolute and relative. Visitors from Outside are sometimes surprised to see Yukoners and Alaskans wearing just nylon windbreakers at 10 above. But when the temperature reaches 25 below, a bare hand on a metal doorknob leaves behind flesh no matter whether you're from Circle, Alaska, or Circle Drive, Miami, Florida.

That's the thing that one must get accustomed to at high latitudes: the range of cold. After that, you can begin to understand that, along with the danger, it can be splendorous.

In temperate regions, everyone instinctively grasps the difference between 80 degrees and 100. Or between the chill of a 50-degree afternoon and the pleasantness of one at 70 degrees. But when the thermometer drops deep into the minus range, newcomers are left with only a stammering vocabulary, unable to say much more than it's cold, or really cold, or really, really cold. The words are spoken in awe and fear. Jack London left us that legacy. The cold is awful. It is a foe to be contested.

By contrast, residents of the Far North, particularly those who live in the bush or otherwise spend long hours outdoors, often regard the cold as wonderful. Yes, they have developed a keen understanding of the thermometer. Just a brief taste of winter provides a convincing lesson that one's comfort and sometimes one's life depend on the ability to manage the cold. Even the most remote, backward cabin will have a thermometer nailed outside somewhere so that it can be read through the window from inside. No greeting, whether between friends or strangers, is complete without a discussion of the cold. But on the other hand, winter is the time of greatest outdoor mobility here—the lakes and rivers and bogs have frozen over and the dog teams and snowmachines have free range. The cold brings with it a delicate, astonishing beauty that is so rarely appreciated by Outsiders as to give locals the feeling of knowing things beyond what other people can even imagine. The climate that Jack London regarded as uniformly forbidding is greeted by today's Yukoners and Alaskans as adventurous. To journey out in winter requires finesse and proficiency, but one is rewarded with the satisfaction of entering a universe that can only be described as pristine.

My first summer here, I was startled to read an essay in the Denali National Park tourist newsletter by a woman named Kathy Berry. She was a janitor at the park, a dog musher, and journalist. Her story told of the subtle altering of one's senses at 40 below. At this temperature, you have no nose for smell, because everything is frozen and odorless. But

your other senses become more acute. The air holds virtually no moisture at this temperature, so your vision is noticeably clearer; everything
is rendered in ultrasharp contours. The slanting sunlight of the Far
North hits things at unfamiliar angles, so even the layer of snow on a
spruce bough appears exotic and captivating. Except for the occasional
sounds of airplanes or bursting trees, the snow muffles almost all noise,
and your ears grow acute. The snow is so crystalline and dry that it
does not squeak as you step. It makes no more sound underfoot than
beach sand. Soon you are hearing only the blood gurgle inside your
body. And this sound makes you feel so very much alive. Kathy
described the wonderland of the subarctic winter as a mind-arresting
exercise in the extremes of scale. Her eye was drawn to the glinting play
of sunlight on the snow covering a twig at her feet, a sparkling dance of
refracted colors that might be likened to a string of diamonds. Then she
gazed at the galactic uprise of mountains all around her, spindrift blowing off their peaks and mysterious translucent blue glaciers hanging on
their shoulders. This was a portrait of the other side of 40 below, when
it is tranquil and inviting. I had never read anything like it.

Later I met Kathy and we became friends. She is petite and soft-
skinned, and every time I see her I find myself wondering if the bristly-
jawed gold miners of the Klondike didn't secretly wander out on clear
afternoons to find themselves likewise dumbstruck by the serene natural wonders surrounding them, but Jack London forgot to tell us.

The cold puts a grip on some people's hearts and never lets go.
Earlier this winter at Joe May's cabin in Trapper Creek, Alaska, I met
explorer Norman Vaughan. Colonel Vaughan mushed dogs with
Robert Byrd during his famed 1928 expedition to Antarctica. He
mushed dogs for a search-and-rescue team in World War II. He has run
the Iditarod thirteen times. In 1994, sixty-six years after the Byrd expedition, he returned to Antarctica and climbed the 10,302-foot peak that
Byrd named in his honor, Mount Vaughan. Last year, he rode a snowmachine from Nenana, in the Interior of Alaska, to the coastal town of
Nome to commemorate the 1925 relay of diphtheria serum that saved
the city. Tonight at 10:30, after dinner, with the temperature about 10
below, Vaughan and his wife, Carolyn, will drive fifteen miles to a trail-

head. They will unload two snowmachines and a pickup full of provisions and bounce down a trail for another ten miles to a remote cabin that the colonel likes to call his retreat. They will build a fire, and by morning they will have raised the inside temperature to above freezing.

Vaughan is now ninety-two. He uses a cane, to which is affixed a spike for the ice.

"Why do I spend so much time in the cold?" he said. "I guess I don't like to be hot."

Vaughan's motto is eloquent: *Dream big and dare to fail.*

Any appreciation of the Far North winter requires the proper gear. Prior to the Quest, I sought out an expert on the subject, Dick Flaharty, a onetime Alaska mountaineer who founded Apocalypse Design, the tiny Fairbanks company that manufactures the cold-weather parkas that are so popular here. Apocalypse—named after an unclimbed six-thousand-foot granite wall in the Alaska Range—made the Fulda parkas that most of the Quest mushers wear, as well as my own parka. It also happens to be the company where Liisa Penrose is general manager. Cold-weather gear was my introduction to her. Apocalypse clothing is deceptively plain—none of the pit-zip, triple-laminated, space-age gimmicks found on most of today's high-priced outerwear. Dick chooses ordinary high-grade nylon for his shells and fills them with spun polyester insulation that has been in use, and proven, for more than twenty years. He makes nothing from down feathers.

"Down is death," he says, emphatically. "Imagine taking all your gear and throwing it in the river, pulling it out, and then making camp. If it won't work under those conditions, leave it home."

An eccentric who has decided, contrary to the polite advice of his employees, to wear his parka for a sixth winter without washing it—just to see how long it will last dirty—Dick is one of those people who comes alive in winter. That's when he heads outdoors. I asked him to walk me down the thermometer.

From about 10 degrees above to zero, he begins, that's just about T-shirt weather. You can treat it casually. You've got plenty of room to make mistakes. You're not going to die. Deep water and overflow are not problems, just inconveniences. Life is easy except that you can overheat if you have to work very hard. Dogs with dark coats are particularly vulnerable to overheating.

From zero to 10 below is the optimum for being outdoors in winter. "Life is good; it's my favorite," Dick says.

At 20 below you have to start paying attention. You don't have to be rigidly focused, but you do need to be mindful. There is still room for a mistake. You might get cold, but you can get warm again. It's not a critical temperature. At 30 below, the stakes get higher. At 40 below to 50 below, conditions are critical. You cannot let your attention drift. If mistakes start happening, things can go downhill fast. At these temperatures it takes an hour to build a fire and get any warmth from it. Propane and white gas will not vaporize unless warmed. A cup of hot coffee tossed into the air will hiss and atomize into a frozen cloud before reaching the ground. "If you're expecting your gear to take care of you, you're in trouble."

At 60 below, there's no screwing around, no margin whatsoever for error. If you were trying to refuel your airplane and splashed gasoline on your skin, you'd freeze the flesh. Any mistake will hurt you.

Everywhere I go I'm confronted with stories about cold-weather blunders that it would never have occurred to me to avoid. Several years ago, a Quest musher had to scratch and seek emergency medical treatment after eating M&Ms that he kept in a pocket in his sled bag. Without thinking, he gulped a mouthful, hoping to gain a burst of energy. Instead, he seriously frostbit his throat. I was saved from a similar fate a few months back when Joe May stopped me from taking a first gulp of rum that had been sitting outside all day. I remember thinking how oddly thick the rum appeared as it poured into the thermos cup. But I still added a single ice cube because . . . well, because that's how I always drink good rum. And because I'm an idiot.

Now, at least, I know better. I know that an ice chest serves half the year as a warmer, keeping important things, like beer, from freezing right away. I know that Gary Nance spends more money on heating lettuce than cooling it in his wholesale food business. I know that after a few years here, the body adjusts to the seasonal extremes and auto-matically begins to add weight just as the leaves turn, ruining all the hopes of preholiday dieters. Residents say there is nothing you can do about it short of starving yourself. I have also learned, belatedly, that when your bunny boots freeze because you left them on the cold floor of a cabin, you do not expect the warmth of your feet to heat them up. If you can, you bring a pan of water to near boiling. You pour the water into your frozen boots for a minute, then drain them and let them dry for a few seconds. Your feet will be warm all day and no wetter than from your own perspiration.

After a while, you accept the fact that meeting strangers usually requires two introductions. You shake hands and exchange pleasantries outside, but you have to be introduced all over again when you meet indoors, where people look seventy-five pounds thinner and don't have heads sprouting beaver fur. Both men and women grow wary of romantic attractions that begin outdoors. Before long, these can lead the new couple indoors to seek a fireplace. Off comes the parka and the fleece and the puffy insulated bibs. "Let's say, there's been quite a num-ber of disappointments at that point," an old sourdough explained.

Then, no matter how good your gear is, there's the matter of how much of it you are willing to leave behind. Dog mushers judge one another by how little they require. You may come to the starting line with the tiniest sled in the race, with the brake stripped off as excess weight and the sled bag limp as if there's nothing inside. Still, an old-timer may eyeball it and ask, "So, what ya got in there?"

Oh, just a spare pair of socks.

"Well, you'd better get rid of that shit if you're going to be competi-tive."

As a race judge, Joe May traveled the 1,023 miles of the Quest with a sleeping bag and a vinyl ditty the size of a sack of potato chips. My outfit weighed fifty pounds at the start of the race and forty at the end. I used up some batteries, but the rest of it I must have lost along the way. In the end, I didn't miss a thing. I'll bet I could now get my duffel down to thirty-five pounds.

Traveling light requires certain special techniques, however, and occasional daring. Even at 20 below and 30 below, mushers sometimes face large, deep pools of overflow with no way around them, such as in a canyon with narrow cliffs. The strategy for proceeding can involve stripping naked, putting all your clothes in a garbage bag, and hauling ass right through it. Just make sure you remembered to put dry kindling and matches in the bag for when you reach the other side.

If the cold is a matter of the right gear and attitude, another challenge in long-distance dog mushing cannot be overcome by equipment or training.

In 1996, musher Bill Stewart was forty miles from the finish line and running smoothly in third place. He was, of course, exhausted. But everyone was. He'd been depleted for days. With a secure grip on the handlebars and a forgiving trail, mushers sometimes allow themselves to snooze. They talk about it in terms of distance, not time, as in, "I think I got about five miles' sleep." But who knows what happened to Stewart that time? He says he met the old veteran Frank Turner on the trail, and Frank was not happy. Frank claimed this was his private trail and said Stewart was encroaching. "Besides, you're going the wrong way," Frank told him.

Bewildered, Stewart turned his team around and mushed off the way he'd come. A while later, he met another dog team head-on. "Hey, you're going the wrong way," the driver told Stewart. Damn, this is a confusing trail, he thought. Again he dismounted, grabbed his lead dogs, and turned around. By now Stewart knew he was tired, probably too tired to continue. He dwelled on that thought, and then came upon an old friend standing by the trail. Sensing that Stewart was about to collapse, the friend pointed him to a guest lodge located nearby in a grove of trees.

Thank God, said Stewart. Without regard to his place in the race but obsessed with the idea of a warm bed with sheets, Stewart trod to the lodge and checked in to the best room in the house. Musher Mark May, who was running behind Stewart, found the man later, sprawled unconscious in the snow. May discovered him only because Stewart's abandoned dog team was sitting in the trail. May followed the boot tracks and found Stewart lying on his back, snoring at 25 below in the cozy warm bed of his dreams with a pillow of drift snow. Stewart had hallucinated the lodge. He had not really seen Frank Turner. His friend was five hundred miles away, at home. It was all a delirium.

Perpetual motion, relentless cold, and long hours of darkness are nothing compared to the agonies of going without sleep. Mushers suffer the most, but race officials and veterinarians share the hollow-eyed look of lepers.

"People asked me before the race what I dreaded. I couldn't think of anything," says John Schandelmeier. "Now I remember. It's being tired like this. . . ."

A musher looks at his watch. He sees the big hand. Then he looks for the little hand. But he has forgotten what the big hand said. With helpless anguish on his face, he holds his watch before a stranger and asks, "What's the time?"

Later, when they have rested, mushers will talk about their hallucinations and how they cope. Suppose, for instance, you are a guy and you're moving down the trail and a naked woman walks out from behind a tree and asks you for a ride?

Well, is she good-looking?

She's a peach. So do you let her climb on the sled?

Hmmm. Sure would be nice to have some company. And she's naked, you say?

Stark naked. So you let her on?

Hell no, I don't need that kind of extra weight.

Ha. Ha.

One musher told me about watching the northern lights and then realizing he was seeing the reflection of a train's headlamp in the clouds. Then he could hear the engine and the ground started shaking, and he realized he was not on the trail but had wandered onto a railroad right-of-way. Suddenly the train came around a corner and . . . and it passed right through him, its whistle screaming. I'll have to be more careful next time, the musher told himself.

In his study for the U.S. Army, the Mayo Clinic's Peter J. Hauri found that the first stage of sleep deprivation, which prompts the body to grab a sequence of microsleeps, is followed by worse. After several days, brain waves of sleep and brain waves of wakefulness are generated simultaneously. At this stage, it is impossible to tell whether people are awake or asleep even as they walk and talk.

"The result is a twilight state in which people feel as if they are in a fog but not really there," Hauri writes. "There have only been a few clear-cut hallucinations and psychotic states documented when three- to five-day sleep deprivation experiments were carried out in a laboratory. However, if one adds stress to the equation, then psychotic states—delusions, hallucinations, illogical thinking, etc.—become quite frequent."

One of the treasures of my first trip down the Quest trail was this mysterious entry in my notebook:

Breezy and 25 below. Jerry Louden lumbers through fifty yards of shin-deep snow. His boots are like lead.

"You want me?" he asks.

No.

"Oh. Okay."

My gloved hands are clumsy and pencil leads become brittle in the cold. I must have broken one because the next few pages are filled with scratch marks. Louden is weary. Me too. I wonder what I am missing on these blank pages. What did we talk about?

Louden is so incredibly shy that his overture is itself a rarity. "Ain't so good at expressing myself," he told me when we first met. But I have gone out of my way to cultivate him. I like the way he treats his dogs. He overpowers them with kindness.

I do vaguely remember his telling me a story. He was riding the sled, the dogs were loping easily through a birch forest, and his mind was wandering. He couldn't remember the details. Suddenly the team burst into a full run. He scanned into the blackness ahead with his headlamp and realized his dogs were chasing something. When the team reached a clearing, the northern lights illuminated the shadowy low-slung, head-down figure of a wolverine galloping ahead. Wonderful, thought Louden. The dogs are running like the wind and this beautiful, shadowy animal ahead urges them on. What a scene. Then a realization slowly takes root. If the wolverine tires before the dogs do, it will stop and fight. And at least some of his dogs will be mauled. Horrible, awful, something must be done. But what? Well, he could try to stop the sled. Yes, that's it. Stop. Let the wolverine go. Rest the dogs. Now, let's see, we need to stop. I need to move my foot to the snowmachine track that drags between the runners, the drag brake. That will slow the team. Yes, move the foot down there. That's it. We're slowing now. The dogs are alive. Are we still on the trail? Seems so. The wolverine is gone. Are you sure it was a wolverine? Wonder what time it is? Why aren't we going? Oh yes, now I need to lift my foot off the brake. Okay, I can do that. Now we're moving again. Is everyone all right up front? Is my headlamp dimming? Are the batteries going? Where did I put spares? Have to warm them up. I should reach inside my parka to see if I put them there. Yes, move my hand. Okay, but I cannot feel any-thing. I have to take off this mitt. Just don't drop it. Don't worry, it's tied on. Okay. Yes, here are batteries. Now why did I want them . . . ?

17

Well, do we live or do we die? That won't be known until the very last moment.

—A mountaineer on Kanchenjunga

When aligned on the floor, the government topographical maps covering the route of the Yukon Quest stretch for fifteen feet— too big, even, for some mushers' cabins. If you mark the trail in pink highlighter, it follows a curving, hiccuping, zigzag path, as if it had been scrawled by someone recovering from a hangover—except for one place. Covering a distance of about eleven inches on the map after Circle, Alaska, it looks as if the hangover victim had a seizure. According to the scale of the map, the climb up Birch Creek is about twenty-eight miles. But straighten out the fluttering helix of oxbows, and the mileage might be twice that.

On the ground, the coils of tiny Birch Creek are so tight that dog teams double back on themselves and mushers can look into the eyes of their lead dogs. For hours they snake back and forth, traveling gently uphill, following the course of the old gold mining stream through a quiet, willowy valley. It is one of the most intimate places on the long trail, a cozy contrast to the raw, wide-open Yukon.

Having rested his team and allowed Andre Nadeau a substantial head start, Bruce Lee summons his ten dogs to their feet and aims them in a western trajectory away from the village of Circle, through an overgrown and frozen marsh. After three bumpy miles, the dogs scamper down a bank and onto Birch Creek, which is only about twenty-five feet wide. This is the northernmost point of the Yukon Quest—one hundred miles farther north than Nome and the Iditarod finish line, and just forty-eight miles below the Arctic Circle. Here Lee's team makes a ninety-degree turn to the left—Haw!—and sets sight to the south, toward the direction of the sun. Except there is no sun today, just the gloomy, dull, closed-in feel of overcast. It is 4:00 P.M., but not yet growing dark. Bruce can tell that the days are getting longer now. Rather than seven hours of light, there are nine. Today the sun will remain above the horizon eight minutes longer than yesterday. The sun will not set until 5:30 P.M. But there is no discernible gain in warmth— that will not occur for a month or more. Down here on the creek bed, the temperature is 15 below, and cloudlets of ice fog hang in the willow thickets like brush strokes.

Bruce thinks to himself how, after the big river, Birch Creek feels strangely snug and sheltered, but at the same time vaguely Moorish and haunted. He applies himself to muscling the sled around bends that are so tightly wound, his team is never stretched out straight. He concentrates on the surface of the river, looking for signs of overflow— disruptions in the patterns of snow covering the ice that may indicate a live spring underneath. Most of this work must be left to the lead dogs, however, because they are already around the next corner when Bruce and the sled come from behind the last one.

At times like this, a man's mind grabs onto thoughts and then loses them as quickly as if they were tendrils of fog. Bruce momentarily wonders if he is being overconfident. His spirits sag. Mushing is a moody undertaking. The next checkpoint, at Central, lies seventy-five miles away—maybe more, considering the twisting route of Birch Creek. Bruce will have to rest his dogs once. They could probably make the trip with only a couple of quick stops for snacks. But Bruce has not trained them for seventy-five nonstop miles and resolves not to try. Andre, on the other hand, just might plod along without a long rest. That strategy, plus his two-hour head start, might give him an edge for the next stage. Hell, it might give him an edge in the race. Bruce's confidence sags. He has to cue off Andre with his every decision, but what if the stout little French Canadian starts to gain strength? Bruce cannot ask much more of his dogs. Every one of them has been trained for the Quest since the first day he put them in harness as puppies. But he's trained them for fifty-mile sprints with plenty of rest. Now this maniac keeps going like the Energizer bunny on less rest than anyone thought possible. You know, Bruce decides, Andre just might win this—and if he does, the key will be right here on this seventy-five-mile stretch.

This worry slips from his mind as easily as it arose, and Bruce again concentrates on the trail. All the dogs are looking good. Real good. They are running smart, even without the seasoned leadership of old Miles. But, my, how he misses that dog. The big climb over Eagle Summit begins just after the next checkpoint. That's when a dog like Miles, a natural-born, one-in-ten-thousand kind of leader, could make a difference. When his head is right, Miles can shoulder up the glaze ice, digging in his nails for traction, and the rest of the team will follow along, never realizing that what they're doing is impossible. A dog like Miles can make you cry because he is so undaunting. But, look, these guys are doing okay without him. Cross your fingers.

Bruce lets his mind drift to the idea of a cup of coffee. Wouldn't that taste great? Hot and rich. But not now. For the race, Bruce has sworn off coffee. He loves it, but caffeine alters body chemistry. It dilates the blood vessels and makes him more susceptible to cold. It may ruin his ability to fall asleep when he should and, more important, to awake exactly when he is supposed to. No rolling over in the sleeping bag for another five minutes that accidentally lapses into two hours. No, if he's asking this much of his dogs, Bruce will give up coffee. But, damn, wouldn't it be great to reach down and pull out a thermos and have a cup? Nothing on earth like coffee.

One thing that does not cross Bruce's mind is comfort. His red-and-black parka is dusted with snow; his ruff glistens with hoarfrost. But inside, he's toasty, downright warm, in fact, from exertion. The ice caked on his mustache, the snotcicles hanging from his nose, the frozen rind of moisture on his neck gaiter all serve as insulation. A stranger taking a first look at him might think he's a man who is just about to freeze to death. But Bruce, burrowed deep in his own mobile environment, couldn't be more cushy comfortable. The tongues of his dogs hang down and swing rhythmically with their loping strides. They are nice and warm, too. To himself, Bruce thinks, Wouldn't it be wonderful to know what goes on in their minds?

Suddenly, there is movement ahead. Through the willows and the winding path of the creek, Bruce cannot tell what, really. He watches intently. Then . . . no, it couldn't be. Yes, sure enough. It's Andre Nadeau, barely crawling along. Bruce has been on the trail only a little more than an hour, and already he has made up the two-hour difference. He's shocked at how slow Andre is traveling. Once again, Bruce's mood takes a bounce. For an instant, he almost feels bad for his rival. All along, everyone said that those Siberians could not keep their pace with so little rest.

Andre stops, and the two mushers mumble greetings in languages that neither fully understands. Andre uses the time to pass out chunks of frozen fish for dog snacks and then lumbers on. Bruce snacks his dogs and rests a little longer. He did not expect to see Nadeau for hours, if at all. He wonders to himself whether Andre is deliberately slowing down to fake him out. Finally, Bruce moves out. In a half hour, he catches Andre a second time and passes him without hesitation. Once again, Lee's tracks are first down the Yukon Quest trail. He's got a notebook in his pocket with a plan written out in pencil. The plan does not necessarily call for him to be in front, but it tells him that if he keep moving, nobody will catch him again. If only he'll be lucky and have good weather for the trip over Eagle Summit, or at least not god-awful weather. If only his young dogs will lead when the going gets rough.

At 4:17 in the morning, with the temperature 20 below, Bruce Lee mushes into the checkpoint at Central, Alaska, and beds down his team.

If there was ever a one-man town in the Far North, Central is it. The

one man in this roadside burg is Jim Crabb, a bearlike, pot-bellied, profane old sourdough who runs Crabb's Corner, a restaurant, gas station,
and ten-room roadhouse right at the intersection of two gravel roads,
one leading to Circle and the other to the old gingerbread resort known
as Circle Hot Springs. A few summer tourists and a colony of suspicious gold miners keep Central from disappearing into oblivion.
Crabby, as he's known, endures the tourists as long as they pay with
cash and don't say anything to piss him off. But his heart is with the
gold miners. A sign in the restaurant proclaims his right to refuse service to anybody working for the federal government. He is at least half
theatrics, maybe two-thirds. But I suspect if you pushed him, he could
produce a short-snouted pistol from underneath the cash register. A
film crew from Japan passed through Central a while back, and Crabb
came roaring out, the screen door banging, and ran them off because
you don't go sticking cameras in people's faces here.

Crabb supervises the checkpoint in Central. His roadhouse serves as
race headquarters and as the collection point for the local characters, a
whiskery clannish group with a penchant for plaid wool shirts, extra-
wide suspenders, and weather-beaten fur hats. Like most miners, they
collectively curl their tobacco-stained lips and glare at all strangers as
if they might be claim-jumpers or, worse, water-quality inspectors from
the Environmental Protection Agency.

"When the Quest gets to us, it's a sign that the cold weather is pretty near over," says Crabb. "People here really look forward to it. It gets
them looking in a new direction. It breaks them out of their cabin fever,
they start up their snowmachines and begin moving around again. It's
a boost in the butt for people in the bush."

Thus, almost every stranger who passes through the blue haze of
cigarette smoke inside Crabb's Corner can regard the silent, suspicious
greeting they receive today with a measure relief. Luckily, they didn't
come last month, before the locals worked themselves into a party
mood.

An hour and ten minutes behind Bruce Lee, Andre Nadeau arrives
in Central. He has lost more than three hours to his rival over seventy-
five. Still to go: 177 miles.

, , ,

Lee holes up for seven hours. Weather reports are ominous. Dog handlers driving the road over the 3,750-foot Eagle Summit say they were battered by winds and blowing snow with almost zero visibility. Eagle, the second-highest climb on the trail, is the only one that parallels an all-season road. By "road" here I mean a two-rutted pathway through the blown snow where you are as likely to see a moose as another car. On a good day, you can stop at the summit and watch the teams struggle, slip, and claw their way up a wind-scoured 30-degree headwall that leads to the bald top of the summit. When the sky is clear, the sight in all directions brings a longing to soar in the restless air like a long-winged bird over hills and mountains that end only because the horizon clips off the view. All of it, for the tens of thousands of acres, appears clean and white and untouched except by the hands of God.

But winter on Eagle Summit is seldom so benevolent. These hills are a convergence zone. To the north lies the valley of the Yukon Flats, to the south the Interior plains of Fairbanks. Only when these two vast land masses are in absolute equilibrium is there peace on the summit. The slightest variation in temperature or pressure sends torrents of wind spilling over the ridge in one direction or another as nature strives to balance its two preserves. At the very top, the wind is compressed into a screaming sheet that can scour away snow and carry away small rocks in a blinding fury. Mushers have been knocked right off their feet.

At 11:30 A.M., under gray skies, Bruce is the first to depart Central, driving his team across the roadway and up the gentle rise of Crooked Creek. After thirteen easy miles, the trail turns left and veers up a side canyon and quickly begins to steepen. The mountain in front of him is lost in the low-hanging clouds, but Bruce can sense its looming presence. The clouds are dense and blotchy on their underside and he is about to head into them. The breeze is growing stronger in his face, but Bruce tells himself that it does not signify much. It might not be much worse up higher. Or it could be plenty worse. He's got two-year-old Hawk and three-year-old Clovis in the lead. Hawk is a dark-coated dog

with the hanging ears of a Labrador retriever. Lee calls him the Michael
Jordan of the team for his natural agility and heart. Clovis, whose silly
ears point sideways like stubby wings, was a surprise dog—a single
pup with a white mask and chest whelped from a female that Bruce
didn't even know was pregnant. He believes that Clovis is the offspring
of his dropped lead dog, Miles. Earlier in the year, Clovis picked up a
virus and was unable to run in any preliminary races. This is his first
competition.

From the 932-foot elevation at Circle, the Eagle Summit trail grows
progressively steeper, until Bruce Lee finds himself climbing into the
whirl of clouds. The lead dogs are not only ahead of him but noticeably
above him. With each foot gained in altitude, the wind intensifies.
Blowing snow stings his eyes. Even through the thick padding of his
hood, he can hear the roar and the gunfire rattle of his nylon clothing.
The team slows but does not falter. The visibility worsens and now
Bruce cannot see his leaders in the swirling merger of snowpack and
wind. He searches anxiously for a glimpse of a wooden stake that will
tell him that his dogs have not wandered off the trail, perhaps to the
edge of a cliff. Bruce is not conscious of time or of distance, but only of
the wind in his face. The dogs appear to be moving forward, but there
is no way to measure progress. The surface of the mountain is being
blown from underneath him. For all he can tell, the whole team is striding in place, getting nowhere. Then he feels the grade lessen, and the
line of dogs levels out. He has reached a tiny plateau, and the dogs
stop. He is at the bottom of the mountain's headwall—a sequence of
two unbearably steep pitches with a gentle slope in between. Here the
dogs must claw their way up glaze ice for several hundred feet. The
slick, exposed climbs are wind funnels, and Bruce can barely stand
against the force, even hunched down.

The dogs stop. He crawls down the gangline and tries to reassure the
team. When he finally gets back to the sled, he gives it a push and yells
out for the dogs to go. They refuse. He shouts louder. Nothing. He tries
to stay calm. These dogs have never been in a situation like this. Hell,
I've never faced anything like this, he reminds himself. But he cannot
allow his worry to show; he must not give the dogs any reason to lose

confidence in him. Mental stress is a contagion in dogs. He switches leaders and gives the okay call. They pull ahead ten feet and stop. He puts another pair into the lead. They won't budge. He is already breathing deeply. The dogs turn their heads away from the wind and lie down in the snow. Their survival instinct has switched on. Because no one is moving, they hunker low.

"If you let those dogs bed down, they'll never go," Bruce tells himself. "They will quit at the exact point they lose confidence in me."

Besides, this is no place to ride out the weather. Not with that flinty tough French Canadian behind him. Challenges like this determine races. Those who persevere will be drinking champagne straight from the bottle in Fairbanks. The others will be blaming their bad luck with weather.

Bruce digs his boots into the windblown crust for leverage and heaves on the sled. It skids forward. He pushes until he is about to run into his wheel dogs. Then he shoulders ahead on foot until he is at the front of the team. He grabs the necklines of the leaders and hoists them to their feet. He pulls with all his might and they acquiesce and stagger behind him. When the whole line is straight, he has moved about eight feet. He walks back to the sled and pushes it ahead again. Then he lumbers forward and pulls his dogs. After several relays, the trail becomes so steep he cannot push the loaded sled any higher. So he unsnaps the buckles and empties it, kicking platforms in the ice so that everything will not tumble down the slope. Then he goes back to work: eight feet ahead with the sled; eight feet with the dogs; back to the sled. With paralyzing slowness, he drags his team up the slope in a blinding gale. After a while, he realizes he can no longer see the food and gear he unpacked, so he fixes a snowhook to the sled and slides back down the icy path. He begins shuttling dog food, cooker, sleeping bag, ax, snowshoes, spare clothes—all of it—back up the hill. He carries each load forty yards and returns for another, sometimes carrying a load in one arm while he uses the other to scratch his way forward on the ice. In some places there is no ice. The wind is so fierce here that it has scoured everything right down to the frozen stubble of summer grass. At least these bare areas give him a place to kick out a foothold.

Perhaps halfway up, dizzy with exhaustion, Bruce begins to think about the stories of mushers who gave up, turned back, and lost. "Well, I want to win," Bruce says to himself. "And I'm going to get over this mountain even if I have to carry everyone and everything up it myself."

After a while, Bruce tells himself that he must be near the top of the first pitch and things will get easier. No use, then, even thinking about going back. It is so steep now that he must push his sled forward and then tip it sideways and wriggle it into the snow to keep it from sliding back. After each round, his dogs wait patiently for him to crawl forward and lead them the next eight feet. Then they stand in place while he glissades down on his backside to right the sled and push again.

Almost simultaneously, two things occur. He feels the ground level out, signaling the top of the first grade, and the weather lifts; he is standing in bright sunshine—a hole in the towering clouds. The wind still howls, but most of the snow has already been blown off, so he can see the stakes ahead, marking the route to the second agonizing pitch toward the summit. He makes one more series of shuttles to bring his food and equipment up from down low, then repacks the sled. His lead dogs seem thoroughly demoralized. They have never been mushing like *this*. But Bruce tries. He takes hold of the sled and shouts, Okay, let's go! The team bolts forward, but not toward the markers. The dogs veer off and head downslope. There are drop-offs and cliffs all over this mountain, and he slams the snowhook into the icy surface to hang on to the gains he has made.

Struggling to keep his head, Bruce does not hesitate. He flings open the sled bag and unpacks it again. He'll carry it all, and drag the dogs, too. He tells himself it's not their fault. But he does not convince himself entirely. With the weather still holding and the dogs watching him with puzzled expressions, Bruce shuttles the frozen dog food, rattling stove, and loose equipment up the gentle slope toward the next climb. Not only is he short of breath but he realizes he's drenched in sweat. It would be poor bushmanship to soak his parka in this cold. Up this high, the temperature is probably about zero, but the wind makes it much colder. He's going to need that parka. He tells himself he is lucky he realized this before everything got even wetter. So he strips off his parka and the fleece layer underneath, which is sopping. Damn. The wind bites into his wet polypropylene underwear, but he decides to move faster, work harder, stay warm, and get his layers dried out.

At the moment, his decision seems logical. Before long, he will regret it.

He hurries back the fifty yards to the team, grabs another load, and huffs it to his cache. Then back to the team. Why won't they go? Why can't I get them to go? Bruce is panting, and he can feel the sweat start to freeze like hardening candle wax whenever he stops.

He looks once again at the team and sees Clovis with those goofy horizontal ears standing, looking back at him. There's something in those eyes, Bruce thinks. He unclips Clovis from his position in the middle of the team and moves him into the lead. He returns the other dog to Clovis's open spot on the gangline, and then taps the handlebar on the sled. Clovis shoulders forward, and turns into the wind. They're going for the trail. They're all loping along like it's no big deal. In just his double layer of underwear, Bruce lopes by his pile of food and equipment. He should stop and get his parka, he tells himself. But what if they quit again? No, this is too good. He'll ride with them as long as they'll pull and then he'll come back and get everything.

Clovis reaches the bottom of the steep grade, and Bruce holds his breath. The dog springs forward without hesitation. The whole team follows, pulling like hell, clawing and skidding and lunging. Bruce jumps off the sled and pushes. He's stretched out with his arms above him, pushing with all his might, his feet stumbling. He drags behind the sled, regains his balance and pushes again, fighting for traction. They are barely crawling now and the wind slams them in the face. But Clovis will not give up. The young dog with the silly airplane ears paws ahead a couple of inches and then throws his weight against the harness, and then paws forward again. The others do the same. There is no rhythm to their movements, just a drunken slow-motion, shoulder-forward lurching. Sometimes a powerful heave by several dogs will send a shiver down the gangline and yank another dog right off its feet, sending it slamming flat-faced into the ice. But they're all still getting up and throwing themselves forward.

Bruce is gasping, dizzy for breath. In all the sunlight and white glare, he begins to see spots of black. Waves of nausea rise in his stomach. He stops. Then Clovis stops. Everyone stops. Bruce cannot see the top of the rise, and guesses they are about two-thirds of the way up. He has to catch his breath. He is sweating again, but the instant he is motionless, the wind cuts through his underwear and he feels the heat being sucked away.

He is aware of the danger now. There is no time to rest. He has made a mistake. He's exposed. On his hands he is wearing only polypro glove liners, and his fingers are starting to feel thick. With just two long-sleeved underwear tops, he feels wet and naked in the mountain windstorm. I'm in trouble, he tells himself. We're in trouble. Get a grip.

He speaks to the dogs, "You gotta get us through this. We can't stop. I ran out of gas. But you can't. Okay, boys? Let's go."

Ten sets of ears have rotated back to hear his words. Then with Clovis making the first move, they scramble forward.

They top the summit. Bruce brings them to a halt, grateful and amazed. You never know about dogs. Clovis almost did not make the team. It was a choice between him and other dogs in the kennel. Clovis was the last picked to go.

There is no triumph at the crest of the great hill, however. The wind is so powerful, Bruce feels himself losing his balance. He realizes his nose is just a big knob of ice. He touches it, and it feels like grasping a piece of wood. His ears have no sensation. The wind is gaining strength and now he sees dusk coming. The temperature is falling again. The wind is maybe forty or fifty miles an hour, with the temperature down around 10 below. That would put the windchill at minus 70. As he reaches for the snowhook to hold his team, he realizes that his hands are numb.

After twenty-one years of living in the Alaska bush, after thousands of miles of mushing in all extremes of weather, after just completing this miserable climb up Eagle Summit, Bruce Lee is not prone to panic. But he feels it rising in him now, uncontrollable, the same panic you experience when a stranger closes in behind you on a darkened street and you see a knife in his hand. Bruce will give up his nose if he has to and his ears, but not the hands. Without hands, a man cannot take care of himself. That's the first rule of the cold. Break that one, and all the other rules of survival don't matter. Oh, man, how many stories has he heard about just this kind of thing—the one mistake that snowballs into disaster. He has never been this scared. He has never been so cold. He has never been as close to disaster.

His heart pounding, Bruce skid-slides back down the icy chute. He uses his elbows when he falls, banging them on the ice, trying not to injure his hands. He struggles to squeeze his fists, but his fingers are going. He tries not to think about it, but instead concentrates on getting back to his gear. Scrambling down the last hundred yards of the headwall and onto the gentle slope, he trots as fast as he can, the wind behind him and blowing him toward the pile of equipment. There is nothing wrong with Bruce's computerlike brain, and he calculates that he has five minutes, at the most, to get himself dressed in arctic gear and gain control of the situation. Otherwise, he tells himself, you're not going to win the Quest. You're not going to finish the Quest. You're going to start losing body parts.

Panting, he reaches his stash. He begins methodically to put on every layer of clothes he has. All the underlayers and then the parka. It is a clumsy process with hands as dexterous as two rib roasts. He struggles for a long time with the zipper on his parka and the cinch of his hood. He draws on his heavy mitts. His five minutes have long lapsed. Then, despite the exhaustion of all his other efforts, he begins to windmill his arms and trot in circles, trying to build up body heat and circulation. He realizes that he has not just frost-nipped his nose and ears but frozen them good. His hands are slow to regain movement. But when the burning and blood-pounding throb finally comes, he is overjoyed.

Now all he has to do is shuttle all this food and gear back up the ice chute, load by load.

When he has completed that and he's finally packed and pulls the snowhook, his dogs bolt wildly across the barren dome of Eagle

Summit. On level ground, they seem to fly. And then the team is heading down, going faster still. Bruce does not see any trail markers. Maybe they missed a turn. The team splashes through a surprise pool of overflow, and they race on. Even if he's lost the trail, he's in the right canyon and heading down. Somewhere around here is the road, and down the road four or five miles is a ten-by-twenty foot shack known as Mile 101 checkpoint.

Bruce sees the lights. Then he can hear a generator. Then there are people. He is overcome. If there were anything left in him, he'd probably sob at having reached the safety of other people and this under-sized, overcrowded drafty old plank cabin.

"It was the greatest sight in the world," he says.

It has taken him six hours and thirteen minutes to travel thirty-three miles. Nearly four hours were consumed climbing up the two ice pitches to the top of the summit.

Tomorrow's *Fairbanks Daily News–Miner* would devote most of the front page to the story: LEE SURVIVES. America's threat to attack Iraq is relegated to minor play.

18

A four legged friend,
A four legged friend,
He'll never let you down.

—Roy Rogers

The scene comes into view: just inside the schoolhouse, a man sits slumped on a bench, his beard crusty from the trail, his hair matted and greasy, his cheeks swollen and blistered with frostbite, his mouth hinged open and leaking a string of drool. His puffy, red-rimmed eyes are shut, and his head bobs as if it will detach itself any second and fall on the dirty floor. On the card table in front of him, his palms encircle a Styrofoam cup of coffee, long cold. Then, sensing he is being watched, the man involuntarily snorts—a big, rattling draw of air through thick mucus. His head regains its balance and the bloodshot eyes squint open. He collects the drool with two swipes from the back of his hand and attempts a smile. With the other hand, he tips over the coffee, which runs into his lap.

Thus Liisa Penrose greets the man who presumes to be courting her.

To her credit, she does not flee outright at the sight of me. After nine winters in Alaska, she is not easily frightened. And, as I'm about to learn, a man who has not bathed and drools on himself is not automatically placed on the reject list. She has just driven alone over Eagle Summit in a windstorm at night in a strange rental car full of beer, smoked salmon, cream cheese, a box of music tapes, and, in case she slides into a ditch, a snow shovel. I'm afraid, at this point, her choices are a long drive home or the gamble that a shower and a few hours of sleep will return me to something resembling tolerable.

She brings me up to date about the Quest, at least insofar as is known. Which isn't very much.

Mushers are spreading out, with a gap of 266 miles between the front and the back of the pack. The last she heard, Bruce Lee remained in the lead with Andre Nadeau shadowing him. Twelve hours behind are John Schandelmeier and Rick Mackey. The next mushers are strung out in intervals: Frank Turner, Paddy Santucci, Jerry Louden, and Dave Dalton. The leaders are thinking ahead to Angel Creek, a roadhouse northeast of Fairbanks. Race rules require an eight-hour layover there, as a safeguard against any muddleheaded temptation to push teams too hard without a good rest.

After that, the trail makes a sixty-eight-mile, looping run through spruce forests and low-lying hills, skirting a Fairbanks suburb with the absurd name North Pole—so designated by the city fathers to attract highway tourists, even though North Pole is roughly two thousand miles from the real north pole and offers nothing whatsoever for tourists except an RV park, a McDonald's, a tacky "Santa Claus" house, and an oil refinery. If your child mails a letter to Santa Claus, North Pole, Alaska, it lands here, God forbid. The Quest trail then makes a right turn onto the Chena River, a serpentine midsized stream with a long Gold Rush history. Following its twists and oxbows for thirty-two miles, the trail passes through the U.S. Army's cold-weather training base, Fort Wainwright, and enters Fairbanks proper. Spotters along highway bridges call local radio stations with live reports of the approach of the first musher. When the team rounds the last bend and lopes for the Cushman Street Bridge in the center of town, the bells ring out at Immaculate Conception Church. Saloons empty and people scramble down the steep and eroding riverbank to crowd under banners strung across temporary scaffolding. For some reason, everyone uses the Quest finish as the occasion to show off their finest and most garish fur hats, giant pelts of fox and wolf, many with the tails and paws still affixed and dangling jauntily. Some of these hats are three times as big as the heads they cover, as if there had been some horrible outbreak of water on the brain in the Alaskan Interior. The voice of an announcer, cranked up extra-loud to penetrate the fur, booms through the streets of this hunkered-down, low-rise city, giving thanks to local sponsors.

We're still in Circle, however. "Let's go catch up," says Liisa. She adds, "Oh, and you might want to wash off that face."

I have noticed this before. Women in the Far North adapt various mannerisms to deflect the rampaging, big-bore, sub-idiot-IQ macho that infects a significant portion of the male culture here. One tactic is to apply a lead foot to the gas pedal until a male passenger whimpers for mercy. Liisa has the Ford Contour up to about fifty miles an hour on the glaze ice of the meandering one-lane road leading out of Circle City. There is no shoulder here. I could reach out and touch the spindly trees that scoot by in the darkness. Through corners, I feel the car lift as though it is about to be released from the grip of the ground.

I feel perfectly secure. We will not attempt to return across the summit tonight. Instead we will join the massed Fulda press corps at the Circle Hot Springs resort eight miles away.

This is a winter oasis in the Alaska Interior. Located . . . well, located precisely nowhere, it really does have hot springs, which bubble up and fill a large raw-concrete swimming pool just outside the lobby. Steam rising from the pool coats the lodge and the surrounding birch forest with a fantastic glaze of ice. In summer, the faux-chalet architecture looks a little weather-beaten and out of character, but when frosted in winter white, the lodge looms as an inviting interlude from the boxy cabins and prefab Atco units that dominate this part of the state. To my surprise, the lodge has a vacant suite. The shower is barely a dribble. The two bedrooms are separate. I have no intention of complaining.

Gathered in the low-ceilinged saloon, the German reporters are downcast, and roaring drunk. They welcome me to their tables. As I accept their hospitality and take a seat, I find myself contrite. The Quest has taught me a lesson—a belated one, I'm afraid. All the pre-race anxiety about this enlarged press corps and Fulda's sponsorship is now taking on a different and much less alarming perspective. I should have known better. Residents of the Far North always resist and fear newcomers. But when newcomers are put through the paces of subarctic winter, they rise in standing and quickly become more "us" than "them." Lounging in the old bar, these reporters now seem part of the scene. What was I thinking? And who was I even to have such thoughts? The ordeal of the Quest has brought us all closer to what matters in life, which of course is the best part of honest adventure. If these colleagues bear me ill, they do not show it.

I lend a sympathetic ear to their woes. Editors back home are still clamoring for more speed, more thrills, more spills. I had wanted the press corps to fill in their reports with stories about the indigenous culture of the Far North, and was shocked when they did not. But now I understand that all the time they were battling editors who seemed to think that if they just worked harder they could capture stories of sleds crashing into crowds at breakneck speed. Real action! While these journalists followed the struggle of the race with awe, editors insisted there must be more to mushing than dogs dancing along in the snow at half the speed of a good track-and-field sprinter. And what about these mushers? How do you explain to an editor that they're so groggy they can barely grunt a profanity or two, let along string words into sentences? How can you get a good interview with a musher who answers every question with, "Huh?" I feel sorry for my friends. This great adventure will earn them grief. Think of the teasing they'll get back home, they say. Hey, Stefan, how would you like to cover the budding of the trees in the Black Forest next spring?

Leaving Circle, Paddy Santucci worries that he has frozen his nose. It's only 30 below, but it seems damp, which makes it more dangerous than 50 below and dry. He worries about the noses of his dogs, too. For the first time in days, the sky clears after midnight and a vast, shimmering

curtain of northern lights materializes overhead, glaucous green and
trimmed in red. When he reaches Central, he oversleeps. Somewhere
he got the idea that Rick Mackey was going to wake him up. The mistake costs Santucci two hours. The mind plays funny tricks on you. . . .

Before dawn, Rick Mackey and John Schandelmeier meet inside the
Circle City café for coffee. This is the third consecutive year that they
have run most of the Quest within striking distance of each other. But
for the first time these former champions are not in front. Now, as they
talk, they concede all hope of a come-from-behind victory. They give
the race to Bruce Lee and figure Andre Nadeau will hang on for second
place. They look at each other and agree it's a race for third.
Surprisingly, their spirits lift even as their tired faces droop.

Neither man makes easy excuses or blames his dogs for Bruce Lee's
commanding advantage. "We've got comparable dog teams. If I hadn't
screwed up, who knows?" Mackey tells a reporter. In retrospect,
though, Rick knows how it happened. He let himself get in the habit of
stopping at cabins, even if it meant cutting some runs short for the sake
of a warm stopover. Bruce wrote out a race plan that disregarded the
placement of these cabins. He stretched himself to take advantage of
the capacity of his team, even if that meant camping in the cold time
after time.

"He was right. He had it all down. . . . That's where we blew it,"
Mackey concedes. "I was stuck on the same routine I've been stuck on,
and that John's been stuck on."

Mackey leads the pair out of Circle, but he has to double back. He'd
forgotten to sign out with the checker. Even the pros are stumbling.

Somewhere in this race, there was supposed to be a crisis over dog
booties. For a while, it threatened to bring everything to a halt. But no
one seems worried any longer. One musher withdraws his official
protest. Those entrants who dropped out have donated their surplus to
the cause. More booties, at first hundreds and now thousands, have
poured in from outfitters and other mushers. A round-the-clock effort
by Quest volunteers and the selflessness of fellow dog mushers has
paid off. Teams now advance, knowing they are almost sure to receive
an adequate issue of booties at the next checkpoint. No doubt a

wonderful story of perseverance and remote logistics lies behind the outcome, but anyone who knows it is too worn out to tell it.

Dave Dalton, the Fairbanks cab driver, has been stuck in the middle of the pack. He's thinking to himself that he should be doing better. But goddamn, this is a tough field of mushers. No one is cracking. He's fought heavy snow. He's been through sixty-mile-an-hour winds at 10 below. But he cannot seem to gain. And now, approaching Circle, things get really tough for him. Maybe his diet of Power Bars and Gatorade isn't quite enough, because he is cold now. Cold to the core. For three hours in the predawn darkness, he runs and kicks behind the sled to try to keep from freezing. "When it's that cold, you can't stop. You know that when you do, it's going to get really cold," he says. "But, shit, it's really fucking cold out here anyway."

His luck has been spotty so far. He got lost at his last rest stop. When he finally found the cabin he was looking for and got it warming, another musher arrived and heated some horrible energy-food concoction on the woodstove and stunk the whole place up. They had to open the door and let out all the heat along with the stench. His fingertips are cracked and swollen from exposure. He recalls passing one musher who was standing by the trail with his pants pulled down. Dalton could think of nothing to say except, "What the hell are you doing?"

"What the hell do you think I'm doing?" answered the pantless man.

Exhausted, frozen, stuck in the middle, and sick to death of frozen Power Bars, Dalton figures it's the perfect time to make his move and try to advance in the standings.

Tim Mowry is running faster than he ever has, but he too is stuck in the middle of this highly competitive pack. He and the other mushers have heard, by word of mouth, about Bruce Lee's horrible climb over Eagle Summit. Mowry has talked himself into the certain knowledge that his dogs won't pull up the headwall either, and he'll have to shuttle his gear, sled, and dogs just like Bruce did.

Beset with gloom, Mowry lies down in Central. Before leaving, he calls home. He tells his wife, Kristen, that he overslept and has been in Central nine and a half hours

"What are you doing? We need the money!" she screams.

' ' '

Up ahead, Bruce Lee recovers from his struggle over Eagle Summit with a five-hour rest, curled up in the far corner of the Mile 101 shack, where cotton mattresses have been randomly strewn on the drafty floor. He sleeps alone on the mattresses with his lead secure. Andre Nadeau is a flat-land musher. He may know about Newfoundland's rotten winter weather, but he's inexperienced on big climbs. Bruce snores easily. He even allows himself a moment of worry about his rival's safety on the high ground behind him.

Andre arrives two and a half hours behind Bruce, looking no worse for the experience. He feeds his dogs and checks them carefully, spreading straw on the ground to give them insulated beds—a sign that he plans a long rest here. True enough, he's not a man at home in the mountains. What bothered him, though, was not so much the climb up but the furious descent, where his big enthusiastic Siberians stretched out and galloped like pups. Andre gives them ninety minutes to make certain no one has sprained an ankle or pulled a muscle from the unaccustomed speed. Satisfied that the team is sound, Andre whispers to the checker that he's leaving and he tiptoes out of Mile 101. No one except his wife notices when he wriggles on the handlebar and the dogs trot ahead. The Energizer bunny looks like he found a charge. Inside, Bruce snores contentedly, his notebook with the winning race plan zipped in his pocket.

With Liisa driving and fresh coffee in the thermos, we depart Circle Hot Springs in the morning, climbing the empty road toward Eagle Summit in high spirits. I promised the German press that I'd throw one helluva party for them in Fairbanks at the end of the race. I feel we've patched over most of the raw feelings, and that pleases me. Liisa, deputized by the Fairbanks Convention and Visitors Bureau, has elicited promises from the foreign press to at least keep an open mind about Alaska, even if Fulda regards it as hostile territory. So she's pleased too. Plus, the drive is spectacular. Almost immediately, we are engulfed in a forbidding blue fog driven by howling winds. As we ascend the ice-covered road, winds buffet and slam the car with the force of a linebacker in shoulder pads. I crank up the stereo and try to keep from spilling the coffee. The heater whirs at maximum output and keeps us warm in shirtsleeves. As we round the summit, there is a break. The fog swirls below us, and angry clouds scud overhead to the left and right. But directly ahead is a hole of blue sky, through which a dazzling spray of sunlight touches the landscape, fantasy-like—a view of clouds and earth more typically encountered from an airplane than a car. In our surreal, guilty comfort, we watch in the distance as Jerry Louden and his dog team battle their way across the exposed summit top, looking something like a centipede struggling in a wind tunnel. At this moment his world is so far apart from mine that it cannot be measured in anything like distance.

For some reason—habit or confusion—I forgot to get much sleep last night amid all the free-flowing Fulda whiskey. I look in the car's visor mirror and see the face of a vagrant. But I'm cleaner than I've been in two weeks, and warm. My plan is to deposit Liisa back at her job in Fairbanks, check in with the race officials, and then head back up the trail to follow the finish of the race.

Bruce Lee has lost the lead, but not his incredible discipline. On autopilot, he yanks himself from a deep, slow-breathing sleep—a hibernating sleep—precisely on schedule. Some mushers need to be kicked a couple of times with a heavy boot just to get them to sit up. For Bruce, any interval spent between the mattress and the latch on the door of the shack at Mile 101 is a waste of time.

Stoically, he receives the news of Andre's surprise leap for glory. He begins preparing his team. The thing is, no matter how close you are to the finish line and how desperate you are to catch up, the process of getting going remains preposterously tedious. Water must be heated, dog food cooked and ladled out, booties put on—always carefully, so that a foot doesn't get rubbed. That means working bare-handed or with only a thin glove liner, so your fingers ache almost from the start. Each dog needs attention and encouragement; just like with a class of kindergartners, no one can be left out. Bruce takes another long look at his notebook and puts fresh batteries in his power pack. Then the feeding pans have to be collected, the stove broken down, the sled packed again. Once more, Bruce walks through the team to connect necklines and tuglines. He pulls his neck gaiter up and fits his hands into heavy mitts. He nudges the handlebar. And they call this racing.

One hour and fifteen minutes behind Andre, at 10:45 P.M., Bruce departs into the ground fog that has settled over these hills, his halogen lamp reflecting a faint rainbow in the ice crystals. From here, the trail aims mostly south. For ten miles, Bruce travels downhill, paralleling the road. He uses the drag brake to keep his dogs from running too fast and risking injury. Then the road proceeds straight and the Quest trail turns to the left, up a small creek and over some lumpy hills. After another descent, the trail winds steeply uphill again toward the 3,600-foot summit known as Rosebud. Despite its height, this mountain does not receive fanfare as one of the three major climbs, King Solomon's Dome, Eagle Summit, and American Summit. Still, mushers must battle their way up two headwall sections to uncertain weather up high.

Bruce worries that his team is mentally fragile after the experience on the last mountain. Back there, his dogs had lost confidence in him—that's how Bruce sees it. And this trust cannot be won back in only hours. He finds himself downcast, replaying the little mistakes and misfortunes that he figures could cost him victory. He's come so close so many times—his résumé is swollen with top-five finishes—yet he's never won a big dog race. Now this one seems to be slipping away. He hasn't felt this lousy since way back on the trail when he was forced to drop his best lead dog, Miles. On the other hand, Bruce notices that his remaining team is running strong in Andre's tracks. Maybe it is a good thing that the dogs have the smell of another team to follow. Maybe they won't quit on the mountain if others have gone ahead of them.

As the trail grows more vertical and the wind begins to stiffen, Bruce's anxiety rises. At the first steep pitch, sure enough, the team hesitates as if this is the end of this day. He dismounts and walks forward. This is no time to scold the dogs and surely not the place for a musher to lose his cool. These animals are spooked by climbs and not sure that their master has command, that much is clear. What Bruce needs to do is give them a reason to believe in him and themselves.

He walks to the front of the team and begins the climb up alone. He looks back over his shoulder and says, "Okay, boys, let's go." They follow.

"They weren't going to do it with me on the runners," Bruce says. "We agreed on that. But they said to me, If you'll walk we'll go with you. So I said, Okay, if you'll come, I'll walk."

The pitch is short, and on the level ground above is Andre Nadeau, taking a quick break. Now, this is a race, thinks Bruce. His gloom lifts, but his confidence does not return. There's no time for these kinds of moody distractions.

Two men with machinelike intensity now eye each other across the small, windblown snowfield. From different countries, speaking different languages, with entirely different kinds of dog teams and strategies that are the opposite of each other, they have managed to leave all the champions and favorites behind. How fast can Bruce's mottled mix of sleek Alaskan huskies cover the remaining 112 miles? How long can Andre's ghostly gray Siberians go without rest?

Bruce assumes the lead and travels the short distance to the base of the next headwall pitch. Again his team balks. Andre drives by with a barely perceptible nod, and his dogs lunge and begin the scramble up. Slowly they climb, slipping and then throwing their weight against the shivering gangline. Andre's voice carries over the rising wind, coaxing them on. Bruce dismounts and follows on foot, kicking toeholds in the crusty snow and balancing himself on his hands. This new two-legged lead dog turns his head. "Okay, boys," he says. The team, eyes blinking against the wind, shoulders forward and follows.

Twelve miles to Angel Creek.

It is of no consolation, but Aliy Zirkle is informed that the necropsy on the body of her dog Prince found absolutely no evidence of mistreatment or negligence. The animal was determined to have been in prime condition, with plenty of fat reserves. University of Fairbanks veterinarian John Blake says that such mysterious deaths sometimes result from preexisting liver or heart deficiencies that would be undetectable in prerace physical examinations.

Zirkle is now cruising along in a rhythmic trance, her entire existence reduced to the tiny scope of this family of dogs and the cyclical routine of motion, camping, resting, and moving. She looks ahead only as far as the next bend in the trail, the next meal of dog food, the next hard-frozen cookie she fetches from her sled bag when her stomach growls. She has no memory. The Quest is all she has ever done, all she will ever do.

When she arrives at Circle City, 150 miles behind the leaders, no one seems able to penetrate this world. Reflecting later, after the finish and four days of sleep, she will put her elbows on the bar and drop her chin into her hands and speak softly about how impossibly difficult it all was. But she gives no sign of it now, crabbing down the gangline on her hands and knees, removing booties from the feet of her dogs, rubbing balm into their pads. She works soundlessly, but all the time she and this team, this family, are communicating at some other level. The dogs watch her, and she meets their eyes. When she stands and a person approaches her and speaks, Aliy gives a start as if a stranger has intruded on her dream. Her cheeks dimple and she smiles automatically, but she walks on purposefully.

Overall, she is running seventeenth among the twenty-six remaining mushers. She is first among the women, but that is no cause for celebration. A woman has never won the Quest, and that remains a frustration. Everywhere else in the sport, women have triumphed. Thirteen years ago, Libby Riddles was the first to win the Iditarod. Susan Butcher is a multiple winner of the Iditarod and the most famous name in mushing. As a consequence, some of the men who compete in the Quest have taken to calling the Iditarod the "girls' race," but they say it quietly and are careful to see who is in the room before they open their mouths.

Mushing has done much for the self-image of women in the Far North and has also done much to temper the redneck bluster of the local male population. Women's success in dog driving has earned them a degree of honest equality that feminists elsewhere could envy.

By the standards men here set and hold dear, women have proved themselves equal.

Your average Tennessee mountain garage mechanic can chug his Budweiser with the smug satisfaction of knowing that real character is measured on a football field or a NASCAR track, where men alone compete. But here, even an illiterate hermit gold miner must contend with the realization that women yield nothing to men when it comes to the Far North's most demanding test of character: mushing dogs long distances, alone through the winter wilderness—in all cases except, so far, the Yukon Quest.

With his ropy muscles and compact build, Paddy Santucci is a naturally graceful athlete. And like all graceful people, he has become slightly vain about it. So he is a little nervous when he leaves Mile 101 for the fast downhill run. Right at the end of the first ten miles, where the trail turns from the road, a couple of photographers have set up positions overlooking an ugly pool of overflow. This standing water has accumulated from the pressure of a natural spring, pumping frigid water through pressure cracks in the ice. Before it freezes, the overflow glimmers in strange, picturesque hues of aquamarine. Here the trail is pinched by the steep banks of a creek, and the overflow is hard to avoid. Paddy fails to avoid it. The photographers want an action shot. They get it: a splashing rooster tail at 20 below.

Unfortunately, they also watch as Paddy must stop his team to remove wet dog booties and replace them with fresh ones.

Paddy tops Rosebud fourteen hours behind the leaders. But he is only four hours behind John Schandelmeier and Rick Mackey, and only minutes behind Frank Turner. His dogs are loping like crazy, and it's a wild son of a bitch of a ride on the down slope to Angel Creek in the pitch black of night. The trail winds down the sidehill of a canyon, and every so often a spring has burst through the ice. The fan of released water freezes into glaciers, angled patches of ice as slick as a skating rink. With downhill speed and momentum, Paddy whip-snakes crazily over them, exhilarated and perpetually on the edge of catastrophe. He is set up low for the next glacier, but the dogs veer high and his sled fishtails. Before he can recover, the runners bite sideways into the ice and the sled flips onto its side, slamming him into the unforgiving surface. The crash pulls his dogs into a tangle and a fight breaks out in the middle, dogs lashing out in fear at the only thing they can reach, one another. Into the fury of snapping jaws, Paddy staggers, his headlamp throwing a beam into a writhing mass of dog flesh, trying to yell over the shrieks of an angry team, pulling dogs apart by the collars and hind legs. No one is hurt, but the whole team, including Paddy, is left dizzy and panting on the trail. He rides with his foot ready near the brake for the final few miles into Angel Creek.

Here the mushers have eight hours to size one another up and lighten their sleds of everything that's not absolutely essential for the last hundred-mile dash home. There won't be any spare socks along the way from here on.

19

*To one who lives in the snow and watches it day
by day, it is a book to be read. The pages turn as
the wind blows. . . . It is a shadow language.*

—Alaska poet John Haines

It should come as no surprise to find that the Far North has two
faces. But, of course, such discoveries always come as a surprise.

Here is one face of the Far North: in mid-January, sixty miles southwest of Fairbanks near the town of Nenana, a cabin burned down. It
belonged to a little-known, hand-to-mouth dog musher named Tony
Browning. This happened on a Tuesday. Before the last embers smol-
dered out, the scene was being surveyed by his neighbor and fellow
musher Dick Mackey, the Iditarod champion and father of Quest racer
Rick Mackey. By Thursday, with the temperature 20 below, Mackey had
ordered lumber and wiring, trucked everything down from Fairbanks,
and mobilized a dozen men—and the frame of a new cabin had been
hammered together. By Sunday, the cabin was insulated, heated, and
wired for electricity, ready for Browning to move in. Rural Alaska, it
should be noted, is unburdened by building codes, permits, or inspections. Browning asked for the price list of materials and was told to pay
it off whenever he could. By Monday, Browning was back on the train-

ing trails, preparing his dogs for a mid-distance race the following weekend. He hoped to pick up some prize money to start paying his neighbors back.

Another face of the Far North greets me when I reach Fairbanks: the accusatory glare of race marshal Dave Rich. I didn't quite catch it at first. My brain was misfiring from weariness and the strange confusion of returning to civilization. But the gist was this: I am being blamed for the loose dog that chased after Bruce Lee at Biederman's cabin. The story had grown so that now the wayward dog from my team either attacked and bit Bruce or tore into his team and caused a mess. I had disrupted the race. I had warned the press against this very thing, and now I was guilty. Apparently the tale had a satisfying I-told-you-so symmetry for Rich. The Outsider from L.A. got in over his head. That's why he'd discouraged me in the first place from taking a dog team on the trail. The story was untrue. In the days ahead, I had Bruce and other witnesses remind Rich that I was a half day behind on the trail and that my dogs had at no time caused anyone grief. But Rich had made his call. And he stuck with it. Some of the people caught in the middle, like Joe May, felt they had to choose sides. Joe, who gave me so much, sided with Rich. And I can't blame him, as much as it stings. Rich is a local, and he had responsibility for the race. If he says something went wrong, it must have.

I never did determine what lay beneath Rich's resentment. I am not unaccustomed to watching ordinary people swell in importance behind the name tag of authority—clerks who become commissars when made coach of the neighborhood Little League, that sort of thing. I suppose this can happen in Alaska the same as elsewhere. But I'd like to think that something else was at work. I'd like to think that, down deep, Rich was trying to safeguard the Quest from the snooping intrusion of Outsiders. After all, American adventure outfitters are now taking trekkers into the hallowed and once forbidden mountain reaches of the Himalayas—for a price. American Indians are selling tickets to sacred dances. And now the pressure of commercialism threatens to distort the Yukon Quest, this private ritual by which Far Northerners anneal their links to the mythical past. I'd like to believe that Dave

Rich, formerly of Miami, Florida, just could not shake the hand of any man who was part of the intrusion. For that matter, I'd like to think I wouldn't, either.

I have spent two winters and one summer with these people, fallen for one of their women, wandered their country, mushed their dogs. I have slept on the floors of their cabins, shared their moose stew, taken turns when the whiskey came around, and gloried in their stories. But now, near the end, it's apparent that I'm not one of them. The Quest belongs to the people who live by the myth, not to those who live from a suitcase.

For a musher slip-sliding down Rosebud Summit, speed trumps endurance. Bruce Lee drives his lanky dog team to the roadhouse at Angel Creek just at sundown, twenty-nine minutes ahead of Andre Nadeau.

In a snowfield behind the kitchen, he gives his dogs beds of straw. They receive a final once-over by the veterinarians. A quiet room out back is set aside for mushers to rest in. The eight-hour layover proves to be exquisite torture. Without the mandatory stop, competitive mushers would have no choice except to push on, perhaps too hard. So they are grateful to see their dogs paw out nests in the straw and snow, curl down, and tuck their noses under their bushy tails for a long sleep. But eight hours is a prolonged interval during which to dwell on the perils of the remaining one hundred miles.

In his mind, Bruce turns over two worries. For the next sixty-eight overland miles, the Quest trail intersects dozens of local trails—a whole spiderweb woven through the forested rolling hills by snowmachiners, cross-country skiers, recreational dog mushers, and wandering moose, of which there is a dense concentration in the wildlands around Fairbanks. A single wrong turn could ball up the team and cost him his half-hour lead just turning around. A vandal who pulls up a single marker stake for a souvenir could mean a wrong turn and the difference between the $30,000 winner's purse and $24,000 for runner-up. By now, the dogs know the scent of other teams running in the race, and can be counted on to chase them. But when you are in front, there is no familiar scent to follow. Bruce will start the final leg out front. What if a recreational musher crosses the trail and one of his female dogs is in heat? If Bruce's concentration drifts at that moment, he'll wind up lost on a side trail.

Bruce finds it equally worrisome that he must ask of his dogs something they have never given and were not trained for: a hundred-mile dash without rest. For more than nine hundred miles, they have been traveling legs of about fifty miles and then sleeping. Now the race plan in his notebook calls for a straight-through run. He will stop periodically and snack the team, but there will be no bedding down. That means at least ten hours at top speed.

In training, Bruce twice ran his dogs down the final thirty-two-mile stretch of the Chena River into Fairbanks. All of his dogs had a chance to lead, "just in case." After both runs, when they arrived in Fairbanks, they were rewarded with food and their familiar beds inside their dog truck, imprinting the idea that this section of trail, at last, meant home.

Dogs have astonishing trail memories. One year on the Iditarod, Joe May's team surprised a family of bison crossing the trail and gave chase, right into a nasty thicket of willows. The next year there were no bison, but the dogs veered off the trail at precisely the same place and into the very same willows. Bruce plans on driving his team the sixty-eight miles to the Chena River more or less as just another day on the job. Then he's counting on the team recognizing the familiar river and perking up for a second shift, forgetting they haven't gotten any rest and running home to the dog truck. The uncertainty in this strategy, as he thinks about it, is that his team, without Miles in the lead, has already cracked going up the big summits. Will they hold up now under added stress? One thing seems sure: Andre Nadeau's Siberians are prepared to go all the way. "They'd walk to the end of the earth for him. . . . They're the best marching-type dogs I've ever seen," Bruce says with a shrug. Then he adds, "But, hey, they're just dogs."

The two mushers wait out the clock without any company. At midday, both men are packing their sleds and installing fresh plastic under the runners while their nearest challengers still climb the slick trail toward the Rosebud Summit. Lee decides to drop a dog, reducing his team to his nine fastest dogs. Andre also harnesses nine.

At exactly 1:00 P.M., Bruce sounds the Okay and shoves his sled forward. His team bounds into the spruce forest. They are fresh, the sled is light, and they lope along at twelve miles an hour, tongues flying. His balance is solid on the runners, and he begins the tedium of scanning ahead for trail markers. Andre is clocked out at 1:30 P.M. His Siberians have their tails up. Happy dogs. The temperature is 5 above and the winter sun throws long shadows through the trees.

From Angel Creek, the trail is wide and well packed from local use, and it encourages speed. Bruce's dogs respond and urge each other on. Every ten miles he calls a halt, stomps the double-jawed hook into the snow with his boot, and hurries down the line with treats. Food is packed in separate bags in the sled—chunks of fish, balls of fat, frozen hunks of meat. He varies the selection. Then they're off. Each time, he looks back. The woods behind him are empty.

To a newcomer, this forested trail that rolls and follows a gentle slope toward the great Tanana River valley of Fairbanks looks as wild and forbidding as wilderness anywhere. The footprints ahead are as likely to be from moose as from a snowmachine. But for Quest mushers, after so many days alone with their dogs over brutal and untouched terrain, the landscape has a reassuring, almost civilized feel, like a hunter might find in the distant cornfields of a farm.

Darkness falls, with stray cloudlets draping over the treetops in an utterly still, hard-blue sky. Stars pulse above as bright as flashes from the wingtips of an airplane. The temperature drops to 5 below, and the dogs stride on. There are lights ahead, and people. According to Bruce's notebook, it should be 7:30 P.M. But he is almost an hour early to the checkpoint at the summer boat landing at Chena Lakes park. He has surprised even his wife. Jeralyn hasn't arrived yet. He is elated as he ties on the red sponsor's bib with No. 12, his starting number, for the race finish. He signals the dogs on. They move. And then, for an instant, the team hesitates. They are not fools, even if they are mere dogs. They know a checkpoint. And checkpoints are places to stop, to lie down on straw, to eat and take a rest. They are tired. Their bellies have had nothing warm all day. They slow to a walk, looking over their shoulders as if to ask, *Do you realize that you just passed a checkpoint?*

"Let's go, boys. Come on. Okay." He coaxes them on, trying to add fresh excitement in his voice. "Let's go!" Their heads swivel forward and they begin to trot, not quite as enthusiastically as before but not reluctantly either. Every so often, one of them looks back again, just to make sure the boss isn't asleep or something. "Keep it up," he replies.

They are on the Chena now. Bruce no longer worries about losing his way. By straight line, he is only twelve miles from downtown Fairbanks. But the corkscrew path of the river lengthens the trail to thirty-two miles. Bruce stops to give them another frozen snack. They cross under the first of a half dozen highway bridges. A few spectators wave. One of them calls KFAR radio with a position report. An hour later, the dogs get a final snack. Then they enter the military base at Fort Wainwright and the realization clicks in their heads. They are going home. They rise tall in the harness; their trot becomes a snappy lope. Bruce grips the handlebar and looks behind him once more for any sight of a following headlamp. The river is empty.

"I told myself, This is the moment. Savor it—you're going to remember this. You're going to remember this team. They're the best I've ever run. I turned off my headlamp and just watched the dogs. Because I knew that just around a few bends, all hell was going to break loose. It wouldn't be just winning, but coming back from losing all my other dogs, and rebuilding. This was the moment. . . ."

Church bells peal. The last of the saloon habitués chug their beers and scramble down the riverbank. Several hundred people have gathered under a bank of spotlights, stomping their feet to keep them warm. A bass voice echoes through the P.A. system. "He'll be coming into sight in just a minute, folks . . . folks. Bruce Lee, winner of the Yukon Quest . . . Quest . . ."

Then there is the far-off dot of a headlamp. In the still air, a string of bobbing dogs materializes as the beam grows closer. Camera lights catch their tiny vapor clouds and the greenish glint of paired eyes. For a moment there is quiet. Everything in mushing happens in slow motion, even the dash to the finish. Then a cheer comes from the crowd. It is a half hour before midnight. Bruce Lee is first in a big one for the first time in his life—1,023 miles in eleven days, eleven hours, and twenty-seven minutes.

Surrounded by people and blinded by TV lights, the dogs stand in place with slightly stunned expressions. A couple of them roll in the snow to cool off. Bruce and Jeralyn move through the team, dog by dog. It is unclear to me whether dogs understand gratitude, but there is no question that what passes from dog eye to human eye, from glove to stringy neck, from nose to nuzzle is the deepest kind of love. When Bruce reaches the front of the team, he takes hold of a lead collar and turns the team in a U, and they trot up the riverbank to a parking lot and their waiting dog truck. When the animals are snugged in their stalls behind latched plywood doors, Bruce steps before a knot of reporters. His eyes are fierce, alert, still attuned to the trail.

"Long-distance dog racing is about two things," he says. "It's about dog care and it's about rest. . . ."

Twenty-one years ago, Bruce Lee came north. He finished his last class as a wildlife biology student at Michigan State, married Jeralyn, and the two drove to Alaska for their honeymoon. They put on snow-shoes that first winter and shouldered seventy-pound packs for a long exploration of the Alaska Range. Bruce pulled another seventy pounds behind him on a mountaineering sled. It was not much fun. Near the end of the hike, he had a realization: Alaska was different country, huge country. Why not join the others up here? Get some dogs. Within a month, he had two. Then five. Same old story. But no musher worked harder, and none suffered like he did, losing an entire kennel at its racing prime. So now he stands here in a church parking lot, the new champion, barely managing a smile, too full and too empty at the same time.

By 3:13 A.M., the crowds and reporters are all but gone and the saloons closed when Andre Nadeau drives into the finishers' chute. Having dropped one final dog at the Chena Lakes checkpoint, he finishes with eight.

Rick Mackey arrives at 9:09 A.M. while morning commute traffic rolls across the Cushman Street Bridge. John Schandelmeier is one hour, ten minutes, behind him. John's good nature was tested earlier, when he was surprised on the trail by four snowmachiners. His frightened dog team knotted up. The gangline looped around the leg of a big dog named Oscar, who began to limp and had to be dropped. Like all of John's dogs, Oscar is a working dog, a member of a race team, and a pet. Oscar resented being left behind and howled. Frank Turner finishes fifth at 1:25 P.M., the first Yukoner to Fairbanks. Frank always orders a big package of beefsteaks, and now he runs down the team handing them out in the finishing chute. It makes for great photographs, the black-bearded veteran in his greasy yellow-and-black parka, kneeling in the snow putting both arms around a dog with blood dripping out of its mouth.

Paddy Santucci, who persevered with only eight dogs for the entire second half of the race, approaches next. He makes one final stop. In the glare of the afternoon sun, the temperature has risen to 10 above, and his dark-coated dogs are overheating. He unties the straps and opens his sled bag. He grabs an ax and chops furiously into the river ice. When he reaches running water, he ladles out buckets and douses the team. The dogs shake happily, and tiny rainbows hang over them in the spray. Friends have come out to see him. His dogs zigzag through knots of people. He crosses the finish line at 3:08 P.M. School is out and waiting children crowd his sled. He hands out souvenir booties and shyly signs autographs. Paddy has vaulted himself into the elite—undaunted by early setbacks. For the last year, he's devoted three-quarters of his energy to this race. Now his lips are cracked, his face bristly and red, his eyes heavy, his hair long and stringy. A reporter asks the inevitable question: How do you feel? "They did good," he replies.

Behind the leaders, seven mushers are bunched in a close race. Bruce Lee's harrowing story of Eagle Summit has filtered back, and some in the pack reduce their ambitions. Now they just want to survive. Dave Dalton, however, advances from twelfth place to eighth by bulling his way up the mountain. Which is to say he walks. His dogs follow him fifty feet up the headwall. Then Dave must stop to catch his breath. He continues another fifty feet, and so on. When it becomes slick, Dave removes the booties from the feet of his dogs so they can dig their toenails into the ice. He pulls himself, hand over hand, kicking toeholds with his boots as a mountaineer would. At the summit, the wind reduces his visibility to just a few feet. His dogs seem to know where they are, so he grabs on and lets them run. He cannot brace for unseen bumps or corners, so he keeps a tight grip on the handlebar. Still, he is knocked off balance and sometimes finds himself dragging loose-footed behind the careening sled.

After a rest at the Mile 101 checkpoint, Dave rides the drag brake down the steep descent and splashes into overflow. Dogs can towel off by rolling in the dry snow, but Dave is soaked and his mukluks freeze as solid as tree stumps. His movements are clumsy now, and he skids down an inclined glacier into willows. Hand over hand through the brittle trees, he pulls his sled back toward the trail. He urges on the dogs, and when they lunge, they jerk him off his feet, facedown onto the hard ice. At the top of Rosebud Summit, a vicious sixty-mile-an-hour crosswind blows his dogs off the trail and sends the sled skidding into exposed boulders. All the while, he slaps and kicks his feet, trying to loosen the ice and keep blood circulating.

On the final run down the Chena River, Dave runs side by side with Canadian Mountie Doug Harris in a sprint for tenth place. Harris wraps his sled bag with a piece of rope and pulls ahead. Dave Dalton, who drove to Alaska in 1982 in a $400 Pontiac in the company of a beagle and a German shepherd, finishes his ninth Yukon Quest in eleventh place—nineteen and a half hours behind Bruce Lee. Dave's share of the purse is $2,900. At the finish line, he loads his dogs into the truck, downs a Budweiser, and then treats his handler to a steak dinner. He showers, sleeps thirteen hours, and awakens, already thinking of his strategy for next year's race.

"I have loooved you girl-l-l-l..." Ta-dah, dee-dah. Walter Newman, dog handler and guitar player, belts out old country-and-western ballads in the hoarse, whispery notes of an Eskimo.

I take Liisa's hand and recoup the dance we missed in Dawson City. The crowd stomps out the beat. It is Friday night and nearly half the Quest teams are still on the trail, but our little traveling press corps assembles anyway at the Dog Sled Saloon, a log-sided Fairbanks hangout where the walls are festooned with dollar bills that customers sign and leave behind, along with a collection of unsigned panties and brassieres that other patrons departed without. There are maybe twenty in our group—mostly Germans with a few Yukoners and Alaskans. I had promised the Germans a party, and Fairbanks wanted to show them hospitality. Walter assembled the pickup band.

I have made my peace with the Germans. Tonight I'm buying. And the townspeople of Fairbanks are buying. Yes, the foreign press may have overlooked the culture of the Far North. But they glorified the landscape and they celebrated every mile of hardship down the trail. That will have to be good enough, at least for me. Many North Americans believe that the vast spaces of the Far North are valuable only for the timber and minerals and oil they hold. Majorities in the U.S. Congress and Canadian Parliament frequently act as if the wild has no value except tamed. The thirty million or so Europeans who watched the Yukon Quest on TV and read about it in newspapers and magazines know better.

I'm afraid I've lost Liisa tonight. After our dance, she drifts away. When the music ends, she and the Germans head off for the late-night haunts of Fairbanks.

This traveling carnival is coming to a bittersweet end.

Tim Mowry, the newspaper editor, tops Rosebud Summit in the bright sunshine. Even after twelve years in Alaska, the scenery takes his breath away. Coming down the hill, he crashes on a fan of overflow and his head slams into the ice. He staggers to his feet and recites the names of his dogs, trying to determine if he has knocked himself silly. For his final run down the Chena River, Tim feels tears freezing on his cheeks. It happens every year. The dogs are so beautiful and noble, and they've given so much.

"They've done it again," Tim says, "and that makes it all worthwhile—the whole two weeks out there wondering what in the fuck am I doing this for."

As he approaches the finish line, his dogs are spooked by the crowd. He has to dismount and lead them across on foot. Waiting for him is a twelve-pack of Labatt's beer from his wife, Kristen, and a check for $1,800 as the fourteenth-place finisher.

On Sunday, just a single musher arrives in Fairbanks: Aliy Zirkle. Her elapsed time is thirteen days, twenty-one hours, and forty minutes. She is seventeenth, two places out of the money and five behind her kennel partner, Jerry Louden. But Aliy's huge smile and aw-shucks ruggedness have won her a following. The quality by which she judges others she has proven in herself. Just nine years ago, she saw that advertisement in the back of an adventure travel magazine. GO TO ALASKA AND FIND YOUR DREAMS, it said.

"The Quest turned out as hard as I thought it would be," she says. "And that was goddamn, fucking hard."

She would never again need to invent stories to make her life sound interesting.

For the mushers who have reached the finish line by the weekend, Fairbanks hosts a banquet, an emotional affair in which memories already have begun the miraculous process of sifting through the agonies to remember the triumphs.

"There was this one morning when the sun was coming and there was no wind," Alaskan Larry Carroll tells the crowd. "I stopped and I talked to God for fifteen minutes."

Bruce Lee recalls a conversation with his wife. "I said to her, Jeralyn, wouldn't it be great, just once, to have a magic-carpet ride? Well, this was it."

Under Bruce's table, his lead dog Clovis snoozes. By tradition, the winning musher brings the dog that meant the most in his victory. Clovis is presented with a ceremonial harness. A waiter brings out a cooked steak on a plate and puts it on the floor in front of the dog. Clovis sniffs and turns away. "He only eats raw meat—which is no reflection on the restaurant here," says Lee diplomatically.

I stand at the banquet bar behind Yukoner William Kleedehn, who finished seventh despite his prosthetic leg. He is trying to cash a check in advance of collecting his $5,000 purse. "I don't have a dime," he confesses. And tonight, he feels like buying the beer.

Like most competitions, the Quest finds ways to recognize achievements other than winning. The Sportsmanship Award, voted by the mushers themselves, goes to Rusty Hagan for his spirited good nature and his concern for the safety of other teams. For the first time, the winner is not on hand to accept the award, because Rusty and the party pack are still back on the trail, struggling to make their way to Fairbanks.

And, to be frank about it, Rusty Hagan does not feel very sportsmanlike at the moment. The tensions that flared between one group of rookie mushers and another after that horrible night on American Summit have not abated. Rusty is fuming again. As before, he is traveling in a loose, easygoing group with Brenda Mackey, Thomas Tetz, and Keith Kirkvold. Sometimes Amy Wright joins them. And again, they are hopscotching down the trail with two other rookies, Bill Steyer and Walter Palkovitch, who seem to find the clubby clique an irritant. News reports lump the group together as the party pack, but Bill and Walter are not part of the party.

"Those guys had played games with us all the way," Rusty says.

Or, as Walter puts it, "I tried my best for six hundred miles to get away from the party pack. . . . Everyone talked about the steep hills, the pack ice—I add the party pack to my list."

Together, the massed mushers climb up the last of the great mountains, Eagle Summit. As dusk grows to night, they string out for the chaotic descent. Bill Steyer is ahead of Brenda Mackey, with Rusty following. The run is so steep and fast that stopping is difficult, but Bill stops. Rusty jumps on his brake with all his weight but still overruns Brenda's team, and the runner of his sled rides over one of her dogs. The animal is unhurt, but Rusty is livid. Then it's Walter Palkovitch's turn to get on Rusty's nerves. The trail levels out just before the Mile 101 cabin, but Rusty still expects the string of dog teams to proceed in orderly fashion. But Walter stops. He stops twice. As Rusty attempts to pass, the two teams ball up in a growling, snarling mess. Words are exchanged.

"It was weird and he was kind of insulting," says Rusty. "I asked him to set the hook. I was ready to do battle with him, much as I hate to admit it."

Walter wants no part of this, and summons his dogs to move out. Rusty follows on his heels.

At the Mile 101 cabin, the two mushers stop. Rusty tears off his parka and sends it flying into the snow. He lumbers up to Walter and they resume their quarrel. "Walter," I said, "I'm going to take this a step farther. You're a jerk!"

The absurd little scene becomes uncomfortably quiet. Walter does not respond, and Walter's wife walks to his side. Some of the anger drains from Rusty, and he turns away. There is work to do; the dogs need food. Brenda Mackey is shivering cold. Rusty puts on his parka and hugs her like a father would.

That night Rusty and his allies make a resolution. They will continue to travel as a group to Angel Creek, one hundred miles from the finish. At that point, they'll be on their own. They'll race like hell to see which of them can beat Bill Steyer and Walter Palkovitch. They want a race? They'll get one.

At midafternoon, Rusty, Brenda Mackey, and Thomas Tetz leave together. Bill Steyer follows five minutes later. The others are an hour behind. They race through the night—pride now as strong a motive as if they were running for the winner's trophy.

It is the closest finish of the race. Just before 2:00 A.M. on Monday morning, Brenda Mackey reaches the Cushman Street Bridge less than a minute in front of Rusty Hagan.

"It was the best, and the worst, of my life. I can't be more direct than that," says Brenda.

Bill Steyer is nearly an hour behind. Next are Keith Kirkvold, Walter Palkovitch, and Amy Wright. All of them are more than three days behind Bruce Lee.

What should have been a rookie celebration is spoiled, however. Thomas Tetz drives into Fairbanks and learns that race officials have honored him with the Challenge of the North Award for helping the other rookies during the brutal storm on the mountain. But he is missing one dog. Nigel had not been running well, so Thomas took him out of the team and let him ride in the sled basket. Just around midnight, perhaps fifteen miles from the finish line, Thomas stopped his team to untangle a line. Nigel squirmed out of the sled bag and disappeared up the riverbank and into the woods. Quest rules disqualify any musher who cannot account for all dogs.

Thomas turns his nine dogs around and heads back upriver to begin the search for Nigel. Only if he can find the dog will he earn the prized finisher's patch. Even before dawn, word of the missing dog spreads through Fairbanks. KFAR radio broadcasts an appeal for help, describing Nigel and the color of his harness. Snowmachiners swarm over the river and trails. Cab drivers, veterinarians, military police at Fort Wainwright, and race fans of all types join. Without sleep, Rusty Hagan heads back into the woods on a snowmachine. The search continues through the day. Then, at 6:00 P.M., the North Star Borough Animal Control office receives a call from a homeowner. A strange dog wearing a harness is sleeping in front of the garage. Tetz is reunited with Nigel and must return to the spot where the dog escaped. Exhausted, he makes camp and rests. He finally finishes at 8:09 A.M. Tuesday. Gwen Holdman, the blond tennis player from Alaska, drives in smiling an hour later. Friends surround her and announce they're planning a party in her honor on Saturday. "Great," she says. "What day is it now?" Just after noon, spectacled Fairbanks writer Brian O'Donoghue sets a record of sorts—the first man to finish last and collect the red lantern in both the Yukon Quest and the Iditarod. Sixteen days and eight minutes after it began, the Yukon Quest is officially over.

Twenty-six mushers and 227 dogs completed the journey. Added together, they traveled a distance greater than the circumference of the globe.

20

*He pitted his puny strength in the face of things and chal-
lenged all that was, and had been, and was yet to be. . . .
"Hi! Ya! Chook! Mush-on," he screamed.*

—Jack London

I am compressed into a familiar space—the cold, undersized back seat of Gary Nance's Super Cub. We float-buzz at a hundred feet above the tops of the snow-frosted spruce and over the braided, ice-covered pathways of the streams that drain the great valley between Fairbanks and the Alaska Range to the south. We happily smoke cigarettes and try to make sure we don't blast ourselves out of the afternoon sky. Huge haystacks of cumulus clouds hover over the mountains behind us, broken here and there with shots of canted sunlight. Passing beneath us: a winter shadowland of blacks and whites, snow-covered hills that tumble out of the mountains and gradually lose their energy in the one hundred miles of flat lands ahead. To our left stands the snout of Little Delta glacier, which snakes for miles out of the rising peaks and then ends right here, in a corrugated cliff face of translucent blue. Look there! Off to our right, Gary sights a moose cow and her yearling calf, lunging awkwardly through powder snow to escape our noise. Boxes on legs, moose are the hardest animals of all for the cartoonist to caricature because nature already has. There, look, I say to myself, gasoline in the measuring gauges of both wings!

Minutes later, Gary slams the stick over to the side and presses the rudder pedal and the little plane banks onto its side. I am squeezed into the dinky seat by the force of a corkscrew turn. Wolves below. Two of them, both black as night. Then three, and finally six. The entire pack, coal black. They explode in all directions, panicked. Wolves are shot from airplanes in Alaska, and they wisely scatter for their lives at the sound of an engine. Gary, a third-generation Alaskan, still relishes the wonders of home—and he cannot get enough of the sight of free-ranging wolves. We circle and follow two as they hurtle through the trees as if dodging bullets. Imagine, killing animals from an airplane. But the Alaskan tundra is bloody from it. Once, Alaskans massacred coastal brown bears with airborne machine guns with the idea of making the valleys safe for farming. At least, that has stopped. But wolves still feel the rain of lead—the same as they have ever since man took wing in the bush planes of Alaska. The wolves, you see, kill the moose and caribou that rightfully belong to the car salesmen and lawyers in Fairbanks—at least, that's how they view it. Unfortunately, although much of the country here is held in deed by all Americans, we Outsiders are inattentive absentee landlords and the bully politicians here always have their way. But unless you've seen the majesty of wolves on their own terms, calmly on foot in the wild, where you pause and look at each other eye-to-eye without threats, both of you mysteriously aware of an ancient bond; until you've heard the serenade of their haunting music in the moonlight outside your tent; until then, when you size them up to be five times as large as a sled dog with legs like hickory posts and feet like saucers, you might not appreciate how melancholy it is to see them dashing and darting below you, with the panicked memory of the guns that boomed the last time a big noisy bird swooped down on them. In fact, I'm feeling uncomfortable as Gary continues the chase. But he thinks it's good for them, survival practice against the next airplane with the government agent out on his nine-to-five rounds "managing" the wild with a rifle bore. Besides, Gary has never seen a pack of all-black wolves.

Every bit as astonishing as the wolves is the sight just over our shoulders. Look there! The right stabilizer wing of Gary's airplane has not detached itself from the tail of the Super Cub, the bolts from the junk pile seem to be holding fast, along with the splint sawed out of a stray piece of pipe. And the duct tape is not unraveling from where it is wrapped around the precious airfoil, replacing the plane's torn skin. Now, there's a wonder for you.

Just a few hours ago, the little Cub was in bad shape. The Quest had been over for a week, and we were en route to visit John Schandelmeier at his cabin near Paxson, which is situated in the Alaska Range about halfway between Fairbanks and Anchorage. In addition to John's skill as a musher, fisherman, trapper, and all-around woodsman, he is also a bush pilot of renown, a specialist in short takeoffs and landings. He builds and repairs his own airplanes. He also happens to be a boyhood friend of Gary's, and taught Gary a good deal of what he knows about wilderness flying. Gary is telling me all this as we wind up the gorge of the Delta River, a quarter-mile-wide canyon with steep mountain peaks on both sides. The farther we fly, the worse the weather gets. We go low to stay out of the clouds. I watch behind us while Gary looks ahead. One of the rules of flying VFR in mountains is Never lose sight of the route back. When the weather starts to close in behind you, turn around. Right now, the weather behind us is not looking good. Gary is jabbering away, the Cub swaying to the left and then the right, following the winding path of the river. Below us are big jumbles of ice, close enough that I can see their sharp edges. To our right are the cliff faces of the mountains; to our left, a flood plain covered in trees. Somewhere beyond that is a two-lane road known as the Richardson Highway—the road to Paxson. Gary is telling me what a great pilot John Schandelmeier is. Naturally, he is doing this, as pilots are wont to, by recounting John's most memorable crashes. There was the time, Gary says, when John spent the winter surviving in the bush after his plane went down and nobody could find him. No problem: John lived off the land. He kept a single pot of food going all winter, just kept adding to it. In the middle of one such story, we round a bend and a full-on blizzard engulfs the Super Cub. We are blinded by snow and buffeted by the squall winds. We are, I'm afraid, going down. . . .

I can only describe the days since the Quest as dreamlike. In between long, strangely long, intervals of sleep I have followed some of my mushing friends back into their everyday lives, trying to reconcile their memories with mine, to sort out the confusion and find some perspective in the tall tales of the trail—not always successfully, I admit, but the work allows me to cling to the experience. And like most of those who made the trip from Whitehorse to Fairbanks, I find I cannot just let go. The Quest simply doesn't end right away.

One night I have dinner with Aliy Zirkle. She selects the fancy dining room of the Two Rivers Lodge, a roadhouse plopped in the middle of basically nowhere. Here, for a change, she can be served instead of working as the server. We order pitchers of Alaska Amber, a fine, gently hopped ale. And soon the backdrop of white tablecloths and clean china vanishes. We are back on the trail, and her face tightens as she relives the awful moment when Prince's feet went out from under him. "I thought he took some breaths, I really did," she says. Her memories are like the experience itself—moments of indelible clarity followed by long, indistinct intervals where motion, time, and scene are left intertwined in an ice fog of consciousness. Sometimes I lose her entirely. She stops talking in midthought, her reddened hands tighten around her beer mug, and her eyes take on the thousand-yard stare of the trail. I can almost feel the cold coming off her plaid work shirt. Then passing acquaintances stop at the table with congratulations and she snaps alive, flashing her dimples and her smile, rolling her shoulder as if to say, Aw shucks.

Later, I will see her out on the town with some of the roughest characters around, hotshot smoke jumpers preparing for summer. She's surrounded by five of them at the table, with their ropy muscles and hairy chests. Still, she's got them outgunned. They fawn at her smile, but warily.

Another night, I spread out huge maps of the Quest trail, and Dave Dalton talks me through his run, from start to finish, with the same kind of photographic recall that some people have after a World Series baseball game. I confess that I'm sometimes distracted. We have decided to patronize his longtime Quest sponsor, a bar called Reflections. Locally, it is known as a titty bar. But actually, the college women from California and Arizona who come to Fairbanks and work five- to ten-week stints are swaying directly in front of us, stark naked. They are putting on a good show because the boss, Connie Kerns, is sitting with us. And so are a couple of the Quest veterinarians and a handful of other volunteers, who have decided that this work is too important to be left to Dave and me alone.

Dave looks as wholesome as a high school swimming coach, with a trimmed mustache and short-cropped red-blond hair. One minute, I'm listening as he tells me about his first dog team—a few pups from an Airedale-husky cross, two mutts from the pound, and an assortment of giveaways from the kennels of friends. The next minute, I'm looking up at the close-trimmed labia of a smiling brunette who explains that she can pay her tuition after five weeks here, plus have enough for spring vacation. "Please don't put my name in your book. My dad would kill me," she adds.

Connie and Dave reminisce about their days driving cabs together. She would fix him lunches for the long waits at the airport. Otherwise, he'd forget to eat. Dave sold his old Pontiac back then to pay the rent. He borrowed Connie's pickup when he had a chance to homestead some land opened up by the state. Dave remembers the time he found a gold nugget in the back seat of his cab after one shift. He used it to buy materials to put a roof on his cabin. Connie has sponsored him in every Quest.

Later, I have a farewell dinner with Paddy Santucci. The more time I spend around him, the bigger he seems: a man whose skills and accomplishments are perfectly honed for a way of life on the very frontier of civilization, a man of astonishing fortitude whose center is himself and whose universe is the wild, a man who won't give an inch but will guide for miles and miles. His countenance is calm, but I sense there is much bottled up inside him. Some men talk a lot and reveal themselves to be bores. Paddy is the skillful opposite. For three months this winter, he was one of the best teachers I met because he told me nothing but welcomed me into a world that made it possible for me to learn.

I am feeling sentimental this night at the Dog Sled Saloon, and my head is light with ale. Paddy is one of the most colorful men I know, and one of the most impenetrable. He is both generous and withholding. I look at him, at his long dark hair and his fierce eyes, and realize that if I tried to go deeper, I would be guessing. I'll spare him that. So I listen. His sentences come in short bursts, spoken in a pitched growl by way of a lower lip swollen with tobacco. He is precise, and he is lyrical. Dog mushing is animal husbandry. Dog mushing is like music, it is something you do. It's like having a voice in your mind—like wide-open country, like coming to a hill and taking sixteen steps, sixteen beats. It's like breathing. It's the wind.

More than anyone I met, Paddy reveals and dissects the mistakes he made on the trail. In truth, he made few. But that's where his thoughts are: at what went wrong, so he can understand how to prevent trouble next time. I believe Paddy will win the Quest before long. I hope so. He will do it with great flair, and it will be good for dog mushing.

Joe May departs this story in a hurry. One afternoon I see him in a parking lot as he is about to leave Fairbanks, and I invite myself into the cab of his little Toyota pickup. We have driven a few thousand miles together in this truck, listening to B. B. King and Willie Nelson on the scratchy tape player. Paddy was my teacher, but Joe was my professor and my mentor. He did more for me than anyone else because, like all storytellers, he believes in the power of a good story. For a while, we were friends. I know that he understands I did nothing on the trail to disrupt the race. But I suspect that he was overwhelmed by the European press and the swaggering presence of a corporate sponsor in what had been a homegrown and private pursuit. Like Dave Rich, he saw the Quest changing, and not in ways to his liking. He once expressed a nightmare to me: a vision of the Yukon Quest transformed into a spectacle like the Iditarod, where hundreds of snowmachiners fan out to follow the race, where private airplanes and helicopters are thick overhead like mosquitoes, where sponsors and executive committees of business leaders try to wring from it every kind of commercial

advantage, where the press hounds you at every stop. Where everything that's important gets trampled and where strangers track mud
into the house.

Like most everyone here, Joe once was an Outsider. He was born in
Sturgeon Bay, Wisconsin. But that was a lifetime ago. When you hear
stories about Joe May, they're always centered in Alaska. Like in 1982
when he got a call. The Dutch government had just finished a railroad
spur and wanted to inaugurate it with a big party. They wanted to
honor people worldwide who were involved in transportation—a
London bus driver, a Sydney tugboat captain, a San Francisco cable-car
operator, and an Alaska dog musher. So Joe got a passport, picked up
his free KLM ticket, and went. He came back with a woman from
England who drove through the parks of London in a cute three-
wheeled cart pulled by a team of Siberians. In the middle of a conversation about dogs, he asked her, "Say, how do you feel about getting
married and coming to Alaska?" She said it sounded like fun. That
winter he put on a tie—the last time in his life—and married Sandra.
Then he pulled a parka over his sports coat, zipped his bride, gown
and all, into a sleeping bag and put her in the sled basket, and they
mushed to a saloon for a reception, dragging tin cans and old shoes
behind the team.

"There are many things up here that are different," Joe once told me.
"If I hold a little thing in my hand that can do a task, someone in L.A.
would say, Neat, where'd you buy it? Here, people would say, How'd
you make it?"

It turns out that I was a fool. I thought I could find a middle ground
between these two worlds—between the myths I treasured and the
reality of fifty German reporters who were put in my charge. I learned
too late that the middle ground is where you fall into the ice.

Sitting in his pickup that afternoon, I told him: Joe, I wish to God I
had hung on to that job as a vet tech, shoveling dog shit.

He nodded, shook my hand, and drove off.

At the controls, Gary Nance reacts instantaneously to our loss of visibility in the mountains. He dives for the deck and banks in the direc-

tion where he knows there is a road. On the ice of this river, we could not possibly land without crashing. The trees are deadly, too. We cannot turn around. The squall has us socked in. I can barely see the tips of the wings in the blowing snow. Ahead of us, through the windshield, it's flat white. I can see the tops of trees passing now just under the fuselage. Where the trees end is a long ribbon of white. Gary circles tightly and aims for it. Our visibility is now practically zero.

Please bear with me here. The Federal Aviation Administration has ponderous rules and requires endless paperwork in the event of what might be called a flight incident. So, let's spare everyone the paperwork. Let's say that Gary reduces the throttle and we touch down on the shoulder of the Richardson Highway with nothing more than a jolly bounce or two. Let's say that an airplane parked alongside a road in a blizzard is a potential hazard to drivers, so we hoist the Super Cub around by hand and Gary taxis neatly to the driveway of a snowplow station, conveniently situated a couple of hundred yards away. Let's say that we then manually horse the airplane off to the side so it will not be in the path of the snowplow. Let's say that the right elevator—the stabilizing airfoil at the tail—is, ah, dinged by contact with an unmoving object.

One thing for sure: we aren't going to get the goddamn thing in the air again.

Gary has made a terrific save. We are damn lucky to have a road handy. Because it's snowing sideways now and an inch has accumulated already on top of Gary's stupid Dr. Seuss stocking cap. Actually, what appears to be raw luck isn't. Back on the Yukon, Gary knew exactly where he could get fuel when he needed it. It only appeared to me as a miracle. The same with the road. He would have turned back at the first sign of looming bad weather, except he knew there was a road over to his left if we ran into a squall. His plan was to wait for the storm to pass and then fly ahead to John Schandelmeier's cabin, which is only about thirty miles away. But now this rumpled elevator. Hmmm.

If there has been any error in our circumstance, it is mine. The first rule of winter bush flying is this: Don't get into an airplane without your survival gear. Rules No. 2 through No. 5 say the same thing, only underlined. Now I'm standing here in single-ply nylon pants and a fleece jacket. No gloves, no hat, no parka. I could offer a whole tedious explanation for how this happened to be—something about an emergency at home in which Gary's golden retriever started having pups before I could get packed. The dog did not eat my homework, but the dog did start to eat her first puppy and Gary's cell phone started screaming at us, something like that. . . . But, I know, excuses are like assholes; everybody's got one. And they won't get you warm in a blizzard.

Luckily, the snowplow operator happens along. He does not seem particularly astounded to see two shivering men standing by an airplane in his front yard. And he is nice enough to invite us in. It seems that he and Gary know about five hundred of the same people and each one of them is worth a story. So our early afternoon is spent catching up on bush gossip. How this is going to get us home, I'm not sure. But I feel firm ground under my feet, and the snowplow station is equipped with a crusty jar of instant coffee, so I smile and add my approval upon learning that some distant cousin of a guy who once went to school with Gary's neighbor's best friend got married and shot a moose in the same week. A big moose, fifty-four-inch rack. You don't say? Sure enough.

Finally, Gary seems to have imagined a plan. We can't get to John Schandelmeier, so Gary calls John's secret cell-phone number and invites him down here. An hour later, John materializes out of the tail end of the squall in a crew-cab pickup with a couple of his sled dogs along for company. John does not seem in the mood to talk much about the Quest. He's not really thirsty for coffee. But, damn, look at that airplane—that catches his interest.

With his two-bladed Swiss Army knife, he cuts away the fabric of the elevator to inspect the bent tubular frame underneath. It is, unfortunately, bent ninety degrees. Rather than nice and horizontally straight, the elevator is crooked, like a man's arm as he is about to salute a general. And a straight, aerodynamic elevator is an essential part of an airplane. A flight primer defines the part this way: "A pilot-controlled airfoil attached to the trailing edge of the tail's horizontal stabilizers, used to make an aircraft go up or down and to control pitching."

Now that I look, it's not just the elevator but the whole damn stabilizer, too, that is pointing to the moon.

"Oh, no problem," John announces.

I understand then that John does not mean to invite us up to his cabin for a salmon dinner and offer us cots on which to sleep while we await the special order of a Super Cub horizontal stabilizer *and* elevator and a mobile team of mechanics who can install it.

We follow him inside the snowplow station, where he begins rummaging through the tool room. There is a bin of fasteners and a box of scrap pipe and conduit and sheet metal. He calls for a hacksaw, a drill, and a screwdriver. And, of course, that handiest and most ubiquitous fix-it product of all, a roll of silver duct tape.

In a line, we traipse back to the Super Cub. John drops onto the snow in blue jeans with gaping holes at the knees and cuts away more of the fabric skin, saws off the mutilated sections of frame, measures out some electrical conduit pipe as splints, drills holes, and fastens the frame back together with bolts. He heaves on it a couple of times and pronounces it airworthy. Gary slides into the cockpit and confirms that the elevator is still connected to the controls.

Now, in place of the skin, John wraps a single layer of duct tape until the frame is covered. He gives it a stroke, like he would a dog.

"No problem," he says again.

Who am I to be skeptical?

I see the weather has cleared, although towering clouds still sit on the peaks. But we're in no rush for that final fireball at the end of the road . . . er, in no hurry to get home. Let's go inside and bring John up to date on the fellow who got his moose and married in the same week, and a few dozen other forgotten friends. You don't say?

Presuming that this airplane flies, we are an hour from Fairbanks. Gary waits until there is only an hour of sunlight remaining; then he rises, scratches, stretches his neck, and says, "Well, better be off."

One more delay: The storm deposited snow on the wings. When we brush it off, we find that the wings were warm enough to melt the first flakes. Then it got cold again, so the wings are covered in a thin layer of ice.

No problem.

Gary has a Visa card, I have an LAPD press card, John has a driver's license, the snowplow operator has a ladder. With our cards in our hands, we scrape the layer of ice off the wings. I squeeze myself into the miniature passenger compartment, then Gary follows, grinning like a wild man and slamming his seat into my knees. The engine catches and he taxis to the road. He looks both ways for traffic, guns the engine, wriggles the elevator once more, spins the plane 180 degrees, and fire-walls the throttle. As we rumble down the icy road on landing skis, John gives us a thumbs-up. The Cub lifts gracefully and we clear the trees ahead. I am through being worried when Gary is flying.

Hey, you got a match?

It is dark when we touch down at the private landing strip known as Chena Marina. Gary ties down the airplane and calls home. When we took off, the golden retriever had four pups. Now there are seven. Including the one whose foot accidentally got nibbled.

From the bar at the Dog Sled Saloon, I call Liisa Penrose. I leave her a message.

After an experience like today, I tell her, I'm going to consider each and every day from here on as bonus time. And I'm going to try to live it right. How'd you like to go to Mexico and see if we can't fall in love?

Soon enough, we're on our way. We stop in Anchorage and, just for fun, buy tickets to the Iditarod starting banquet. Instead of hundreds, there are thousands of people. The auditorium has the sterile feel of a bankers' convention. It is a multimedia extravaganza—booming loud-speakers, an emcee straight from Toastmasters, slick videos. I don't see a single pair of Carhartt overalls. But I see mushers wearing neckties. And that's the truth. It's definitely time to leave.

The Far North won't leave me, however.

For months to come, I'll feel pangs of emptiness, a yearning that I cannot answer—the call of far-off friends, the beckoning of unbounded spaces, the elegant simplicity of woodstoves and log cabins, the easy evenings with storytellers, the glorious dance of phosphorescent colors on a cobalt sky, the long trails into the wild. Some nights, I still bolt awake at random hours on the sagging floor of a cabin or in a one-room native schoolhouse. Nothing seems stranger than blinking and finding myself in a bed with clean sheets, without the song of the dogs or the melody of the cold wind. Mush on.

1998 Yukon Quest
Order of Finish

POSITION/NAME	ELAPSED TIME	PRIZE	DOGS @ FINISH
1. Bruce Lee, *Denali National Park, Alaska*	11d 11h 27m	$30,000	9
2. Andre Nadeau, *Sainte-Melanie, Quebec**	11d 15h 13m	$24,000	8
3. Rick Mackey, *Nenana, AK*	11d 21h 09m	$18,000	7
4. John Schandelmeier, *Paxson, Alaska*	11d 22h 19m	$12,000	10
5. Frank Turner, *Whitehorse, Yukon*	12d 01h 25m	$ 8,000	11
6. Paddy Santucci, *Fairbanks, Alaska*	12d 03h 08m	$ 6,000	8
7. William Kleedehn, *Carcross, Yukon*	12d 03h 40m	$ 5,000	9
8. Keizo Funatsu, *Two Rivers, Alaska*	12d 04h 53m	$ 4,200	9
9. Brian MacDougall, *Whitehorse, Yukon*	12d 05h 44m	$ 3,700	8
10. Doug Harris, *Whitehorse, Yukon*	12d 06h 33m	$ 3,300	7
11. Dave Dalton, *Fairbanks, Alaska*	12d 06h 41m	$ 2,900	10
12. Jerry Louden, *Two Rivers, Alaska*	12d 08h 48m	$ 2,500	9
13. Dave Olesen, *Hoarfrost River, Northwest Territories**	12d 09h 36m	$ 2,100	7
14. Tim Mowry, *Two Rivers, Alaska*	12d 23h 10m	$ 1,800	8

15. Larry Carroll, *Willow, Alaska*	13d 00h 21m	$ 1,500	9
16. Louis Nelson, *Kotzebue, Alaska**	13d 03h 45m		7
17. Aliy Zirkle, *Two Rivers, Alaska**	13d 21h 40m		8
18. Brenda Mackey, *Nenana, Alaska**	14d 13h 47m		7
19. Rusty Hagan, *North Pole, Alaska**	14d 13h 48m		11
20. Bill Steyer, *Fairbanks, Alaska**	14d 14h 39m		9
21. Keith Kirkvold, *Fairbanks, Alaska**	14d 15h 13m		12
22. Walter Palkovitch, *Two Rivers, Alaska**	14d 15h 41m		9
23. Amy Wright, *Tok, Alaska**	14d 17h 04m		9
24. Thomas Tetz, *Tagish, Yukon**	15d 20h 09m		10
25. Gwen Holdman, *Fox, Alaska**	15d 21h 35m		9
26. Brian O'Donoghue, *Two Rivers, Alaska**	16d 00h 08m		7

SCRATCHED	REACHED
Cor Guimond, Dawson City, Yukon	Fortymile
Tony Blanford, Two Rivers, Alaska*	Stewart River
Dieter Dolif, Trebel, Germany	Stewart River
John Nash, Nenana, Alaska*	Stepping Stone
Terry McMullin, Eagle, Alaska*	Stepping Stone
Dan Turner, Haines, Alaska	Pelly Crossing
Jimmy Hendrick, Denali National Park, Alaska	Pelly Crossing
Stan Njootli, Old Crow, Yukon*	Pelly Crossing
Mike King, Salcha, Alaska	Pelly Crossing
Ned Cathers, Whitehorse, Yukon	Pelly Crossing
Kurt Smith, North Pole, Alaska	McCabe Creek
Michael Hyslop, Grizzy Valley, Yukon*	Carmacks

* rookie

Acknowledgments

With My Thanks

Behind the scenes, there is one man who holds the Yukon Quest together. Without race manager Leo Olesen, in Fairbanks, the race would have withered away years ago. Every participant, every volunteer, and every spectator who stood on a riverbank and watched in wonder at the passing of dog teams owes Leo first and most. He gave me the chance. I salute him. Well done, friend. That hardly says enough.

Deb Ryan in Fairbanks and Dee Balsam in Whitehorse ran the Quest offices. To appreciate them as I do, you would have to see the impossible tasks demanded of these women. Burt Zielinski pioneered the blood-screening study that will save the lives of dogs. And we tore the hell out of a few good saloons, too, didn't we, buddy?

Dave Arlen of KFAR Fairbanks shared the thankless chore as press liaison, not to mention all those hours on the trail—a double rum and Coke for my friend, please. Thanks, also, to John McWhorter of KUAC and Bob Eley of the *Fairbanks Daily News–Miner*.

Yukon board president Tom Randall was a lightning rod for controversy, and he dreamed up the nutty idea of making me press liaison,
but ingratitude is not in my nature. Thanks, Tom.

Peacemakers Rob Touey and Tina Sebert spanned the biggest gulf of
all—between the Fulda journalists and the race. Big Al Hallman taught
me, among other things, the wisdom of getting the thermometer warm
before sticking it up the ass of a sled dog. Larry "Cowboy" Smith
turned me loose with his dogs that first time. Kathy Swenson taught
me grit. I tip my hat to race judge Ty Dugger and radioman Brad
Brooks, who got us down the path safely and laughing.

A hundred race volunteers added up to a thousand kindnesses. I say
thanks to one, Tracie Harris of Whitehorse, but I mean it to all.

It seems long ago, but my first call was to Shannon Walley. Thanks
for saying "Come on up."

At home at the *Los Angeles Times*, Scott Kraft gave me the opportunity and encouragement to try. Kit Rachlis made me believe that trying
would be worth it. When it counted, he rolled up his sleeves and made
sure of it. Two pathfinders, David Lamb and David Shaw, inspired me.
Anna Virtue, as always, knew where to find the answers.

And where would I be without the professionals? Editor Tracy
Brown believed in this story and in me. My agent, Bonnie Nadell, ran
in lead for so many long miles from the first day until the last. My
thanks to these two are not casual. I mean to shout them out. I never
met Bonnie Thompson, but we lived together for a while in the editing
of this manuscript. I'll never write another sentence without thinking
how she would make it right.

Last, but by no means least: This story really began in the Brooks
Range Mountains. Macgill Adams is the finest wilderness guide in
Alaska and the most naturally gifted storyteller I've ever met. His tales
of dog mushing lit my imagination. And he was the first to say, "You
ought to check out the Quest someday."

In memory of Benson. For all those good years, he pulled his share of
the load. And for Prince, who tried.

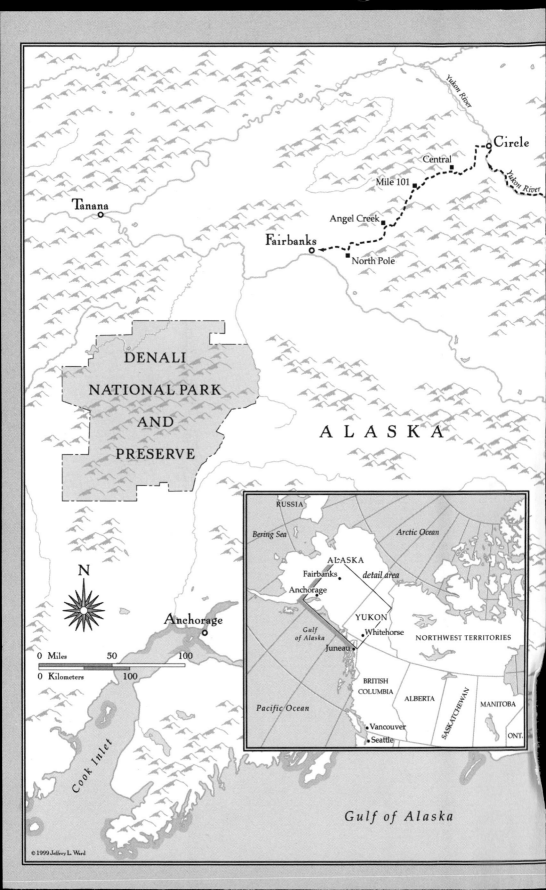

Circle

Yukon River

Central

Mile 101

Angel Creek

Tanana

Fairbanks

North Pole

Yukon River

DENALI

NATIONAL PARK

AND

PRESERVE

ALASKA

N

RUSSIA

Bering Sea

Arctic Ocean

ALASKA

Fairbanks

detail area

Anchorage

YUKON

Whitehorse

NORTHWEST TERRITORIES

Gulf
of Alaska

Juneau

Anchorage

0 Miles   50   100

0 Kilometers   100

BRITISH
COLUMBIA

ALBERTA

SASKATCHEWAN

MANITOBA

ONT.

Pacific Ocean

Vancouver

Seattle

Cook Inlet

Gulf of Alaska

© 1999 Jeffrey L. Ward